The Return of Hans Staden

The Return of Hans Staden

A Go-between in the Atlantic World

EVE M. DUFFY *&* ALIDA C. METCALF

Johns Hopkins University Press
Baltimore

© 2012 Johns Hopkins University Press
All rights reserved. Published 2012
Printed in the United States of America on acid-free paper
2 4 6 8 9 7 5 3

Johns Hopkins University Press
2715 North Charles Street
Baltimore, Maryland 21218-4363
www.press.jhu.edu

Library of Congress Cataloging-in-Publication Data

Duffy, Eve M.
The return of Hans Staden : a go-between in the Atlantic world /
Eve M. Duffy, Alida C. Metcalf.
p. cm.
Includes bibliographical references and index.
ISBN-13: 978-1-4214-0345-8 (hardcover : alk. paper)
ISBN-13: 978-1-4214-0346-5 (pbk. : alk. paper)
ISBN-10: 1-4214-0345-5 (hardcover : alk. paper)
ISBN-10: 1-4214-0346-3 (pbk. : alk. paper)
1. Staden, Hans, ca. 1525–ca. 1576—Travel—Brazil.   2. Staden, Hans, ca. 1525–
ca. 1576. Warhaftige Historia und Beschreibung eyner Landtschafft der wilden, nacketen,
grimmigen Menschfresser Leuthen in der Newenwelt America gelegen.   3. Brazil—
Description and travel—Early works to 1800.   4. Indians of South America—
Brazil.   5. Tupinamba Indians—Social life and customs.   6. Brazil—Early works
to 1800.   7. America—Early accounts to 1600.   I. Metcalf, Alida C., 1954–   II. Title.
F2511.D84   2011
980'.01—dc22   2011013721

A catalog record for this book is available from the British Library.

*Special discounts are available for bulk purchases of this book. For more information,
please contact Special Sales at 410-516-6936 or specialsales@press.jhu.edu.*

Johns Hopkins University Press uses environmentally friendly book materials,
including recycled text paper that is composed of at least 30 percent post-consumer
waste, whenever possible.

For our students

CONTENTS

It is an enormous pleasure to express our appreciation to all those who assisted us as we sought to make sense of the story of Staden's return in the context of the opening of the Atlantic world. Because this work was a true collaboration, we would like to begin by thanking each other and acknowledging longstanding mutual support, from our initial conversations to our sustained writing, always across great distances. Trinity University provided the initial institutional context for our work, and our gratitude goes to Anene Ejikeme for first suggesting that, as historians of Germany and Brazil, we should write this book together. We especially recognize John Martin, who not only encouraged the project at every stage but has given us many insights into the early modern world.

We are grateful to our respective institutions for providing settings in which to write and work. Our wonderful librarians, especially Anna Shparberg at Rice University and Claudia Funke, curator of rare books at the University of North Carolina at Chapel Hill, have provided tremendously rich resources and helped us locate essential texts. Nicholas Shumway, Dean of Humanities at Rice University, and Bill Andrews, Senior Associate Dean of Fine Arts and the Humanities at the University of North Carolina at Chapel Hill, shared a subvention that allows us to include the images that complement our text. Like Staden, we know the value of images to convey meaning, and we are fortunate to have the support of our institutions to enable this enrichment of the text for our readers.

A conference on Hans Staden held in Wolfhagen in 2007 provided Alida the opportunity to visit Staden's native land and to meet many of those who have worked on Staden over the past decades. Our thanks go to Franz Obermeier and Wolfgang Schiffner for organizing the conference and to all of the participants who shared their ideas, especially Neil Whitehead, Vanete Dutra Santana, and Marília dos Santos Lopes. Wolfgang and Barbara Schiffner are remembered fondly for their hospitality in Wolfhagen. A trip to Munich in 2010 enabled Eve to visit the Bavarian State Library (whose digital collections provided invaluable and easy access to rare texts). A special thanks goes to Chuck Weinraub for facilitating her travel.

A wide network of colleagues and friends shared their ideas and served as sounding boards as we wrote the book in 2009 and 2010. The Helm Fellowship program at the Lilly Library at Indiana University supported two weeks of research in residence in Bloomington during the summer of 2008. Christine Johnson gave us early insights into the historiography on Hans Staden, while Susan Boettcher served as a resource for sixteenth-century Hesse. Carlos Fausto helped us to understand the complex anthropological debates over cannibalism, and Felipe Vieira de Castro and Francisco Contente Domingues lent their expertise on Portuguese ships. Ruth von Bernuth and the students of the UNC graduate seminar on travel writing provided valuable insights into the narrative structure of the *True History* that are incorporated into chapter 3. Likewise, Rice students in Diane Wolfthal's art history seminar Multi-Cultural Europe critically read the first draft of chapter 4; Diane first suggested that we explore the images not as the work of Staden or a single artist but as the result of a collaboration.

Our long-distance collaboration could not have been possible without the online workspace at Rice University created by Angela DeHart Rabuck, which allowed us to easily manage and share scores of drafts and an extensive array of sources. We would also like to thank Kim Ricker and Jean Niswonger at the GIS/Data Center at the Fondren Library at Rice University for extensive training on how to conceptualize maps; Jean Niswonger deserves special recognition for her outstanding work in creating the maps in their final form. At the Rice Digital Media Center, Lisa Spiro and Jane Zhao provided expert advice in assembling the images. Rice graduate students in history Amanda Moehnke and Angela Prattas assisted us in proofreading, compiling the bibliography, and researching the images. Paul Igmundson provided helpful insights as we thought about the significance of Staden's text and the limitations of historical knowledge. David K. Frasier at the Lilly Library at Indiana University was enormously helpful with our requests for images, as was Leslie Tobias Olsen at the John Carter Brown Library at Brown University, and the other institutions who are credited in the text. The late Henry Tom at the Johns Hopkins University Press was an enthusiastic supporter of the book from the start, and we are honored to be among his last authors. Suzanne Flinchbaugh skillfully shepherded the book to its completion with patience and good humor. We are especially grateful to Elizabeth Yoder for her deft copyediting. We thank our anonymous outside reviewer for suggesting revisions that strengthened the manuscript. We thank Daniel Rigney for a careful reading of the final manuscript.

Finally, we acknowledge our families—our husbands, Dan and Kevin, and our sons, August, Benjamin, Cole, Matthew, and Max—who are there whenever we return (often after long stays at libraries, archives, and our desks) and who have listened to our stories of Hans Staden with patience, shock, good humor, and love.

Staden's *True History* is written in early modern High German, a language not easily accessible to most modern readers. The translations that appear here are our own, and we cite an online digitized version of Staden's text for the original quotations provided in the text and footnotes. This text, a reproduction of the original published by Karl Fouquet, is available at the German-language Gutenberg Project, hosted by the magazine *Der Spiegel* (at http://gutenberg.spiegel.de). Given the various editions and translations of Staden's text available, we cite each quotation from the online version of the *Warhaftige Historia* (1978) by book, chapter, and paragraph, so that book 1, chapter 2, paragraph 3, for example, is cited as *WH* 1.2.3. We use standardized English versions for names and places. The sources for quotations, information, and the work of scholars are referenced in combined notes for each paragraph.

The Return of Hans Staden

Introduction

*I*n February 1555, when the hazy blur of the French coastline came into view from the deck of the *Catherine,* the German gunner Hans Staden was probably not thinking about writing a book. After four months spent crossing the Atlantic, Staden, in debt to his French captain, would have been worried about more pressing matters, like keeping the powder for the ship's guns dry. English pirates lurked in the waters beyond the ports in Brittany and Normandy, looking for an easy strike that would deprive the captain, the ship's investors, and the crew of the fruits of their long and dangerous journey. Other problems and deprivations would have weighed upon both Staden's mind and his body: the putrid water in the ship's casks, the rancid rations, and the icy, numbing cold. During the crossing, the winter days had been short and the nights very long. Most of the crew had been at sea at least a year, but Staden had been away from his home longer than that. He had left Spain in 1550 en route for Asunción, the tiny Spanish settlement far up the Rio de la Plata estuary and the Paraná and Paraguay rivers, hoping to cash in on the conquest of lands rumored to be rich in gold. It was his second trip to the Americas, but he never reached Asunción; he had landed instead in Portuguese Brazil (see fig. 1). Now he was returning on a French ship, and from France he planned to return home to Hesse in central Germany. With the coastline looming before him, Staden could perhaps finally believe that his travels might be over.

What does the traveler feel on returning home? Time has passed, and some things have changed. The traveler is different, often quite so, depending on how long the absence has been and the distances traversed. One way to bridge such differences and to lessen the tension between traveler and homeland is to tell stories of adventures, of new peoples and places experienced. The stories help to reintegrate the traveler into the community, and they allow the traveler to share experiences and emotions. Some of these emotions may be vivid and violent: anger over treacheries suffered; a feeling of righteousness over choices made; grief for those lost or left behind. The return home is the narrowing of the lens of experience, and the telling of stories puts those experiences away and leaves them safely in the past.

Many people were traveling in sixteenth-century Europe, both throughout the continent and to lands across the sea. Even during the Middle Ages, often seen as

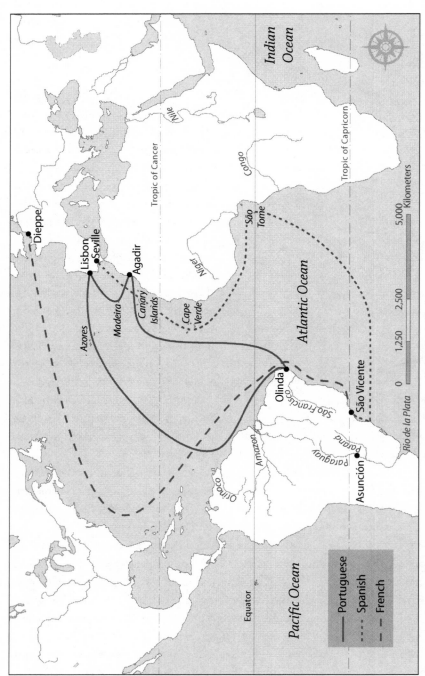

Figure 1. Staden's Voyages

insular and parochial, ordinary people had moved from place to place, supported by a network of people—captains, sailors, innkeepers, or guides—who made their travel possible. Travelers spoke to others of their journeys, and a few recorded their experiences in letters, diaries, accounts, and travelers' tales.[1]

After his return to Hesse, Staden wrote an account of his experiences that became one of the most popular travel books of the sixteenth century. Its popularity rested in no small measure on the fact that it shaped European stereotypes about wild, man-eating savages, fueling popular fantasies about New World peoples that could justify a sense of European superiority. It also became popular in Protestant states because it served as a morality tale about God's grace and the value of true faith.

Staden seems to have begun to formulate his story on his return from Brazil in February 1555, while he was on board the *Catherine*. Hans Staden had joined the French crew in the Guanabara Bay in Brazil with nothing to his name: no money, no gold, no sea chest, not even any clothes. The French captain had taken him on board, the crew had given him clothes, and Staden had survived the long winter voyage across the north Atlantic. Once they anchored and unloaded the ship of its cargo, he planned to stop in the northern French seaport town of Dieppe before turning home to Hesse. In Dieppe he intended to see if another ship had returned. Staden had met the crew of this ship, the *Marie Bellotte,* in Brazil.

In Dieppe, Staden learned that the *Marie Bellotte* was overdue by three months. There he delivered a crushing judgment that became the crux of the story he would tell about his return: "There are some godless people on that ship," he reported to a gathering in the house of the *Marie Bellotte*'s captain. Staden related how he had met the crew when the *Marie Bellotte* came to trade for monkeys and peppers at the coastal village known as Ubatuba, where he was held as a captive of the Tupinambá, a Tupi-speaking group who lived south of the Guanabara Bay. "I escaped from the savages and swam out to them to their ship. But they didn't want to take me. So I had to swim back to the shore to the savages. It nearly broke my heart." The men from Dieppe, Staden continued, "also gave a Portuguese to the savages, who ate him." Staden reported that the sailors "had shown me no mercy at all."[2]

Staden then delivered his most devastating statement: "In the face of all that, I now see that God meant the best for me. I am here now—praise be to God—to give you the latest news. Let them come if they may. But I will be a prophet to you. God will see to it that such cruelty and tyranny as they showed to me there in that land will not go unpunished, whether that will come sooner or later. Because it is clear to me that God in heaven heard my pleas and had mercy on me."[3]

What can we, looking back on this exchange, make of it? Did it really happen? Was Staden telling the truth? Could the French crew of the *Marie Bellotte* have knowingly given the Tupinambá a Portuguese sailor to be eaten? Were the Tupinambá, in fact, cannibals? And who was without pity, in the end—the Tupinambá, who practiced cannibalism; the French sailors who turned their backs on Staden; or Staden, insisting that God's grace had manifested itself in his safe return but not that of the crew of the *Marie Bellotte,* who might have perished at sea, punished for their sins in Brazil?

Staden's anger and righteousness, visible in the story he told in Dieppe, became the beginning of a story he eventually published in a book that appeared in Marburg, Germany, two years later. The *Warhaftige Historia,* or *True History,* quickly became a bestseller, spreading rapidly through northern Europe via numerous reprints and translations.[4]

How does one determine the difference between a good story and a lie? This question haunts the tales of travelers who are known to exaggerate, embellish, and even fabricate their stories. In medieval and renaissance Europe, travelers' accounts shaped how Europeans interpreted and understood distant and unfamiliar lands. Distortions, objectification of different cultures, parroting the descriptions written by others, and bald-face lies are part and parcel of these travelogues; nevertheless, they had a far-reaching influence on how other peoples were seen. The most popular writers became famous for decades, even hundreds of years, whether or not their stories were true. Marco Polo's *Il milione,* the account of what he saw and heard during his years in China, never seemed to lose its appeal. Written before the invention of the printing press, the text has 140 different manuscript versions, suggesting that it was copied over and over again by different scribes. *The Travels of Sir John de Mandeville* (ca. 1375), a hugely popular travel book in the fourteenth and fifteenth centuries, was apparently written by someone who never went anywhere. Another famous traveler was Lodovico de Varthema, who disguised himself as a Muslim and traveled to Mecca with the intent of seeing the hajj and then made his way to India. His *Itinerario* (1510) was the first account published in Europe of the Middle East and Southeast Asia; it gained Varthema great fame. Amerigo Vespucci's published letters were so persuasive about the lands he claimed to have discovered that a continent was named after him.[5]

Whether Hans Staden's *True History* was in fact true has been a focus of intense academic scrutiny because Hans Staden claims to present a true account of cannibalism based on his own eyewitness observation. Scholars have long debated whether the cannibalistic acts Staden includes in his text were an accurate description of local customs, a misreading of indigenous resistance in the form of taunts and lies, pure fabrication, a projection of European fears about transubstantiation in Christian holy communion, or part of an emerging European discourse about the violent and primitive nature of peoples encountered during campaigns, on trading routes, during the age of exploration, or in European metropoles.[6]

At least since the publication of Edward Said's *Orientalism* (1979), scholars have understood that travel accounts reveal as much about the traveler's homeland as about the places visited. Subsequently, scholars have mined travel accounts to reveal how Europeans could project their deepest fears and fantasies on these peoples who are often described as the colonial Other. Those who study medieval and early modern travel writing argue that such stories not only track European encounters but reflect contemporary European concerns, fears, and fantasies. Travel literature has thus often been seen as a source of (mostly European) preconceptions about inhabitants of the New World; a current focus has considered how Europeans' obsession with the Ottoman Empire may have shaped their encounters in the New World.[7]

"But he was very wicked!" a colleague told us when we described writing this book on Hans Staden. "He was such a liar. It was not God's grace that saved him! He just made it all up to sell his book!"

Another colleague told us that Staden is detestable, using the Portuguese verb *odiar,* which comes from the Latin *odi,* "to hate." "Any attention that he gets is undeserved," this colleague said. "It only serves to perpetuate an image of Brazil as a land of savages."

There is much in Hans's story that is disturbing today, more than 450 years after it was first published. On the title page of the original edition, German Gothic letters, printed in a brilliant red, highlight the first word of Staden's title: *Warhaftige,* "True." The rest of the book's title follows, first in red then in black ink: *History and Description of a Land Belonging to a Wild, Naked, Savage, and Man-Eating People, Situated in the New World, Unknown before and after the birth of Christ in the territory of Hesse, until two years ago Hans Staden from Homberg knew them through his own experience, and now puts it in print.* At the bottom of the title page is a woodcut illustration in black ink (see fig. 2). A man sits in a hammock holding a severed human foot to his mouth. He stares at the reader, unrepentant. Beside the hammock is the *boucan,* the original barbecue pit where human legs are roasting. It is a gruesome, gripping, shocking image.

Is this Staden's first manipulation of the reader? Is he molding us, before we read even one word of his story, to view the people he will describe to us as, in the words of one scholar, "fully pagan and Other?"[8] Or is this some sort of sick joke?

Staden's account of his captivity and escape from cannibalism has long been shrouded in controversy. At the center of this controversy is whether or not he can be believed. William Arens argued in 1979 that European depictions of cannibalism

Figure 2. Title Page Woodcut. From Hans Staden, *Warhaftige Historia*. Marburg: 1557. Courtesy, Lilly Library, Indiana University, Bloomington, Indiana.

in sixteenth-century accounts have no basis in fact. Arens specifically debunks Staden's claims of cannibalism among the Tupinambá, maintaining that Staden could not speak Tupi-Guarani, that he did not live long enough among the Tupinambá to observe the cannibalism ceremony (if it even existed), and that furthermore, since he believed the Tupinambá were inferior and animal-like, he assumed they were therefore likely to be cannibals. No firsthand accounts of cannibalism, Arens maintains, can be verified; and the recycling of suspect accounts over and over again by missionaries, traders, or government officials became part of a larger project through which Europeans labeled indigenous peoples as barbarous, primitive, and cannibalistic in order to rationalize and defend the conquest and exploitation of them.[9]

Reports of cannibalism did begin to circulate in Europe immediately following the first voyages to the Americas, and many vague descriptions were repeated as if they were truly seen. Columbus made reference to a group in the Caribbean, whom he did not personally see but labeled as cannibals, in his first letter from the New World, addressed to Luis de Santángel in 1493. A woodcut depicting cannibalism accompanied Vespucci's popular *Mundus Novus* letter printed in Augsburg in 1505; while Vespucci's *Lettera,* first printed in Florence as early as 1504 or 1505, contained a graphic description of a sailor killed and eaten in full sight of his shipmates.[10]

Rumors of cannibalism soon served the imperial aspirations of Spain. Reports of cannibalism, whether accurate or not, became the justification for the enslavement of Indians. Queen Isabella signed a law in 1503 that permitted indigenous groups who were cannibals to be legally enslaved. Thereafter, indiscriminant enslavement of Indians began. Similar views took hold during the Portuguese exploration and settlement of Brazil, where captives supposedly slated for cannibalism could be purchased by colonists and held as slaves. Images of cannibalism and places labeled as "of cannibals" or simply "cannibals" began to appear with increasing regularity on maps of the Americas.[11]

French literary historian Frank Lestringant explores this depiction of and writing about cannibalism in Europe, in particular in France, and finds that it illuminates how European encounters with the exotic Other changed over time. In the sixteenth century, he argues, essayist Michel de Montaigne was fascinated by the Tupinambá whom he met in the French port city of Rouen and with whom he attempted to converse through an interpreter. Montaigne, as well as André Thevet and Jean de Léry, who published accounts of the Tupinambá based on their visits to Brazil, believed the Tupinambá to be honorable, their lifeways worthy of contemplation, and their practice of cannibalism understandable as part of a cycle of revenge caused by war. By the nineteenth century, however, when the French writer Gustave Flaubert paid five *sous* to see exotic Others—Kaffirs from South Africa—in Rouen, the image of the colonial Other was so degraded that there could not be any dialogue between them. The Kaffirs could not speak; Flaubert described them as primitive and animalistic. Their destiny, Lestringant observes, had become to serve as slaves or as mere commodities exhibited at fairground attractions.[12]

What did Staden think of the Tupinambá? Staden's description of his personal struggle to free himself from imminent death and cannibalism was sensationalized, according to some scholars, to sell his book. Annerose Menninger argues that Staden interwove his adventures with his account of cannibalism in order to give his German readers what they were expecting. In her view, Staden's is a carefully constructed book, designed to be a bestseller, which became one precisely because it delivered the tales of exotic, terrifying, and wild peoples readers expected.[13]

The growth of a broad reading public, particularly in northern Europe, had begun with the invention of printing in the middle of the fifteenth century. Fueled by religious conflict—printed broadsheets attacked Catholic excesses, for example, and Martin Luther's printed Bible translated into German what had been a Latin text previously accessible to only a few—the printing press became an agent of change. Books revolutionized how information traveled and was digested even by ordinary men and women. The discoveries made by the Spanish and Portuguese in the New World were accompanied by the printed word, and even in Germany, a land not directly involved in expansive efforts to settle the Americas, ordinary men and women were eager to read news about the wonders encountered by others on their travels.[14]

The rise of Protestantism went hand in hand with the expansion of print culture and increasing literacy, for Martin Luther preached that the Bible should be published in the spoken languages of Christians who could then read it in their own languages. Staden had been raised in the religious ferment of Germany during Martin Luther's lifetime. He identified with Luther's message that Christians were saved by God's grace and not by their good works, as traditional Catholic doctrine held.[15]

Some scholars dismiss Staden's claims as pure fabrication, meant either to appeal to a developing reading public or as part of an attempt to denigrate native peoples by assuming the worst about them. Among these is Gananath Obeyesekere, who sees Staden as "unreliable" and even possessed of a paranoid imagination. For Obeyesekere, Staden was likely a sexually repressed, misogynist Christian, tormented by childhood fears that he projected onto the Tupinambá. His story of cannibalism, therefore, was his way of expressing his fear of the Other (the Tupinambá cannibals) by talking about it with friends and neighbors, who then might embellish the tale even further. When such "cannibal talk" is written down, Obeyesekere maintains, the stories become like ghost stories, an invented genre that the author wants the reader to believe but that cannot be taken at face value.[16]

Other scholars, however, are inclined to accept Staden's account. Recognizing that cannibalism was used as a justification for enslaving indigenous people and accepting that accounts of cannibalism must be carefully scrutinized, these scholars part with Arens's nearly universal denial of cannibalism or Obeyesekere's characterization of "cannibal talk" as tending toward pervasive fantasy. Even if accounts are fabricated and reprinted as truth, this does not mean, they argue, that cannibalism did not exist. Donald Forsyth finds that much of Staden's account can be verified with other eyewitnesses of the sixteenth century. Lestringant's careful study of the accounts by Thevet and Léry lead him, too, to accept these accounts as reliable ethnographies, as have Brazilian social scientists such as Florestan Fernandes. Anthropologist Neil Whitehead and historian Michael Harbsmeier argue that *True History* is a rich ethnographic text that is especially compelling because Staden lived among the Tupinambá. According to Whitehead, the text is both fundamental and relevant if it is carefully read to understand sixteenth-century encounters and insights into contemporary manifestations of violence.[17]

Looking for the truth in Staden's account is a complicated matter, for he openly reveals himself to be a liar in his text. While a captive, he continually lies to the Tupinambá. He pretends, he fabricates, he deceives. Some scholars see Staden as an actor who lied and skillfully presented himself in order to survive. He was, H. E. Martel argues, "a practiced chameleon," who in scene after scene "demonstrated his willingness to lie and perform an identity not his own."[18]

If Staden's account is full of lies, does it at the same time tell certain truths? One way to read Staden is to understand the complexities of his cross-cultural experience, as Luciana Villas-Bôas notes. For Villas-Bôas, Staden assimilated much of the Tupinambá ways and became like the mixed-race Portuguese and Indian men who lived on the fringes of the Portuguese settlements in Brazil. Staden described them as "skilled and experienced in both the Christian and the savage ways of fighting and languages," and, as Villas-Bôas argues, the same can be said about Staden himself.[19]

Staden claimed to be an eyewitness observer, and much of his account is taken up with detailed descriptions of the lifeways of the Tupinambá in Brazil. These "ethnographic" descriptions point to an increasing awareness among European humanists of the importance of scientific observation. Beginning in the sixteenth century, whether in astronomy, cartography, or medicine, new insights were gleaned from the direct observations of educated humanists or practically minded laymen. A man like Staden, a soldier who worked on ships, would have recognized the need for accurate observation in order for ships to cross oceans and return to known ports. Travel writers in particular relied on their experiences as eyewitnesses to shore up the basis of their accounts. As Lorraine Daston and Katherine Park show, because these writers were telling tales of such novelty and implausibility, truth was an even greater concern than it had been in the past; and because travel writers could not invoke ancient authorities to confirm their truths, they had only their reputations and their experiences and credibility to testify to the truthfulness of their stories.[20]

We argue that Staden can be best understood as a go-between. Complicated figures prevalent in situations where different cultures came into contact and conflict, go-betweens may be separated into three distinct groups: the physical, the transactional, and the representational. The simple traveler—the physical go-between—connected worlds that had been long separated. While at sea and while living in Brazil, Staden's experience as a physical go-between was a direct and sensory exploration of a new and very different world: he saw, heard, touched, tasted, and smelled.[21]

When Staden was captured by the Tupinambá, he stepped into another common role played by go-betweens in early colonies: the transactional go-between. Usually transactional go-betweens were the cultural intermediaries, the translators and facilitators of the interactions between two different worlds, such as the Tupi-Guarani world and that of the European traders or first settlers. In addition to being acutely aware of the sensory, they also dealt in the realm of language: they talked, translated, argued, and persuaded. Moving back and forth between worlds, they were often caught in the middle, and they could be highly vulnerable, for their loyalties were constantly questioned. As was common with other transactional go-betweens, Staden lied because his very survival depended on it. Transactional go-betweens frequently played one side against the other, invented stories, and changed sides; so, too, did Staden. Transactional go-betweens often possessed a great deal of power at certain moments in time, power that could shape key moments in the interactions between European and Indian traders, European colonists and Indian villages, colonial officials and Indian chiefs. So, too, may have Staden.

Representational go-betweens are those who attempted to explain a different, new, and distant world: its geography, its flora and fauna, its peoples and their customs. Representational go-betweens wrote, interpreted, performed, and recounted their experiences for others, thereby explaining meanings, characterizing peoples, and passing judgments on them. Staden clearly becomes a representational go-between when he tells, writes, and illustrates his story.

Because of their movement between worlds, go-betweens constantly returned, and they undoubtedly experienced many emotions on returning. Sailors, pilots, sea captains—classic examples of physical go-betweens—returned often to ports of call on both sides of the Atlantic. Other physical go-betweens, such as slaves or penal exiles, never could return, but many certainly yearned to. Staden was a physical go-between who traveled to Brazil twice, thereby experiencing three different returns. He returned from Brazil; he returned to Brazil; and, after living there for four years, he returned permanently to his home. Transactional go-betweens were in the business of constant returning. Negotiating, translating, brokering, they continually moved between worlds and thereby returned. As a captive of the Tupinambá, Staden used every stratagem at his disposal to attempt to return to the Portuguese settlement of São Vicente in Brazil. Representational go-betweens returned both literally, when they made their final return, and virtually, through their stories, images, and maps, to places visited. Staden develops his story after his final return, and in telling his story, he returns to Brazil in order to explain and translate what he saw there for his readers.

In this book, Staden is our go-between. There is much about him that we may not like. There may also be things about him that we can admire. We may find him wicked or simply lucky. We may believe him or doubt his honesty. Our challenge is less to judge than to use him to travel back into the sixteenth century, a time when encounters of many kinds forever changed the traditional ways peoples had lived. These encounters, some peaceful, others violent, opened up the Atlantic Ocean and laid the foundation for the emergence of the Atlantic economy of the early modern era. By the middle of the sixteenth century when Staden began to construct his tale, the newly discovered lands had become the foci of regular trading routes and new colonies. Staden's story took place in a world hardly isolated from Europe. When he delivered his message in Dieppe, he underscored that what happened in Brazil did not remain there, that Brazil was connected to Europe. Choices made there bore consequences someplace else.

Staden's lies and Staden's truths are one man's attempt to survive in the early modern world on both sides of the Atlantic. Through his returns, we shall explore emotions that were not unique to him and situations that were common to many ordinary men and women in the sixteenth century. It all began with the fact that towns and villages were no longer isolated but were connected into a much larger world. As Staden put it: "I Hans Staden from Homberg in Hesse, decided, if God were willing, to see India . . ."[22]

CHAPTER ONE

Staden Goes to Sea

Hans Staden went to sea in the spring of 1547, but we don't know why. Years later, back in Germany, he declared that he had "left his homeland" and that he "wished to sail to India." Why would a young German from Hesse want to go to sea? Was the pull of India so strong in central Europe at that time that it needed no further explanation?[1]

Born sometime around 1520, in the generation following Vasco da Gama's successful sea voyage to India (1497–98), Hans Staden was raised and educated, became a man, and learned a trade in several towns throughout Hesse. In the sixteenth century, Hesse was a principality, one of hundreds of states of varying sizes and strength that were bound under what was known then as the Holy Roman Empire. A large political entity consisting of various individual units of various sizes, from small city-states (the imperial free cities—those sixty to seventy cities that owed allegiance to no other lord than the emperor himself) to larger principalities, the Holy Roman Empire stretched from the North Sea to northern Italy and from the Rhine to the borders of the kingdoms of Poland and Hungary in the East. Some areas were ruled directly by the emperor, but most were ruled by counts, bishops, abbots, and others, collectively known as princes. Hesse was one of the more remote areas of the empire ruled by such a prince. United in the thirteenth century, its rulers held the title of landgrave, which meant that they owed direct feudal duty to the Holy Roman emperor himself.[2]

Situated on a fault line between the more important regions of the empire, namely, the imperial cities in the north and the cities of the Hanseatic League (Bremen and Hamburg), the old cathedral towns along the Rhine (Aachen and Cologne), and the urban region of upper Saxony (Leipzig and Dresden), Hesse was divided into four distinct sections, two of which—the upper and lower principalities with the towns of Kassel in the north and Marburg in the south—were important in Staden's life.[3]

The north Hessian landscape was mountainous, and the poor soil of the region made farming difficult. The Oden forest rose up from the Rhine plain from the west and the south, and the forested mountain ranges of the Taunus and the Vogelsberg surrounded a number of river valleys that coursed through both principalities; these valleys were cut by the waters of the Lahn, the Eder, the Fulda, and the Werra rivers, resulting in high hills and steep valleys. The landscape created by these rivers was dense, and not until the nineteenth century did it take on its modern character. Along the riverbanks stretched miles of wetland forests, dark and waterlogged. More than half of Hesse was covered by forests. Fynes Moryson, an English traveler to the region in the sixteenth century, noted the "stony mountaines and woods of oakes" that characterized the countryside. Two hundred years after Staden lived, eighteenth-century contemporaries compared this overgrown landscape to that of the New World, even the Amazon, although the deciduous and pine forests were quite different from the jungles of Brazil.[4]

Hesse contained more than one hundred towns, many of which had been chartered in the Middle Ages. These towns included Hersfeld, Homberg, Korbach, Marburg, Wetter, and Wolfhagen, all associated with Hans Staden and his family. Like most towns in German lands, these were not very large urban centers. The Hessian towns were also not particularly wealthy; in fact, the English traveler Moryson remarked on the general poverty of the area: "The houses were of timber and clay, each one for the most part having a dunghill at the doore, more like a poore Village, then a City: but such are the buildings of the Cities in Hessen." Yet despite their poverty in comparison to towns in other principalities, the Hessian towns were part of a larger network of trade and communication that brought them in contact with lands far across the oceans.[5]

Ringed by fortified walls, these towns had local markets and served as centers of textile production or as posts along the traditional overland highways connecting the important fair towns of Cologne, Frankfurt, Leipzig, Nuremberg, and the Northern German Hanseatic trading cities. Despite their thick protective walls that had survived from medieval times (see fig. 3), the towns of Hesse were hardly isolated from the expanding trading networks that took the capital of merchants from Antwerp, Nuremberg, or Venice to India.

That Hans Staden did not grow up in one place may have contributed to the ease with which he seems to have left his home. The Stadens cannot be linked to any particular town in Hesse, but rather we find evidence of their lives throughout the various small towns around Marburg and Kassel. Although it was cumbersome for citizens to change residencies and move from one place to the next, many people did so; and in fact, migrants to cities generally made up more than a third to a half of the population of any German city. Homberg, where Staden was most likely born, was approximately 60 kilometers north and west of Marburg. It produced wool and was on the major trade routes between the North Sea and the Levant.[6]

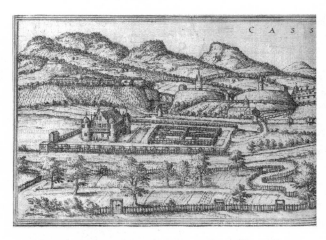

Figure 3. The Town of Kassel in Hesse. From Georg Braun, *Civitates orbis terrarum.* Antwerp: 1575. Courtesy of the John Carter Brown Library at Brown University.

Yet in the period in which Staden lived, one's trustworthiness and one's honor were still tied to one's reputation at home. This reputation followed families even as they moved. "The proverb says that the apple always tastes of the tree," wrote Johannes Dryander, humanist, medical doctor, and professor of anatomy at the University of Marburg, in the introduction to Hans Staden's book, reflecting a commonly held belief that if Staden's father had been an honorable man, his sons would be too. Dryander knew Staden's father in Wetter and Homberg and described him as "an upright, pious, and brave man who is also versed in the liberal arts." Fourteen kilometers north of Marburg, Wetter was the site of a famous humanistic school that Dryander, and possibly Staden's father, likely attended. Dryander went on to study at universities throughout Europe, including the University of Erfurt (where Martin Luther had studied); he later became rector at the University of Marburg, which is generally held to be the first Protestant university in Germany. If Staden's father was "versed in the liberal arts," as Dryander maintains, he would have studied Grammar, Rhetoric, Logic, Geometry, Arithmetic, Music, and Astronomy. He certainly knew Greek and Latin. It seems likely, therefore, that his sons, including Hans, were educated as youths.[7]

Dryander places Staden's father in Homberg, the town Hans Staden claimed as his home. There are few archival records linking the Staden family name to that city, but a certain Gernand Staden appears in the tax rolls of Homberg as someone who had moved to the area in 1528—this is likely Hans's father.[8]

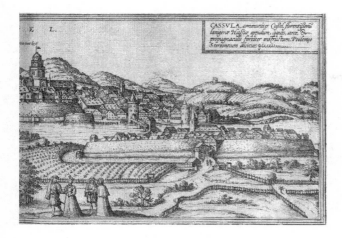

Gernand's travels from town to town may have been related to his marriage prospects. Gernand probably married a widow in Homberg. This would explain the lack of an established record for him there, since any documents connected to his family would have been linked with his wife, and not with him, if he had come from outside the town. As a widow, the future Frau Staden, unlike unmarried or married women, would have had control of her own property. She may not have been old, for widowhood was a fact of life in early modern Germany. Spouses commonly lost their partners after short marriages, and nearly half of children died before the age of ten. Every second adult lost a spouse before ten years of marriage had passed. Mortality from outbreaks of smallpox, dysentery, influenza, and the plague was high in sixteenth-century Europe. If not threatened by illness, individuals also faced threats from disruption caused by war, harvest failures, accidents, and poor weather.[9]

Although the Stadens were townspeople, they did not stay in Homberg, even though Hans identified himself as a native son. This explains the lack of records linking the family to that town. Gernand and his family—perhaps even Hans himself—moved to Korbach in 1551, or even earlier. A Gernand Staden became a citizen of Korbach in 1551 (according to the citizens' roll), and a certain Joseph Staden, who also became a citizen, listed Homberg as his birthplace. Joseph must be Hans's brother. Citizenship, or *Bürgerrecht,* was a privilege that one acquired through inheritance or by outright purchase, and the citizens' rolls listed those people in the town or city claiming such status. As a citizen, one enjoyed the protection of the town or city and could exercise a trade or engage in commerce. Once purchased, the rights of citizenship passed on to all legitimate heirs.[10]

Growing up in Hessian towns, Hans Staden experienced a childhood different from that of most Europeans, who were born into peasant families living on the land. In towns, social life was more complex and stratified. While the household served as the main economic, social, and cultural unit both for peasants and urban dwellers, the artisan's shop and the marketplace distinguished life in the city from that of the countryside. Towns were places where craftsmen produced finished products and sold them at markets. Urban households were more reliant on professional producers for their daily needs than peasants were. Even if city dwellers could grow some of their own food or make some of their own clothes, their jobs as retailers or artisans meant that they had little time to spare. Peasant families wove and spun cloth, raised cattle, dipped candles, baked bread, and made butter and cheese; while urban families bought these products at the butcher's, baker's, or grocer's shops or stalls in town.[11]

Towns—even poor towns like the Hessian towns the Stadens lived in—were places of increasing specialization and exchange in the sixteenth century. Merchants, traveling from town to town, offered outside goods for sale, thereby bringing complex systems of trade to very remote locations. "By the sixteenth century," historian Alison Rowlands writes, "these markets had become the focal points of local, regional, or long-distance trade, ensuring that commercial exchange was a town's defining feature." It would have been in the markets of Homberg and Korbach where Hans was first introduced to the world beyond Hesse. There he would have seen merchants arriving and leaving, and he likely first heard tales of the riches of India.[12]

Many of those living in towns and cities belonged to craft households, producing foodstuffs, tools, leather, and other products. We can assume that Gernand carried out a trade and that he did so in Wetter, Homberg, and Korbach, moving from place to place in search of work. We can also assume that since his son, Joseph, was listed in the town's rolls, he too was a craftsman. Dryander asserts Hans to be trustworthy because "he, along with his parents, comes from this country, and he does not wander around from one country to the next in a gypsy-like fashion, as do vagabonds and liars." We can suppose, therefore, that Dryander thought moving from place to place within Hesse to carry out a trade fell within the confines of "respectable" behavior.[13]

Korbach, where the Stadens seem to have remained to ply their trade, had more direct ties to the sea than the other towns in landlocked Hesse. Korbach, lying 40 kilometers west of Kassel, was a member of the Hanseatic League, an organization of merchants and cities engaged in foreign trade. The larger cities of the League, such as Bremen and Luebeck, were involved with trade along the North Sea. Starting in the fourteenth century, the Hanseatic League began to intensify its trade with Portugal. Ships left the ports of Danzig, Riga, Reval, Bremen, and Hamburg filled with grain and wood to exchange for salt, wine, fruits, and cork in Lisbon. Portuguese salt, from ports such as Setúbal, was not cheaper than salt produced in western France, but it was of much higher quality and thus prized by merchants and customers in Germany.[14]

From the sixteenth century onward, the markets of the Hessian towns would have had spices from the East Indies available for sale all year long. Perhaps it was through spices that Staden was first exposed to the idea of India. Prized by the affluent, spices were luxury goods with medicinal, culinary, cosmetic, and ritual uses. Dried spices (in contrast to herbs, which were used fresh and had little value) came to Germany by land and sea routes from India and remote islands in south Asia. They were expensive, ostentatious, and fashionable displays of wealth. Nutmegs, cloves, cinnamon, black pepper, ginger, and saffron flavored the cooked dishes of the elite, not to cover up the taste or smell of rotting meat (other processes such as salting and pickling were much more effective ways), but rather to proclaim the status of the family who used and consumed them. Spices were certainly part of the lure of India: expensive, mysterious, precious, and increasingly available, they were markers of wealth in the towns in which Staden lived.[15]

Other signs of status also came from India, for the sea trade had made the goods of India, once out of reach to all but the exalted few, accessible to many more. Luxurious fabrics, exotic animals, and new styles of jewelry created by combining gold and gems with new materials, such as mother-of-pearl, rhinoceros horn, and tortoise shell, gradually made their way into European ports, cities, and towns. The fantastic animals brought back from India on Portuguese ships, at first completely exotic, gradually became familiar. The animals from India were especially legendary.[16]

King Manuel of Portugal's embassy to the new pope, Leo X, in 1514 makes clear the power of exotic animals to impress. The embassy delegation sent to Rome was carefully orchestrated to enhance Manuel's traditional gifts of rare textiles, gems, altar ornaments, and richly embroidered vestments encrusted with jewels. The Portuguese delegation arrived in a highly scripted procession with a white elephant with ginger-colored hair, trained to do tricks, accompanied by a cheetah, two leopards, parrots, rare dogs, and a Persian horse. The elephant had left India on the monsoon of 1511, and sometime that summer it reached Lisbon. Two years later, after the new pope had been elected in 1513, King Manuel dispatched his elaborate delegation. Everywhere along the way the elephant caused a sensation, and crowds trampled fields, pushed through fences, and caused roofs and walls to collapse—all to catch a glimpse of it. Once in Rome, the elephant became a favorite of the pope.

Two years later, King Manuel attempted to surpass this feat by sending a rhinoceros. The rhinoceros had been given to the Portuguese governor in India by the sultan of Gujarat, and the governor, in turn, sent it to his king. Surviving the long voyage to Lisbon, the rhino unfortunately did not make it to Rome. When the ship en route to Rome sank in the Mediterranean, the rhino drowned along with the rest of the crew. The carcass was recovered, however, and the king ordered it skinned, stuffed with straw, and mounted. Even dead, the rhino was still deemed exotic enough to be presented to the pope.[17]

Stories of these unique animals spread, and as they captured the attention of artists, they became even more familiar. Parrots, not seen in Europe since Roman times, now regularly arrived on ships, as did wild cats—leopards, lions, and cheetahs. Albrecht Dürer incorporated parrots and monkeys into his woodcuts and drawings; his famous woodcut of Adam and Eve (1504) features a parrot drawn so closely to life that it can be identified as a Ring-necked Parakeet from Asia. Dürer's famous woodcut of a rhinoceros (1515) is based on a sketch of the animal made by a colleague in Lisbon before the animal left on its ill-fated journey for Rome.[18]

The luxuries of India became things to own, display, and study, even by ordinary people in German towns. Central European princes and scholars began to collect all manner of novelties, organizing them into cabinets of curiosities, known as *Kunstkammern*. These cabinets are the precursors to modern museums and laboratories. Animals once so unique that only the king of Portugal could use them in processions to burnish his royal image began to appear in zoological gardens in Europe and in affordable naturalistic prints that could be purchased, while parrots had become common enough to own as pets.[19]

The Staden household likely contained images of such exotic creatures, if not the animals themselves. Woodcut images of monkeys, lions, parrots, and peacocks adorned playing cards, which were to be found in the houses of townspeople, as historian Laura Smoller has shown. Resilient even in the face of Protestant bans on gambling, card playing was an important part of everyday life in Germany. Exotic beasts had filtered down into popular culture to such an extent that we can imagine some members of the Staden family using cards decorated with parrots.[20]

The foreign, therefore, was becoming familiar to the townspeople of land-locked Hesse. Spices from India and images of exotic animals appeared on the tables of the learned and the low-born alike. These products may have been alluring, and they signified the existence of a wider world beyond the confines of Homburg, Korbach, Hesse, or even the Holy Roman Empire. Were they enough to entice a young man to go to sea?

A lack of opportunity may have propelled Staden to leave the towns of Hesse. If Joseph Staden, who appears in the citizens' roll of Korbach, was the older son who stood to inherit his father's property, that left Hans to look to other opportunities to earn his livelihood. Given that he was later hired in Lisbon as a *Büchsenschütz,* which means a shooter of guns (from *Büchse,* "box; rifle," and *Schütze,* "marksman"), it seems that Hans Staden's chosen profession was soldiering. Marching off to war meant that Staden had already left home before he later set out to sea, and this experience might also have had something to do with why Staden left home again in 1547. By becoming a soldier, Staden left the landscape of Hessian towns behind him, entering more directly into the worlds of politics and religion, areas of increasing conflict in sixteenth-century Germany.

As residents in territorial cities, citizens had a great deal of control over their own affairs (and enjoyed freedoms in the city that peasants living on the land did not possess). Yet the citizens of Hessian towns were ultimately answerable to their territorial lord, the landgrave (or ruler). Landgrave Philipp, to whom Staden later dedicates his book and whom he acknowledges as "my gracious Prince and Master," had faced particular challenges in consolidating his rule over Hesse and therefore was in need of soldiers.[21]

Landgrave Philipp (1509–67) "the Magnanimous," as he came to be known, had a difficult early life. His father William II died of syphilis when he was only five, and a long struggle ensued over who would take over the regency for the young boy and whether the family could hold on to the disparate lands that William had brought together through both diplomacy and skill on the battlefield. Philipp's mother ruled on his behalf until he was thirteen, when the emperor declared him to be of age. Once a ruling prince, Philipp wasted no time: he proved himself in battle, subdued the nobles who were competing for power in the kingdom, and consolidated his territorial gains.[22]

Landgrave Philipp initially needed an army to defend himself against upstart nobles, but he later came to rely on troops in a religious war against his own lord and master, the Holy Roman emperor, Charles V. A Habsburg, Charles inherited kingdoms and city-states in Europe, such as Burgundy, Austria, Tyrol, parts of southern Germany, Sicily, Sardinia, Naples, and, most importantly, Spain. In 1519 he was elected Holy Roman emperor. As the most powerful monarch in Europe, Charles believed that it was his God-given duty to lead Christian Europe against the growing power of the Muslim Turks of the Ottoman Empire. Charles V saw Luther and the movement for reform within the church as an internal threat that needed to be subdued.[23]

As Staden was growing up, Hesse was becoming a center of Protestantism and the locus for some of the first battles in the religious wars that soon engulfed all of Germany during the Reformation. Homberg, Staden's declared home, was the location for an early Protestant synod, while Hesse in general was one of the first places where the established state church followed Protestant teachings. Philipp's acceptance of Lutheran ideas assisted him in bringing Hesse under his control. As the first major principality to introduce the Reformation within its borders, Hesse became a model for other territories; changes to beliefs were accompanied by a seizure of church property and the establishment of state-sponsored sites of learning. Scholars have argued about whether Philipp's embracing of Lutheran ideas was simply a way to increase his own power and authority or an expression of true faith. He was acutely aware of the power of religion to pacify princely subjects. As he wrote to his envoys in 1526, "Nothing will help hold all subjects in peace, unity, and obedience [more than] to have the holy gospel preached to the people, clearly and purely, and to provide the subjects with pious, godfearing, learned preachers." As an early follower of Martin Luther, he soon joined forces with the imperial cities within the empire to unite against the forces of the emperor, Charles V. Philipp's Schmalkaldic League was a defensive alliance of Protestant territories in Germany.[24]

It seems likely that Staden acquired his knowledge of guns fighting as a soldier for Landgrave Philipp of Hesse in the Schmalkaldic War, one of the religious wars that consumed Germany during the Reformation. Armies were growing in size in the sixteenth century across Europe, soldiering was becoming a profession, and towns and villages were often engulfed in larger conflicts. In Staden's childhood the German Peasants' War (1524–26) swept through towns and villages before it was finally suppressed. The Ottoman Turks under Suleiman the Magnificent (1520–66) laid siege to Vienna twice. As historian Steven Gunn writes, during this period, the scale and rules of war were changing from the practices of the medieval period. Charles V possibly had as many as 150,000 soldiers in his pay in 1555. Cannon and arquebuses (muskets) were becoming the norm on sixteenth-century battlefields, and as a result, mercenaries had become "indispensible for serious warfare because of their mastery of the new weapons and of the drill necessary to coordinate pikes and arquebuses against hostile cavalry."[25]

The German lands in the center of Europe were often battlefields, and German woodcut prints from the period frequently depict battle scenes and soldiers in action. So common was the "siege-piece" print that it became a distinguishable genre of woodcut and even, according to art historian J. R. Hale, "a cliché-ridden one." Produced for urban audiences, the siege-piece also served to distribute news. Erhard Schoen's three-block print of the Siege of Münster (1535), for example, is an

Figure 4. A Lansquenet with Harquebus. Woodcut by Erhard Schoen. In Walter Strauss, *The Illustrated Bartsch*, XIII: 383. Reproduced with permission of Abaris Books, Norwalk, Connecticut. Location of original woodcut unknown.

elaborate panorama that shows burning buildings, advancing armies of pikemen, smoking guns, and the wounded being carried away on stretchers. A legend under the scene carries the news, reading in part: "A great many nobles and other soldiers on both sides fell; as we can honestly say, nearly three thousand men were left dead on the field."[26]

Landgrave Philipp led the final attack against the German city of Münster. The radicalism of the city, which had expelled its bishop and had become an Anabaptist encampment led by a prophetic leader, John of Leiden, had become threatening to Protestant and Catholic leaders alike. In a subsequent version of the Siege of

Münster, a seven-block print that took the form of a long strip, Schoen shows in striking detail the soldiers at work during the siege (firing the canons, standing at attention, and marching in formation) as well as at leisure (cooking their food, drinking, and throwing dice).[27]

Soldiers, known as *Landsknechte* (lansquenets) in Germany, became the subjects of an innovative genre of drawings and prints in the early sixteenth century. German and Swiss artists project a fascination with the lives of soldiers—their costumes; their weaponry; their temptations to drink, gambling, and sexual encounters; their flirtation with death. Artists used the soldier's life to express a variety of moral views, and their interest in soldiers lay partially with their otherness, the sense that soldiers were necessary but frightening figures. When the novelty of drawing the soldiers wore off for the artists, printers ran off newssheets and illustrations that fell somewhere between art and illustration. Schoen's depiction of a *Büchsenschütz* (see fig. 4) shows a man armed with a sword attached at his waist and an arquebus resting on his shoulder. The woodcut image is stylized with several common features found in the depiction of lansquenets in woodcuts, such as the slit breeches and sleeves (suggestive of swordplay) and the plume curling down from the headpiece.[28]

The soldier is shown with his right hand extended and his eyes following his hand, as if he were speaking on a stage. And in fact, the woodcut includes a ten-line verse that gives voice to this generic soldier, highlighting his moral laxity, free-wheeling nature, and potential dangerousness:

> I'm a "Büchsenschütz" so free
> And have shot gunpowder aplenty
> And I haven't too far strayed
> At dice and cards I have played
> The suffering I've endured has been great
> The better to leave the ladies of late
> I've moved from Brabant
> From Sweden into England
> And I don't have a ruler anymore
> I think something's missing in war.[29]

Possibly, Staden was a reluctant soldier taken in by the promises of recruiters. Or perhaps he was a soldier fighting for a religious cause. However he became a soldier, if we compare the chronology of Staden's departure from Hesse with the fate of Landgrave Philipp, it does seem most probable that Staden practiced the art of war while fighting on behalf of the Schmalkaldic League.

The Schmalkaldic War was closely connected to the famous Council of Trent, summoned in 1544 by Pope Paul III. Convened in large measure to deal with the threat that the spread of Protestantism posed to the established church, the council began meeting in 1545. Through long debate and compromise, the delegates began to hammer out the Roman Catholic Church's response to Martin Luther, among other key rulings on the foundational principles of Christian faith. As the Council met, Charles V took advantage of the moment and banned two German princes, one of whom was Landgrave Philipp of Hesse. The Schmalkaldic War then broke out and was fought in 1546–47. While the Schmalkaldic League initially held an advantage, by January of 1547 the tide had turned against the German Protestants. At Mühlberg, Charles V defeated the Protestant princes in the spring of 1547. Since a decisive victory in sixteenth-century wars required the capture or killing of the enemy ruler, Landgrave Philipp of Hesse subsequently became Charles's prisoner in the Netherlands.[30]

Staden places himself in Bremen in the spring of 1547. Bremen was one of the members of the Schmalkaldic League and one of the last to submit to Charles V. At this time, the fortunes of the Protestant forces looked bleak, but Charles had not yet sealed his decisive victory over Philipp. From Bremen, Staden followed the Weser River to the North Sea and then to Holland, where he boarded a salt ship and, after four weeks at sea, arrived in Setúbal, Portugal, on April 29, 1547 (fig. 5). This means that he would have left Bremen at the beginning of April or at the end of March just before Charles V's defeat of the Protestant princes at Mühlberg on April 24, 1547.

Had Staden deserted? Was he fleeing for his life? Or perhaps he was in debt? Wanted for a crime? Leaving behind a woman? His religious faith shattered by his prince's demoralizing losses? Is one of these the reason he "wished" to sail to India? Whatever his motivation, it cannot have been a simple choice. To go to sea in the sixteenth century was even more dangerous than serving as a soldier in Germany. It made the soldier even more of an outsider as he left his homeland. Perhaps Staden did dream of making his fortune in India, the place from whence came spices, jewels, and other luxuries he had seen in the fairs of the Hanseatic towns or possibly in the homes of the wealthy citizens of Hesse. Whether fueled by a desire for adventure or by a lack of opportunity, or fleeing because he was in danger, this urge to the sea would fundamentally mark him as different if and when he ever returned. Yet he was not alone. The regular crossing of oceans had opened opportunities for trade, economic ventures, military expansion, and evangelism that lured men and some women to sea.

These sea travelers became the physical go-betweens who linked islands, coastlines, forests, swamps, mountains, deserts, and the peoples who inhabited them

Figure 5. Staden Leaves Hesse

into an ever more integrated world. Physical go-betweens were the sailors and crew members of ships that carried gold, slaves, and ivory from trading posts in Africa; or the gems, silks, and spices from India; or the sugar grown and milled on islands in the Atlantic, to ports in Europe. In remote anchorages or in open markets, individuals captured or purchased as slaves also became physical go-betweens as they were transported long distances locked in chains on deck or held in the dark, dank hold below. Colonists, some forced, others freely embracing the role, embarked on ships, thereby becoming physical go-betweens bound for new locations, carrying guns, clothes, seeds, animals. All of these men and women, serving as physical go-betweens, spun the web of an emerging new maritime world, and Hans Staden was about to become one of them.

If we don't know why he left, we do know how: he boarded a ship headed to Portugal to pick up a cargo of salt. The salt trade between Portuguese ports such as Setúbal and northern European ports was an old one, and there was nothing unusual about this voyage. What Staden did on board—whether he was a passenger, a gunner, or an ordinary sailor—is unknown. However, this experience at sea, presumably his first, taught him enough so that he was confident that he might acquire a place on a ship headed for India. Arriving in Setúbal at the end of April 1547, Staden abandoned the salt ship and set his sights on Lisbon (fig. 6), the gateway to India.

The city of Lisbon lay on seven steep hills that sloped down to the Tejo River, which flowed directly into the Atlantic Ocean. The primary port of the kingdom of Portugal, the westernmost kingdom of Western Europe, Lisbon was at that time home to the most advanced knowledge and technology in seafaring. The city's population was estimated in 1551 at 100,000, and according to that estimate over a thousand men worked directly as seafarers—as sailors, pilots, and masters of ships. The city was crowded with merchants, sailors, free blacks, and slaves; and it pulsed with novelties, not just from India but from Africa, Asia, and, increasingly, from Brazil. More than seven hundred ships left Lisbon for India in the sixteenth century, and most were largely financed by the Portuguese crown. The trade with India upgraded the image of Lisbon in Western Europe; no longer the port of a peripheral Iberian kingdom, it had become famous as a city that rivaled Rome, Venice, Paris, and Cairo.[31]

The caravels, carracks, and galleons returning from the Atlantic Islands, Africa, Brazil, India, and the Spice Islands turned into the Tejo and sailed triumphantly up the river to anchor by the Casa da India. There they lay until all merchandise was received, inventoried, taxed, stored, and sold. The quantities and diversity of the spices unloaded—peppers and ginger from the Malabar coast of India, cloves from the Moluccas, cinnamon from Sri Lanka, mace and nutmeg from the Banda Islands of Indonesia, and sealing wax from Sumatra—must have been remarkable. So, too, would have been the sight of the heavy, sticky *caixas* (boxes) of sugar lifted from the holds of the ships returning from Madeira, São Tomé, and Brazil.[32]

What did Staden think of the nearly ten thousand slaves who lived in Lisbon, comprising approximately 10 percent of the city's population? What emotions did he feel when he saw slaves unloaded from ships? He could not have failed to see such sights, for on average 5,500 slaves arrived from Africa each year between 1510 and 1550. Men, women, and children from Arguim, Benin, Kongo, and Angola came ashore in chains, but they were not alone. It is likely that Staden also saw

Figure 6. The City of Lisbon. From Georg Braun, *Civitates orbis terrarum.* Antwerp: 1575. Courtesy of the John Carter Brown Library at Brown University.

men, women, and children from Brazil and possibly even Asia who were also forcibly brought by sea to Lisbon to be sold as slaves.[33]

The maritime trade in slaves had its beginnings in the Portuguese trade with West Africa in the 1450s and was very well established by the time Staden arrived in Lisbon. Few questioned the morality or the legality of the slave trade. As historian Ivana Elbl has shown, the Portuguese crown was a significant investor. The slave trade was, however, in the midst of a shift that would affect millions of Africans over the next three hundred years. Whereas the Portuguese had first transported slaves from West Africa to Lisbon and subsequently from Benin, Kongo, and Angola to the trading post at São Jorge da Mina in West Africa, by the middle of the sixteenth century slave traders were transporting slaves across the Atlantic. Some of these slaves were headed for the Spanish colonies of the Caribbean, Mexico, and Peru; others were destined for Brazil. While the morality and legality of the enslavement of indigenous peoples in the Americas was being questioned vigorously in Spain by Bartolomé de las Casas, the enslavement of Africans was increasingly viewed as acceptable. The trans-Atlantic slave trade that would become one of the most infamous characteristics of the emerging Atlantic world was taking its shape before Staden's eyes.[34]

Royal officials handled the trade in gold, diamonds, pearls, rubies, emeralds, and other precious stones with strict rules, and Staden was not privy to these secrets. Gold from the West African trading post at São Jorge da Mina entered Lisbon with the utmost of supervision. According to historian John Vogt, returning caravels from Mina were met by royal officials who questioned each member of the crew to make sure that all royal regulations had been followed and that there had been no illegal smuggling of gold. The captain was responsible for the locked chest of gold that typically contained gold weighing between 46 and 57.5 kilograms with the purity of 22⅛ carats. Lisbon's source of West African gold led to the striking of a new coin: the golden cross, or *cruzado de ouro*. Intended to be equivalent to the Venetian ducat, it symbolized not only the new wealth of the Portuguese but their desire to surpass even the merchants of Venice.[35]

The magnificent Rua Nova dos Mercadores, a street more than 300 yards long and about 10 yards wide, showcased the wares of merchants in the more than forty houses, each three or four stories high, that adjoined each other. Walking down this street, Staden would have brushed elbows with merchants and people from all over the world, and he would have seen for sale in the ground-level shops the silks and porcelains from China, the cottons from India, the stoneware from Burma, the sandalwood of Timor, and the elaborate new kinds of furniture such as chests and caskets inlaid with ivory and desks, chairs, and cabinets crafted from teak and ebony that arrived from India. Perhaps Staden marveled at the exotic goods that African, Indian, and Chinese artisans were, by the time he was in Lisbon, producing for an emerging European market by combining indigenous materials and techniques with European religious or utilitarian needs. For example, an export trade in ivory spoons, forks, knives, saltcellars, and hunting horns flourished in Sierra Leone and Benin, while in Sri Lanka artisans specialized in carved ivory caskets that transformed the Portuguese traveling trunk into a luxury item.[36]

These were all fabulous things, but the route to India was long and dangerous. Pilots and captains on the India run in the mid-sixteenth century first set course for the once densely forested lava gorges of the Madeira Islands then planted with sugar cane. Bypassing the Canary Islands, which Spain claimed, and leaving them to the east, the helmsman steered for the Cape Verde Islands, twelve hundred miles farther south southwest. Here they would re-provision and set out to sea again, seeking the trade winds that would carry the ship west, deep into the Atlantic, almost to the coast of Brazil. There was no need to call along the coast of West Africa as scores of Portuguese captains had done since the middle of the fifteenth century when they named every major port, bay, cape, and river. These places—Cabo da Bojador, Rio de Oro, Arguim, Guinea, São Jorge da Mina—were well known to sailors who specialized in the African trade. The most important ports were *feitorias*, fortified trading posts, where the Portuguese first challenged Muslim merchants for the gold of West Africa. Although land-based Muslim merchants had supplied the West African kingdoms for several centuries by developing profitable caravan routes to carry trading goods across the immense distances of the Sahara in exchange for the gold of Guinea, now Western European merchants competed for this trade by nosing their ships packed with trading cargo into ports along the West African coast. The jewel of the Portuguese trade was São Jorge da Mina, built in 1482 to facilitate the exchange of West African gold for Mediterranean goods.

The ships on the India run also bypassed Sierra Leone and Benin in the Bight of Benin, as well as the islands of Príncipe and São Tomé, due south of the Niger River delta and just above the Equator. On these islands, colonists had invested in sugar plantations and become the first to conduct the trans-Atlantic slave trade. A ship en route to India would not call here, however, unless bad weather or the need for repairs required such a stop. Nor did a ship on the India run intend to call at the ports farther south, along the coasts of the kingdoms of Angola and Kongo, where slave traders of São Tomé and Príncipe loaded boatload after boatload of slaves headed for São Jorge da Mina, Lisbon, and, increasingly, across the Atlantic to the Caribbean and Brazil.

Instead, the ships headed to India plowed deeply west before swinging south and later east to round the Cape of Good Hope. The cape, where the Atlantic Ocean conjoined the Indian Ocean, was a perilous place that few pilots besides those of the Portuguese fleets knew well. Two currents converged there: the icy cold Bengala Current, which flowed north from Antarctica and up the west coast of South Africa, and the warm Agulhas Current, which flowed southwest along the eastern South African coast. Beyond the granite and sandstone cliffs of the Cape of Good Hope, pilots gave the east coast a wide berth to avoid sailing against the treacherous Agulhas Current. Reaching Mozambique, Portuguese captains could relax, even though they had entered the range of powerful Muslim princes and wealthy traders, who for centuries had linked East Africa with India, the Middle East, and China. This western edge of the Indian Ocean world was well known to sailors, however, for Indian, Chinese, and Arabian merchants had long traded here, linking the towns and cities of what is today Tanzania, Kenya, and Somalia into an Indian Ocean world. The Portuguese learned from African, Middle Eastern, and Indian sailors how to navigate to India: from Somalia, turning east, India was 2,000 miles, a distance made smaller and more predictable by the cycle of winds known as the monsoons. Beyond India lay Burma, Malaysia, Indonesia, the Spice Islands, China, and eventually Japan.

The India that Staden dreamed of seeing, then, required a long voyage that would log thousands of miles and require months at sea. The dangerous voyage out was followed by an equally hazardous return that could begin only after the winds changed with the January monsoon. Even though the Portuguese had half a century's experience with the India route by the time Staden reached Lisbon, the return

voyage, when ships were overloaded with valuable cargo, was especially treacherous. Disaster could strike with deadly results.

After arriving in Lisbon, Staden, who did not yet speak Portuguese (but would
pick it up on his voyages), found an inn frequented by Germans and run by a German by the name of Leuhr. With the help of Leuhr, Staden hoped to sign on to a
voyage to India. Through the inn, Staden temporarily gained entrance into the
well-established German "colony" in Lisbon that dated from the fifteenth century.
Germans had long been impressed with Lisbon's trade; for example, the Nuremberg physician and humanist Dr. Hieronymus Münzer (1437–1508) published an
account of a trip he made in Portugal in 1494–95, in which he described the many
slaves he saw in Lisbon, the shipments of gold from Africa, the prosperous homes
of Jewish and Flemish merchants in Lisbon, and the "*lucrum incredibile,*" or unbe-
lievable profits, that King João II brought in from overseas trade.[37]

Most Germans lived in the traditional trading center of Lisbon, between the
Rossio and the Terreiro do Paço, the two main squares of the city that lay right
behind the shipyards and docks. Their "factories," or trading houses, consisted
of a building with apartments and storage rooms and generally included space
for accountants, assistants, and the "factor," or head merchant. Germans in Lisbon had their own chapels where they held services and where soldiers and seafarers were buried. The most prominent was the Bartholomew Chapel, and a
second chapel, the St. Sebastian Chapel, began to hold services in the sixteenth
century.[38]

Granted special privileges by the Portuguese monarch, German tradesmen,
blacksmiths, carpetmakers, shoemakers, glassmakers, soldiers, and gunners flourished in the city. Their personal property was guaranteed by the Crown, they were
free from all taxes, and they did not have to serve in the military.[39]

This German community prospered in Lisbon because the Portuguese crown
was unable to exploit all of the opportunities presented by India. When Vasco da
Gama arrived in 1498, India had a rich and thriving trade open to merchants from
all over, and subsequently, the Portuguese crown sought European financiers to
invest in the new prospects. The Portuguese traded their expertise at sea—for they
were the only Europeans who had successfully sailed to India—while wealthy merchants from outside Portugal supplied capital. Florentine bankers, some of whom
outfitted and sailed ships directly from Lisbon to India, sought access to the spice
trade; Germans, on the other hand, were interested in the trade in precious stones—
diamonds, pearls, emeralds, and rubies—as well as spices. The famous German
banking family known as the Fuggers became involved in the India trade by sup-
plying the copper from their mines in Tyrol and Schwaz, Hungary, which was

needed to exchange for spices in India. The connection between German financiers and the Portuguese crown was longstanding and mutually beneficial.[40]

Staden's wish to see India did not come true. Perhaps it was an accident of fate,
for he arrived too late to join the armada sailing for India in 1547. The fleet for India
typically departed Lisbon in March or early April in order to catch the summer
monsoon off the coast of East Africa, and Staden had arrived in Lisbon in early
May, a few weeks too late.[41]

Was missing the chance to sign on to the India fleet a bitter pill to swallow? Staden
could have waited for the next sailing, perhaps finding work in Lisbon through the
German community. Instead, he looked for another opportunity to go to sea immediately, and through Leuhr, his German innkeeper, he was able to gain employment on another ship, this one headed for Brazil. In settling for the Atlantic over
India, Staden was not alone. Portugal may have monopolized the sea route to
India, but there were other opportunities for trade in the Atlantic in the sixteenth
century that demanded far less initial investment. The Atlantic was far easier to
navigate, and on its islands and mainlands less exotic but still valuable spices, such
as sugar or later tobacco, could be cultivated; semi-precious jewels, such as pearls,
could be traded for; and dye-producing woods had already found a ready market
in the European textile cottage industry. Traces of raw bullion—gold and gold
dust—were found almost immediately by Spaniards in the streams of the Caribbean islands; silver began to be systematically mined in Mexico and Peru by the
middle of the sixteenth century.

Supposing Staden had been willing to wait a year for the next armada, or if he
had arrived in time, in February or March, may we assume that he would have
found a place on a ship on the India run? He was, after all, not a sailor, not a merchant, and not even Portuguese. Most likely, he would have. Men and ships were
invariably in short supply in Portugal, given the huge demands of the India trade
and the small size of the Portuguese population. It has been estimated that approximately 2,400 people left Portugal each year, and few of them returned. This
was a considerable annual drain, making it likely that ship captains hired whom-
ever they could find to work their ships. As the Portuguese began to extend their
overseas expeditions, they began to depend ever more on the service of foreign soldiers, especially artillerists, known as *bombardeiros,* or gunners, and men such as
Staden, who were called *espingardeiros* (musketeers) in Portuguese. The Portuguese
king even granted foreign soldiers who served on behalf of the Portuguese pensions
(*tenças*). German *bombardeiros* also had special privileges: they could carry weapons at all times, their possessions were protected, and their housing was provided
free of cost. Likewise, in Spain, Spanish sea captains often resorted to hiring

foreign—German, Flemish, and Italian—gunners in the sixteenth century, and thus the ease with which Staden gained employment is probably not unusual, even in Portugal. Staden's experience in war caught a certain Captain Penteado's eye, and Staden was hired as a gunner.[42]

Who might have been on board Penteado's ship, sharing quarters with Staden? Why did men, and a few women, go to sea in the sixteenth century? Most made the choice, not from a desire for adventure, but from a sense of desperation. These were men and boys from port cities in Spain or Portugal or from poor peasant families needing the income that signing onto a ship's crew brought an impoverished family. Seafarers held low status in the Iberian world, and even in Portugal only a few pilots and shipmasters were granted privileges, patents of nobility, or induction as knights into the prestigious military Orders of Christ, Santiago, and Avis.[43]

Others on board, perhaps even the majority, were penal exiles. Captain Penteado's ship carried these *degredados,* "degraded" persons, as forced colonists to a Portuguese colony in Pernambuco led by Duarte Coelho. Penal exiles had been used by Portuguese sea captains since the Portuguese began to explore, map, and trade with West Africa and to colonize the Atlantic islands of Madeira, the Azores, and Cape Verde in the fifteenth century. Criminal exiles were used in dangerous situations, as surety, and they were deliberately left ashore so that they would learn local languages and become future translators. By this time, however, *degredados* were more commonly used as forced colonists.[44]

Women who went to sea often were penal exiles, colonists, and occasionally wives and daughters of royal officials. In general, professional seafarers were men, while women were more likely to be passengers for one or two voyages.

Other men who went to sea, not as laborers on deck, but as soldiers, crown officials, or military commanders, had aspirations of glory, grandeur, or fabulous wealth. Men from humble origins sought positions of prominence through their service to the Portuguese crown in Asia, Africa, or Brazil, or to the Spanish crown in America; while men from established families hoped to emulate the deeds of forebears who had been knights and servants of the Crown, as told in family stories of the lower aristocracy of Spain and Portugal.[45]

Staden fell between the extremes. In some ways he would have been like the vast majority of those who signed onto the ships of the sixteenth century: life at sea offered an opportunity. On the other hand, as an *espingardeiro,* Staden was a step up from the ordinary sailor. Staden may have made the move to a *bombardeiro* on board the ship, and if so, as a *bombardeiro* he earned the equivalent of the ship's barber, purser, or bailiff. A *bombardeiro* was expected to know how to prepare gunpowder, to load, and to fire the mounted guns effectively in battles at sea, as well as how to maintain them in the difficult shipboard environment. Possibly, Staden had aspirations of being rewarded for services rendered to the king of Portugal. Two other Germans—one, like Staden, from Hesse—were hired by Captain Penteado.[46]

Captain Penteado seems to have been an experienced captain, well steeped in the long tradition of seafaring in Portugal. Beginning in the fifteenth century, royal patronage had encouraged Lisbon's captains, navigators, pilots, and merchants to sail west in the "Mar Pequeña"—that part of the Atlantic ocean that included the Madeira, the Azores, and the Canary Islands—as well as south along the coast of West Africa. Sailing in these Atlantic waters, the Portuguese developed their knowledge of mapping (based largely on Catalan and other Mediterranean sea log and mapping traditions), setting and following courses using charts and the compass, and eventually understanding the patterns of winds and currents. Mastering the "Little Wheel," or the system of currents that connected Iberia, the Atlantic Islands, and the West African coasts, allowed systematic trading with West Africa to begin. As the Portuguese gradually pressed farther south toward the Equator, they made modifications in their system of navigation. While in the northern hemisphere, the Portuguese took measurements of the North Star, using the wooden quadrant or the cross staff to determine their latitude. In the southern hemisphere, where the North Star is not visible, the astrolabe, which took a measurement of the sun at midday, was developed to calculate latitudes.[47]

These innovations in navigation, along with others in ship and sail design and more accurate maps, underlay the Portuguese dominance of the South Atlantic and the India route. Yet hard on the heels of the Portuguese came Spanish, Genoese, French, and English sailors, who used the spreading knowledge of seafaring to trade in the south Atlantic. Increasingly, Spanish and French commercial and political interests challenged the Portuguese in Brazil as well as in West Africa. In 1547, Portugal still retained only a tenuous hold over the lands it claimed by virtue of Pedro Álvares Cabral's landing along the coast of Brazil in 1500. Voyages to and from Brazil were contested, and captains needed gunners to protect their cargoes and passengers.

Portugal's rivals in Brazil at this time were France and Spain. Spain argued that southern Brazil lay within the agreed-upon Spanish sphere set out by the Treaty of Tordesillas. Portugal and Spain signed the Treaty of Tordesillas in 1494, two years following Columbus's first voyage, in order to divide the "ocean sea" into separate spheres: one to the west for Spain, and the other to the east for Portugal. The treaty drew a meridian in the Atlantic approximately 2,300 kilometers west of the Cape Verde Islands. The French king, however, refused to accept the underlying principle of the treaty—that the sea could be owned.[48]

Penteado likely had permission from the Portuguese crown to assail any French ships he met, especially in Pernambuco, the most successful Portuguese colony in Brazil. French sea captains from the northern ports of Honfleur, Dieppe, Rouen, and Le Havre had logged thousands of nautical miles and were savvy traders in Brazil. Since the early sixteenth century, the French had actively trafficked in Brazil; during the reign of François I (1515–47), French ships attacked the Portuguese trading fort in Pernambuco in 1531 and held it briefly. In 1540, twenty-four French ships are known to have sailed for Brazil; while in 1546, the year before Staden arrived in Lisbon, twenty-eight ships had left the French port of Le Havre headed for Brazil.[49]

Sometime in July of 1547, Penteado's ship and a smaller caravel weighed anchor, leaving the Castelo do Belem to starboard, and entered the Atlantic just south of Cabo da Roca, the westernmost promontory of Europe, heading south and west for Madeira. Staden was now truly at sea, and the ship had become his new home. How did he feel? What did he think lay ahead?

Penteado's ship would have been a complex social environment. Then as now, each ship was simultaneously a floating village with elaborate social hierarchies, a warehouse stocked with valuable trading goods, and a powerful weapon of war. Ships of the sixteenth century represented an impressive integration of the latest technology of the day. As Spanish historian Pablo Pérez-Mallaína has written, each ship brought together within its hull "a substantial part of the most effective and sophisticated mechanical inventions of the time," making the ship "the most complex machine of the epoch." Simple machines, such as pulleys, cables, levers, wheels, and pumps, worked together to raise the sails, steer the ship, and empty the bilges; while more conceptual devices, such as the astrolabe, the compass, the quadrant, and the cross staff, enabled the navigator and pilot to judge their position and chart their course. Outfitted with cannons, the ship became a powerful war machine, prepared to battle at sea or to bombard coasts. If the design of ships rested on technological innovation, to sail it successfully required a trained crew who performed a wide variety of specialized jobs, from trimming the sails, to loading and unloading cargoes, to pumping the bilges and firing the cannons.[50]

Even with advances in navigation and ship design, shipboard life remained a risky and violent business, for at sea, nothing was certain for long. Danger lurked in the form of clouds overhead that might portend a storm or a sail on the horizon that might bring battle. Long voyages often brought famine and death when food and water ran out. Diseases spread easily in the cramped, unsanitary quarters on board ship. Pirates lurked along the well-traveled seaways, and even respected captains attacked and looted the ships of other nations. Encounters with peoples in distant lands were not predictable.

Of immediate concern to Staden, however, once he was settled, over any sea-sickness, and had learned his way about the ship, was waging war at sea. As an instrument of war, the ship had obvious strengths and limitations, and Staden and presumably the two other Germans had been hired both to protect the ship and to make it into an offensive weapon. The woodcut of Penteado's ship, one of the first illustrations in Staden's book, shows the ship loaded with an incredible number of guns—twenty-four in three rows on one side alone. This large number of guns, which seem to be too many for an ordinary merchant ship of the sixteenth century, suggests that Penteado's ship doubled as a warship. A decade later, when Jean de Léry, a French Calvinist minister, made the voyage to Brazil, he reported that the French ship on which he sailed had eighteen bronze pieces and thirty small cannons in addition to other arms and munitions. Thus, the French and Portuguese ships sailing for Brazil were well outfitted for war.[51]

One type of battle at sea was fueled by the quest to obtain wealth by any means and led to piracy. When ships met at sea, piracy was a common outcome. Jean de Léry described piracy at sea as equivalent to war on land in that "he who has weapons in his fist, and who is the strongest, carries the day, and imposes the law on his companion." When he and others protested the frequent pillaging of ships of friends as well as those of enemies, the sailors on board had a similar attitude to that of soldiers. As Léry put it, they told him that "it's war and custom" and that he would "have to get used to it." From mid-November to the end of December, while the three French ships in Léry's group were in the Mar Pequeña, that part of the Atlantic around the Canary Islands and the Barbary coast of Morocco, they accosted and robbed two English merchant ships, took kegs of wine and fruit from an Irish ship, helped themselves to dried fish from a fisherman's caravel off the Canary Islands, sank two fishing boats, suborned a captured Portuguese captain to attack a Spanish caravel loaded with salt, and then took all of the food off a Portuguese caravel, stole its boat, and ripped its sails before letting the caravel with its crew drift away.[52]

The Portuguese king sanctioned pirate attacks by his captains on merchant ships off the coast of the Cabo de Gué in North Africa. As a result, once Penteado had provisioned the ships in Madeira, he did not intend to sail directly for Brazil but rather first for the Cabo de Gué in North Africa. Santa Cruz do Cabo de Gué d'Agoa de Narba (today Agadir) was originally a *feitoria* (trading post) constructed by a Portuguese merchant in 1505 and later purchased by the Portuguese crown in 1513. As a Portuguese trading post, supported by a garrison, the factor, or head merchant, collected one-tenth of the goods of non-Portuguese ships trading with southern Morocco and regularly seized the cargoes of ships determined to be trading without permission. In addition, the post received tribute paid in wheat from the hinterland. Mounted slave-raiding expeditions, known as *cavalgadas,* captured slaves who were shipped from the port. Gradually, however, the local Moroccan kings began to resist the Portuguese presence. In 1541, M'hammad al-Sheikh successfully captured the *feitoria* from the Portuguese. Six years later, the permission granted to Penteado to attack shipping off the Cabo de Gué was part of the limited response the Portuguese King João III could muster after the loss of the *feitoria,* now renamed Agadir. Since the new overlords of the port permitted trade with European merchants, the Portuguese king authorized his sea captains to attack any merchants trading with the Muslims at Cabo de Gué/Agadir.[53]

Staden's captain, Penteado, approached the shore of the Cabo de Gué in the summer of 1547 and, meeting a merchant ship leaving the harbor, pursued and captured it, allowing the crew to escape in a boat. The ship in question belonged to Spanish merchants from the kingdoms of Castile and Valencia.[54]

Penteado took his prize, laden with North African trading goods—sugar, almonds, dates, goatskins, and gum Arabic—to Madeira and returned to the Cabo de Gué/Agadir hoping to take a second ship. The weather was unfavorable, however, and on the 31st of October, he was forced to sail for Brazil, pushed by a storm. Ideally, he would have called first at the Cape Verde Islands, where he could re-provision his ship, and from which, as the crow flies, Brazil was sixteen hundred miles across the Atlantic. Instead, they sailed directly from the Moroccan coast, sometimes encountering storms, other times schools of fish—albacore, dorados, and peixe voador (flying fish). They arrived, according to Staden, three months later, in late January of 1548, at the Cabo de Santo Agostinho (Cape St. Augustine) in Brazil.

Soon Penteado's ship was anchored off the coast of Pernambuco, where the settlement of Olinda was the most successful colony in Brazil. The Portuguese presence in Pernambuco began as a simple *feitoria.* Following the pattern they had developed along the coast of West Africa, the Portuguese built a trading post in Pernambuco that dated from about 1501. From this and other early posts in Brazil, trade began in parrots, pelts, medicinal herbs and oils, and native slaves. Each trading post included a small settlement with a church and houses where the agents and scribes of the king and of Portuguese merchants lived. Thirty years later, as part of a plan to reward loyal servants of the crown and to transfer the onus of colonization to the private sector, the Portuguese king granted wide strips of land stretching from the coast inland to where the line of the Treaty of Tordesillas was estimated to cross the mainland, to those individuals who would colonize them at their own expense. Despite the fact that these grants were hereditary and conferred great power to their holders, most failed. Not Pernambuco, however. Its first lord proprietor was

Duarte Coelho, an experienced military leader and naval commander who had made a fortune in India. Coelho received the large grant from the king of Portugal in 1534. Pernambuco prospered even though the Crown retained its monopoly over the brazilwood trade. The economic focus of Coelho's colony became sugar, and using the experience gained in the planting, milling, and export of sugar from the Atlantic islands of Madeira and São Tomé, the early colonists of Pernambuco began to build sugar plantations and mills known as *engenhos*.[55]

After Penteado discharged the penal exiles and unloaded the cargo in Pernambuco, he was preparing to leave to take on a cargo farther north, presumably of brazilwood, when a rebellion erupted in nearby Iguarassú, an *engenho* built outside of Olinda. The first sugar plantations and mills in Brazil were located along the coast, near good harbors (to export the sugar), running water (to power the mills), woodlands (to stoke the fires of the sugar house), and soils considered suitable for cane growing. As sugar plantations spread into more remote locations, they expanded the Portuguese footprint in Brazil and intruded on hunting and fishing grounds claimed by indigenous peoples. Moreover, sugar plantations required a large labor force not only to plant, hoe, and cut the cane but also to work in the mill where the cane was ground, the sap extracted, the juice boiled, and the syrup poured into clay molds through which water filtered to leave behind crystallized sugar. (The thick dark syrup that dripped out of the bottom, which later became known as molasses, was distilled into rum.) Tupi and Guarani-speaking peoples who lived along the coast of Brazil were the first laborers in the sixteenth-century sugar plantations, and many had been violently forced into slavery.

The isolation of the sugar mills in Pernambuco concerned the *donatário* Duarte Coelho, as did the attitude of the colonists who built them, who were, in his view, interested only in their material gain, and who expected him to defend their properties. Moreover, relations with the local indigenous peoples had become strained since they had little incentive to freely work on the sugar plantations. Sugar planters purchased some Indian slaves through a trade with indigenous chiefs known as *resgate,* or ransoming, that transferred Indian war captives to colonists, who considered them to be slaves acquired through just and legal means. Coelho had had no reservations about this practice of ransoming; he was permitted to ship a number of Indian slaves to Lisbon each year without paying duties. But an increasingly common practice—outright slave raiding, similar to the *cavalgadas* in North Africa that pressed men, women, and children into slavery through violence—was deeply destabilizing to Coelho's colony. He was incensed that six boats had raided for slaves along his coastline in 1546. He captured one boat, freed the Indians, and punished the colonists as he saw fit.[56]

With the sugar plantation under assault, forty of Penteado's men, including Staden, were pressed into service. Whatever Staden thought about Indian slavery or the claims of the Indians in rebellion, he was a soldier and behaved as such. Joining fifty armed colonists, thirty North African slaves, and an undisclosed number of Indian slave warriors, Penteado's men went by boat to reinforce the sugar plantation. They found the plantation surrounded by forest fortified by Indians with two forts, deep pits, and channels blocked by felled trees. In this siege Staden encountered familiar war tactics, such as shooting flaming arrows into the straw-covered roofs, as well as new ones, such as burning peppers so as to suffocate those inside the palisade with stinging smoke. The plantation was deeply vulnerable; there were not sufficient provisions, and it was not safe to leave the palisade to dig up fresh manioc roots, the staple of the Brazilian diet. The siege went on for a month before peace was re-established.[57]

After leaving Pernambuco, Penteado's ship sailed north for Paraíba, to load brazilwood and to trade for manioc flour to be consumed on the Atlantic voyage home. There, however, they met a French ship loading a cargo of brazilwood supplied by an indigenous group of Potiguars. Following his orders from the king, Penteado attacked, intending to capture the French ship. However, his ship was damaged— losing its mainmast in the fight—and several of his men were killed or wounded. Unable to re-provision the ship because of contrary winds, in May Penteado began the sail across the Atlantic on rationed water and manioc meal. One hundred and eight days later, in August, the archipelago of the Azores broke above the deep blue waters of the mid-Atlantic; they were nine hundred miles from Lisbon. Here the crew hoped to safely rest, fish, and generally recuperate from the long voyage back. Hailing an approaching ship, Penteado found it an easy target and robbed the ship of its stores of wine and bread. Meeting five ships of the Portuguese king, he joined them to escort the ships returning from the New World—a huge armada of nearly one hundred Spanish and Portuguese ships. Staden arrived in Lisbon in fine style, in October 1548, after sixteen months at sea.

Back in Lisbon and experienced with the ways of the sea, Staden passed up his second chance to sail for India. He decided not to wait for the spring armada, but instead he boarded an English ship heading for Spain to purchase wine. Arriving at the Puerto de Santa Maria, Staden made his way inland to Seville, the city from which Spanish expeditions to the Americas were organized. One hundred kilometers from the sea on the Guadalquivir River, Seville was the undisputed hub of Spanish mercantile activities. Like Lisbon, the city had been transformed by maritime trade, but in its case, by the Spanish conquests in the Caribbean, Mexico, and Peru. When Staden appeared in the city sometime in late 1548 or early 1549, the routine of Spanish shipping was being set and the first organized convoys were sailing for the Americas. By the next decade, two fleets would leave Seville each year, one headed for Veracruz in Mexico, and one for Cartagena on the Caribbean coast of modern-day Colombia. This system of fleets supplied the two great Spanish viceroyalties: Mexico and Peru.[58]

It was also the case that German trade had begun to shift from Lisbon to Seville. By the end of the sixteenth century, the trade in precious metals and spices, which had always been the basis of German-Portuguese trade, had moved to Antwerp so that German firms in Lisbon began to lose their importance. Seville became the center of a new and developing commerce focused on the Atlantic world: copper, lead, and nautical instruments were traded; weapons from Milan and wheat from the Black Sea found their way into the hulls of ships headed across the ocean. At the middle of the sixteenth century, then, when Staden arrived in Seville, he would also have found a German community forming, similar to that which he had known in Lisbon.[59]

Tales of gold and silver from Peru interested many in the Spanish colonies in America. When Francisco Pizarro permitted twenty men to return from Peru to Seville in 1534 with huge shares of gold and silver acquired from their participation in the capture of the Inca Atahualpa at Cajamarca, it was certainly sensational news. Subsequently, the Spanish crown sought to limit the number of fortune seekers heading to Peru. The exploits of Pizarro and the civil war between his men and his estranged partner Diego de Almagro were old stories by the time Staden frequented the inns and taverns of Seville, but there was still talk that "there was an abundance of gold" in a territory that the Spanish crown was still in the process of conquering. This land was reached by entering the Rio de la Plata estuary and travelling up the Paraguay and Paraná rivers into what is today Paraguay. Moreover, the first rumors of what would become the great silver mine, Potosí, located high in the Andes of present-day Bolivia but accessible from the east via Paraguay, were circulating by the end of the 1540s. Because of his previous voyage, Staden knew that "the land rich in gold is called Peru," which together with Brazil "forms one mainland."[60]

In Seville, Staden heard of an expedition headed for the Rio de la Plata to be led by a conquistador, Juan de Salazar y Espinoza. La Plata had long been a priority to the Spanish crown, which was determined to defend its claim to lands in South America that lay to the west of the line of demarcation established by the Treaty of Tordesillas. Since where the line actually bisected the continent was disputed, Spain and Portugal both competed for lands in southern Brazil. Spain sent the armadas of Juan Díaz Solis (1514–16), Diego García (1526–30), and Pedro de Mendoza (1535–37) to explore and settle these lands; while the expeditions of Fernão Magalhães (Magellan, 1519–21), García Jofre de Loaysa (1525), and Sebastian Cabot (1525–30) were dispatched to find a sea route to the Pacific. Meanwhile, the conquest of the interior, what is today Paraguay, had begun.

Staden learned that the recently appointed governor of La Plata had died and that his son, Don Diego de Sanabria, was assuming his father's position and preparing three ships to sail for La Plata under the command of Juan de Salazar y Espinoza. Salazar had previously been in Paraguay; he is given credit for founding Asunción in 1537, and he had served under Alvar Núñez Cabeza de Vaca. When Cabeza de Vaca's men mutinied and sent him to Spain in chains in 1545, Salazar accompanied him. Later, however, the Crown changed its mind about Salazar and appointed him the royal treasurer of La Plata, which is how he came to lead Sanabria's expedition. Don Diego intended to stay behind and bring the second wave of colonists and soldiers on a second set of ships.[61]

For Staden, this expedition must have seemed like a stroke of luck, an opportunity not to be missed. Like countless other young men of the sixteenth century, we may speculate, he wanted to "hacer la américa," that is, to get rich. Quite likely greed lay behind his desire to return to the Americas and clouded his judgment, for Salazar was in no way comparable to Staden's first captain, Penteado, and the expedition was plagued by delays and faulty decisions from the start.

The three ships left Seville in the early spring of 1550, the large ship nearly empty because the river was shallow and dangerous at Seville, and likely traveled at the slow pace of 12 kilometers per day until they reached Las Horcadas. The deeper water there would have allowed at least half of the cargo to be loaded. At the mouth of the river, at Sanlúcar de Barrameda, the final loading was done and the last inspections made. From the mouth of the river, there was one last, dangerous sandbar to cross; then the main pilot set a southwesterly course for the Canary Islands, as did virtually every Spanish pilot heading for the Americas. In the Canary Islands captains took stock, re-provisioned their ships, and then set out to sea due west, taking advantage of the strong trade winds that took them to the Caribbean.[62]

While the ships left Sanlúcar de Barrameda on April 10, 1550, which was the usual time of year to head for Mexico or the Caribbean, Salazar intended instead to follow the Portuguese route to southern Brazil, which required sailing much farther south, to the islands of São Tomé and Príncipe, before setting a course across the Atlantic. Salazar's head pilot, Juan Sanches, was not experienced with this route, and his charts did not have marked on them the major landmarks and colonies well known to Portuguese pilots and captains who sailed the Guinea coast of the south Atlantic.[63]

Since the Spanish pilots generally sailed routes north of the Equator, Salazar's pilots were likely suspicious of the astrolabe, the device the Portuguese used to determine their latitudes in the southern hemisphere. Using the astrolabe required knowing how to take measurements of the angle of the sun overhead at mid-day and how to use tables of solar declination.[64]

In the sixteenth century, mariners still retained considerable privileges and rights with respect to the ship's captain. Even ordinary sailors were persons to be heard when important decisions were made. This was so because the success of sea ventures was still unpredictable enough that the experience and knowledge of all mariners was needed, especially in times of danger. Only in later centuries, after the business of the sea became more predictable, profitable, and routine, did sailors become simple "hands on deck," valued for their strength and brawn, not for their experience.[65]

Pilots stood at the apex of the power structure on ships, and the best pilots in the sixteenth century were generally held to be those with the most experience—those who knew the unique characteristics of coastlines like the backs of their hands. Practical experience still trumped scientific knowledge because the cross-staffs and astrolabes used to measure latitude at sea could still give inaccurate readings, especially in the hands of untrained pilots. As captain, Salazar outranked the main pilot, who held the responsibility for nautical matters—guiding the ship to its destination and keeping the ship safe. Salazar's experience was military, and here too soldiers in the sixteenth century were able to give opinions, as was common during the conquests of Mexico and Peru. On this expedition, however, Salazar seems to have used his rank to command the pilot to sail, even in unfamiliar waters, without adequate charts. This was the beginning of a series of misfortunes about to bedevil Salazar.[66]

The three ships under Salazar's command included the main ship, the *San Miguel*—probably a four-masted carrack similar to the ship on which Staden sailed with Penteado but without the many guns—and two smaller ships that Salazar refers to alternately as brigantines or as caravels. On the *San Miguel* were Salazar, serving as captain; the main pilot (Juan Sanches); Don Diego Sanabria's stepmother, known as Doña Mencia, and her three daughters; and other women numbering some fifty, with three hundred persons among all three ships. This high number of women reflects the intention of the expedition: to settle and add to the new colony at Asunción. Salazar and Doña Mencia and her daughters and possibly the pilot all had their cabins on the poop deck, the most prestigious place on the ship, where they would have been attended by pages, another marker of their status. Surprisingly, Salazar later wrote that they had no doctor, surgeon, or barber.

Of the two smaller ships, one carried fifty men. In his first letter, Salazar refers to these two smaller ships as brigantines. Propelled by oars, brigantines had only one mast and sail. They were maneuverable boats with a shallow draught and were more suited for coastal trade or military engagement than for trans-Atlantic travel. In a second letter, Salazar describes these smaller ships as caravels. Caravels typically had three masts, carried guns, and were well adapted to trans-Atlantic travel.[67]

The ship Staden was on nearly wrecked off Cape Verde, but it then continued on to the island of São Tomé, where they took on fresh water. A former Portuguese penal colony, São Tomé was the key to the Portuguese trade in the Gulf of Guinea and south-central Africa. By the middle of the sixteenth century, São Tomean slave traders regularly acquired slaves along the Kongo and Angolan coasts and carried them to São Jorge da Mina, Lisbon, and Caribbean ports. Between 60 and 80 sugar mills worked on the island, each with from 100 to 300 slaves, with an annual production of 150,000 *arrobas* (the *arroba* was a measure of weight equal to 32 pounds), or over 2,000 tons. Many of the landowners were of mixed race—African in appearance and Portuguese in speech and culture. Among them were the descendants of Jewish children taken by force from their families after the expulsion of Jews from Portugal in the 1490s. The descendants of freed slaves, known as *filhos da terra*, were artisans and small farmers. Many slaves from Angola and Congo labored on the plantations, and Angolares, descendants of survivors of wrecked slave ships, lived freely in the forests. São Tomé was famous for its fevers, and the mortality of Europeans on the islands had always been high.[68]

While Staden's ship called at São Tomé, the main ship, the *San Miguel,* had become lost somewhere off the coast of Guinea. Worse was to come. They were hailed by a well-armed French pirate ship from La Rochelle, accompanied by two smaller boats trading for peppers. Captain Salazar was taken prisoner on the French ship while the *San Miguel* was looted. The French captain promised, however, "that the honor of the women and girls (*donzellas*) would not be touched"—that is, his men would not rape Doña Mencia and the other women. Sailing on again for another two months, the pilot continued to be lost, unable to find the island of São Tomé because it was not marked on his charts. When they finally came in sight of it, Salazar later claimed that they could not stop because they had nothing to offer in trade. Instead, they stocked up on bananas and filled their water casks at the island of Santa Helena in exchange for fish hooks and caught fish and sea birds for their food.[69]

Having agreed earlier on a rendezvous place in South America of 28 degrees South, the ships sailed separately across the Atlantic. Staden's ship was the first to arrive, even though it took four months before it could catch the prevailing winds to carry them southwest across the Atlantic. On reaching the latitude measured by the astrolabe at 28 degrees, they headed west, seeking land. The wind rose, and unable to find a harbor, the ship nearly wrecked on the rocks. The men had reached the southern edge of the Portuguese settlement of São Vicente. Their destination, the island of Santa Catarina, lay farther south. When they finally reached their rendezvous point, they met a bilingual Spaniard living among the Guarani Indians who had been left behind to facilitate future interactions between Spanish expeditions and the Guarani. Spanish captains were permitted to punish recalcitrant sailors by leaving them behind, and if the sailors learned the local languages and later served as interpreters, they were subsequently pardoned. Previous Spanish armadas had also often left behind European men who assimilated into the local indigenous populations. The sailors were overjoyed to meet this man, who became their translator and facilitated trade with the Guarani.[70]

Meanwhile, after crossing the Equator, Salazar's ship sailed for three months until the pilot judged them near the agreed-upon rendezvous point at Santa Catarina, where they met the crew of Staden's ship sometime in late November or December of 1550. The second caravel was never heard from again and was presumed lost off the coast of Africa. A group set out overland for Asunción to notify the Spanish there of their arrival. Those who remained behind were busily preparing for the last leg of the journey to La Plata when a new disaster struck: the *San Miguel* sank, leaving too many for the smaller caravel to carry on to La Plata. Nevertheless, the expedition was making its way slowly south when the last blow fell. The caravel, their last ship, went down, marooning 80 men and 40 women and children at a place Salazar called Mbiazá and Staden, Inbiassapé, today known as Laguna in the state of Santa Catarina, Brazil.[71]

During this grim time, two years in all, the men and women lived along the coast, harvesting shellfish and catching fish, small reptiles, and other small animals. The group factionalized, and Doña Mencia deposed Salazar as captain in favor of her son-in-law, Hernando de Trejo. They sent another expedition overland to Asunción, but with little help expected in the short run, Salazar decided to work on building a ship in order to sail north to São Vicente.[72]

Salazar left with twelve armed men, Staden among them, in 1553. The group experienced one last disaster: a shipwreck. Searching for the harbor at São Vicente during a winter storm in June of 1553, the ship broke apart as it hit a wall of rock; the men were able to save themselves by hanging on to pieces of the wreck and swimming ashore.[73]

Shipwreck was one of the most shocking, distressing, and unpredictable dangers faced by those who went to sea. Shipwrecks laid bare the fragility of human life, the limitations of technology, and the meaninglessness of social status and wealth; they set loose uncontrollable human emotions as each person struggled to survive. One of the most devastating Portuguese shipwrecks occurred at about the same time off the southeast coast of Africa. Told by a survivor, it circulated among sailors in port cities before it was eventually written down.

The mighty Portuguese ship, the *São João,* with Manuel de Sousa Sepúlveda, a Portuguese military leader in India as its captain, left India in February of 1552, late in the season and grossly overloaded with cargo. Nearly 600 men, women, and children were on board, many of them slaves. Sepúlveda was not a sea captain, and he overruled his pilot, who had set a different course for rounding the Cape of Good Hope. The galleon was also suffering from neglect; its sails were badly worn. The rudder failed, and the galleon drifted in the treacherous Agulhas Current and foundered along the coast of Natal in southeast Africa. Approximately five hundred persons survived the wreck and began a long, disastrous trek north, led by Sepúlveda, to the nearest Portuguese settlement in Mozambique. They soon ate through what rations they salvaged from the *São João* and resorted to eating shellfish and fish that washed up on the beach. One by one they fell behind from hunger, dehydration, sickness, and exhaustion. A Portuguese captain later rescued only a handful of survivors.[74]

Salazar and his men fared better than Sepúlveda because residents of a tiny Portuguese settlement known as Itanhaém took in the men, sodden and cold from having struggled ashore in the unforgiving winter storm, and later directed them to the town of São Vicente, thirty miles farther north. There, the Portuguese governor of Brazil, Tomé de Sousa, had arrived in early 1553 to complete his review of all settlements in Brazil. Well informed of the disastrous Spanish expedition led by Salazar, Sousa described their plight in a letter to the Portuguese king: "An armada with about 300 persons left Castile for the Rio de la Plata, and half was lost on the Island of Príncipe, off the coast of Guinea, and part was lost between Rio de la Plata and São Vicente, 60 leagues from São Vicente, at a place called Rio dos Patos." Sousa claimed that he sent ships to bring the rest of the survivors to São Vicente, where he hoped that they would remain, especially the women, and strengthen the Portuguese colony at São Vicente. Staden's expertise as a gunner presented him with the opportunity to work at a Portuguese fort. Salazar and Doña Mencia, on the other hand, still intended to make their way overland to Paraguay; they eventually arrived in Asunción with some of the others in October 1555.[75]

At that time, approximately six hundred colonists lived in São Vicente. It had been the first Portuguese settlement in Brazil (founded in 1532), and twenty years later it was still very much a frontier town. The main settlement, also known as São

Vicente, was located on an island of the same name, and around it were the first sugar plantations. There were six *engenhos* milling cane, including one managed by a Peter Rösel for merchants in Antwerp and another by a José Adorno, a Genoese. The slaves who worked on these sugar plantations were in their majority Indians— Guarani, who had been sold into São Vicente by Spaniards, and Tupi, who had been captured by Portuguese in raids along the coast or in the interior. Some three thousand slaves lived in São Vicente, laboring not only on the sugar plantations but in the households and on the fields of the residents.[76]

In 1550, Jesuit missionaries arrived in São Vicente to begin their mission to the Tupi and Guarani-speaking peoples, and by 1554 there were fourteen Jesuit fathers and brothers living in the Jesuit residence. The Jesuits were pleased with their initial success with Indian slaves and mixed-race children of Portuguese settlers and Indian women. They opened a school, where they taught children to read and write, to assist at mass, to play the flute, and to sing. They preached, taught basic doctrines, heard confessions, and baptized many. The leader of the Jesuit mission for all of Brazil, Father Manoel da Nóbrega, arrived in 1553. The Jesuit leader accompanied Brazil's first governor on his visit along the coast of Brazil, the last stop being São Vicente. Father Nóbrega nearly drowned as the canoe ferrying him from the governor's ship to shore capsized in a storm. Despite this ominous arrival, however, Father Nóbrega was enthusiastic about the mission and began to plan for a missionary overture to Guarani peoples who lived farther south and deeper inland, in Paraguay, the very lands that Doña Mencia and Juan de Salazar were heading for.[77]

Tomé de Sousa well appreciated the strategic importance of the Jesuit mission in São Vicente, given the increasing Spanish interest in La Plata and Paraguay. Yet he judged the missionary overture to Paraguay to be dangerous, and he squelched Nóbrega's plans. Instead, Sousa sought to strengthen the defenses of São Vicente, which he found remote and vulnerable to attack by the Tupinambá, who were allied with the French who traded regularly farther north along the coast of Brazil. This affected Staden's prospects, for Staden soon went to work, not in the walled town of São Vicente or in the newer town of Santos, but on the fringe of the captaincy, at a place where Portuguese control was hardly a given and where an isolated fort had recently been constructed. This fort at Bertioga lay at the overlapping edge of Tupinikin and Tupinambá territorial influence, approximately 30 miles north of São Vicente (by sea) on Santo Amaro Island.

In 1551, a simple fort had been built at Bertioga with the help of the Tupinikin. Several mixed-race brothers, who became friends of Staden, worked at the fort. These brothers, all sons of a Portuguese colonist, Diego da Braga, and an Indian woman (or women), were soldiers; their job was to guard the entrance to the long passage that separated the island of Santo Amaro and the mainland. In so doing, they protected the main settlements on the island of São Vicente, which lay to the south of Santo Amaro Island. Mixed-race men such as the Braga brothers were known as *mamelucos* in sixteenth-century Brazil and many were, like the Braga brothers, soldiers or leaders of expeditions that sought Indian slaves. *Mamelucos* were the quintessential go-betweens of sixteenth-century Brazil; their ability to move between Portuguese and Indian worlds allowed them to broker many exchanges, both peaceful and violent. Staden describes the Braga brothers as Christian converts and as skilled speakers of Portuguese and Tupi as well as experienced fighters in both the Portuguese and Tupi style of warfare. The first Jesuits had high hopes to use the *mamelucos* as interpreters because of their skill with indigenous languages, although at the same time, Jesuit missionaries feared that their hybrid lifestyles meant that they could not be trusted as true Christians.[78]

Defense of the coastal Portuguese settlement at São Vicente was an ongoing concern, making Staden, with his expertise with guns and war, a desirable new resident. The Portuguese had established alliances with the Tupinikin who lived above the coast on the Piratininga plateau, where the Jesuits would soon establish a base that would in time become the town and later city of São Paulo. The enemies of the Tupinikin, the Tupi-speaking Tupinambá, lived along the coast farther north, in the environs of the Guanabara Bay, where they were allied with the French. Long-standing competition between the Tupinikin and the Tupinambá over hunting grounds and fishing rights were intensified by the imperial rivalry between Portugal and France.[79]

The Tupinambá ventured south to São Vicente in August when fish ran, and in November when birds nested and the corn ripened. At these times they also attacked their enemies, the Tupinikin. The new fort at Bertioga restricted their access to spawning fish in August and to the nesting guará birds (*Eudocimus ruber*) in November. In response, two years before Staden arrived in São Vicente the Tupinambá secretly approached in seventy canoes and launched an unexpected attack on Bertioga an hour before dawn. A fierce battle ensued with losses on both sides, but in the end the Tupinambá burned the settlement and captured many Tupinikin. There were only eight who survived in an adobe hut constructed in the Portuguese fashion. The Tupinikin, surprised in their large straw longhouses, were killed or captured.[80]

The colonists rebuilt Bertioga. When Tomé de Sousa arrived in São Vicente in 1553, he described Bertioga as "very badly built by the Indians," which suggests that it hardly resembled a Portuguese town; rather, it was very much a frontier settlement built in the Indian style. By elevating it to a town, he hoped to make it more

Portuguese and to have it function as a bulwark to São Vicente. He had ordered a new fort built across the channel on Santo Amaro Island, but when he saw it with his own eyes, he decided to expand it in another way. He included a drawing in his letter to the king, which unfortunately is unknown today. It was in this stone fort, fortified with cannons, that Staden agreed to serve for two years; and in return, he expected to receive the privileges normally granted to Portuguese gunners as well as a promise of future rewards.[81]

Six years after leaving home, Staden found himself in an isolated fort at the tip of a heavily forested island at the northernmost edge of the Portuguese colony of São Vicente. He was no longer constantly on the move as part of the troop of sailors, gunners, slaves, convicts, colonists, sea captains, and traders who lived at sea. Did he miss that life, with its excitement, dangers, and unknowns? Perhaps he understood that he had been part of something new as he glimpsed landscapes coming into focus, marveled at unfamiliar flora and fauna, or became acquainted with different peoples. Perhaps he felt a kinship with others who by seeking employment at sea had become the physical go-betweens who linked islands, coastlines, forests, swamps, mountains, deserts and the peoples who inhabited them into an ever more interconnected Atlantic world. He had seen firsthand the consequences of this greater integration—piracy, slavery, trade, colonization, outbreaks of disease, shipwrecks, and slave rebellions. Whatever he thought of these things, he was but one of many who made it possible for merchants to transport gold, slaves, ivory, and sugar and for kings to establish colonies, to send expeditions to reinforce them, and to authorize captains and soldiers to engage in war. One in a cast of thousands, his physical presence and movement had helped to string the network of connections in the emerging Atlantic maritime world. But now he, Hans Staden of Hesse, was no longer one of them. He was again a soldier, a mercenary defending a spit of land in a remote outpost claimed by the king of Portugal.

In four months, he settled into a new routine. He spent his time in the stone fort, watching for the enemy Tupinambá who might approach silently in their canoes. Somehow he had acquired a slave, a Guarani, who lived with him in the fort. His closest neighbors lived across the channel at the tiny settlement of Bertioga, where he undoubtedly visited often, perhaps even every day. There he most likely spoke Tupi-Guarani and Portuguese, ate manioc meal with fish, and drank fermented corn beer or raw rum with his mixed-race friends, the Braga brothers.

One day he had two unexpected visitors: a Spaniard from São Vicente, and a German, a fellow Hessian with a Latin name, Heliodorus Hessus, an accountant and scrivener for the sugar plantation owned by the Adorno family. Staden had met Heliodorus before: Heliodorus had come to his aid when he had been shipwrecked.

Now, having heard that Staden had been sick, he paid a visit, with the Spaniard, to see how he was. Perhaps Staden wanted to receive them well and lay on a proper feast, or perhaps it just happened that his Guarani slave had been hunting a few days prior. But for whatever reason, Staden went out to collect the game, and suddenly, amidst the usual sounds of the forest, he heard a shouting back and forth across the trail. He recognized the sounds, but it was too late. Before he could react, he found himself surrounded by a menacing group of Tupinambá warriors. Staden was about to be torn out of the colonial world he had become a part of and brought into the sphere of the Tupinambá. He would soon be further from rural Hesse than he ever could have imagined.

CHAPTER TWO

The Lying Captive

𝔍t happened suddenly. Staden and his Guarani slave were in the forest collecting game, when loud screaming and yelling surrounded them from all sides.
Before they had time to react, Tupinambá warriors—the bitter enemies of the
Tupinikin and the Portuguese—were everywhere, stamping their feet, hurling insults, and brandishing their bows and arrows.

"May God now have mercy on my soul," Staden cried out. And just as the words
were out of his mouth, he was struck to the ground. Arrows flew, one wounding
him in the leg. The Guarani slave escaped, but the warriors quickly began to tear
off Staden's clothes—"One of them took my collar; the other my hat; the third my
shirt"—and they set to quarreling over who deserved the right to claim him as his
prisoner. Two warriors then lifted him up and jogged him down to the shore, where
they joined a larger group of Tupinambá near where their canoes lay hidden. Staden
took more blows to his face before his hands were bound and four ropes were tied
around his neck.[1]

Captivity was an increasingly common experience in the Atlantic world of the
sixteenth century, and it was terrifying. Pirates seized sailors and passengers from the
ships they stormed. Soldiers captured in battle became prisoners of war, their fates
uncertain as they languished, waiting to be freed or ransomed. In parts of Africa,
villages were not safe from outright slave raiding attacks or the less violent but no
less ruthless business dealings of slave traders. By the middle of the sixteenth century,
ships were transporting thousands of captives from ports in Africa to the Spanish and
Portuguese colonies in the Caribbean and Brazil. The Tupinambá who kidnapped
their mortal enemies were therefore hardly unique.

Staden's experience as a captive was unique, however. We know that he had
chosen to leave home and to cross the Atlantic twice and that he therefore had a
greater degree of freedom in determining his future than most sailors. Unlike others
who journeyed across the Atlantic, Staden would publish an account of his experience and thereby convey to an audience of readers how he felt at the moment he
was captured, what he experienced in captivity, and how he plotted to escape. The
vast majority of captives were voiceless and left few accounts of their lives. And, as
historian Joseph Miller observes, the horrors of enslavement in Africa were such

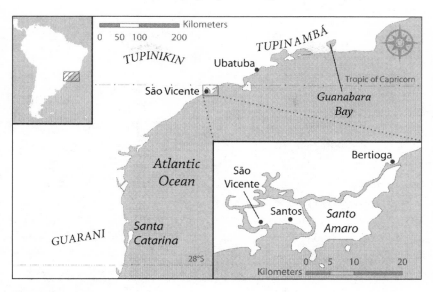

Figure 7. São Vicente

that even those who escaped could hardly give voice to the enormity of the experience, "even if the slaves had left a personal record of all they suffered." Shocking as it may seem, historians today must rely largely on the records of slave traders to reconstruct their experience.[2]

At first Staden felt fear, certainly the overwhelming emotion of the recently captured. In Staden's case, it was not fear of the unknown, however. His knowledge of Brazil at the time he was captured was extensive. His first trip to Pernambuco in 1547–48, his survival for two years along the Guarani coast of Santa Catarina from 1551–53, and his more recent residence in São Vicente in 1554 (see fig. 7) meant that Staden understood much about his captors and the rapidly changing world in which they lived. He even spoke their language, Tupi-Guarani, which was widely spoken along the coast of Brazil. As a soldier posted at the frontier fort of Bertioga, he comprehended the hostilities between the Tupinikin allied with the Portuguese and the Tupinambá allied with the French. Staden's first fear, therefore, was of immediately being "struck down" dead.[3]

Staden's captors were strong, fearless Tupinambá male warriors, any one of whom could have dispatched him in a second. The men in the war party had spent days and nights preparing themselves for this very moment. Their bodies would have been painted and feathered, and their weapons—arrows tipped with sharpened bone, sharks' teeth, or other sharp points and the long-handled five- to six-foot-long war club—had been carefully made ready beforehand. They had approached Bertioga by canoe, paddling south from their villages farther north, camping along the way. They had probably arrived a day or two before and had spied on Staden at Bertioga, hiding in the forest and waiting for him to return for the felled game. When the Tupinambá attacked, Staden's firearm, if in fact he was carrying one, was of little use; there was no time to position, load, prime, and fire an arquebus. Indeed, Jean de Léry, who spent some time among the Tupinambá a few years after Staden, remarked that the Tupinambá could shoot five or six arrows before a single shot could be fired with a gun. Although Staden feared instant death, the warriors carried long cords to tie up their prisoners, for rather than killing them in battle, they preferred to take their enemies alive and to return home with them as their captives.[4]

A chief carrying a club began to pace back and forth among the throng of warriors from several Tupinambá villages gathered around the beached, hidden canoes. Staden recalled that the king "preached (*predigte*)," called him their Portuguese slave, and told him that they would "avenge the deaths of their friends on me." Some of the warriors indeed demanded that Staden be killed on that very spot. Staden waited for the blow from the war club that would kill him, but the chief decided to keep him alive in order to take him back to the village "so that their women might see me alive and have their feast with me."[5]

Tupi chiefs were powerful elders who were skilled at oratory and who used their power of speech to incite men to war. This chief had led the war party south and would have continually exhorted the warriors to be brave and to avenge the honor of their kin who had been captured by the Tupinikin and the Portuguese. Each night en route, the warriors had listened to speeches, danced, and taken note of the chief's admonition to dream well. The chief certainly knew Staden to be an important adversary; he was the soldier, that "Portuguese slave" who shot at their canoes when they tried to slip by the new stone fort to attack their enemies or to reach the nesting grounds of the Guará birds or the fresh waters where the Bratti fish spawned. Staden's capture would be the occasion for a grand feast with plenty of manioc beer for all. Staden knew that this Tupinambá feast, which he called "Kawewi Pepicke," would not end well. After the drinking and feasting, he says matter-of-factly, "all of them would together then eat me."[6]

Whether he had observed one or had only heard tell of them, Staden had to have known before his capture that the cannibalism ceremony was a central ritual for the Tupinambá, as it was for the Tupinikin and other Tupi-speaking groups living along the coast of Brazil in the sixteenth century. It was not about having enough food to eat, nor was it an invention of European observers, as some scholars have claimed. Sixteenth-century Tupinikin and Tupinambá practiced exocannibalism, which is the eating of those from outside their group, most commonly enemies whom they captured in warfare.[7]

Europeans such as Staden initially had difficulty understanding Tupi warfare, so different was it from what they knew in Europe. One European observer of Tupi warfare in the sixteenth century wrote that they "do not wage war to win countries and lands from each other . . . even less do the conquerors aim to get rich from the spoils, ransoms, and arms of the vanquished." The urge to war was instead entangled with the eventual cannibalism ceremony, for, as this observer continued, "they are impelled by no other passion than that of avenging, each for his side, his own kinsmen and friends who in the past have been seized and eaten."[8] Staden, however, would soon notice that the cannibalism ritual was not just about revenge; it was central to how the Tupinambá saw themselves.

The cannibalism ceremony took place in the village, far from the battlefield, unless a war captive had been badly wounded (such captives might be cannibalized on the journey home). In its fullest expression, cannibalism was the culmination of an elaborate ritual that took place in a festive atmosphere that included the entire village, and often guests from surrounding villages, in a carefully planned and, for the Tupi-speaking groups, an honorable ceremony with deep spiritual meaning. Through the cannibalism of the enemy, not only were ancestors remembered, but the memories of past deaths were avenged, new names were taken, the bonds between the living were renewed, and the power of the chief was strengthened. Another German who was in São Vicente at the same time as Staden provided a German analogy to the cannibalism feast: when the Tupinikin returned from war victorious, he wrote, they brought captives to their villages for a great feast, not unlike the weddings he had attended in Germany.[9]

Jesuits in São Vicente were quite familiar with the cannibalism ceremony and described it in some detail in their letters sent to Lisbon, Rome, and elsewhere. The most elaborate description of the cannibalism ceremony was written by one of the Jesuit brothers in São Vicente in 1551, and it foreshadows much of what lay ahead for Staden. Brother Correa, known as the best Jesuit interpreter in São Vicente because he had lived in Brazil since 1534, sought to explain the many facets of the cannibalism ceremony to a fellow Jesuit living in Africa. First a rope was placed around the neck of the captive so that he might not escape; at night the rope was tied to the hammock in which the captive slept. Straps that were not removed were placed above and below the knees. The captives were given women, who guarded them and also slept with them. These women were high-status daughters and sisters of chiefs; they were unmarried and sometimes gave birth to the child of a captive. Some of the captives might be held for a period of time until corn was planted and new large clay vessels—for drink and cooking flesh—were made. Guests were invited to the ceremony, and they often arrived eight to fifteen days in advance of it. A special small house was erected, with no walls but with a roof, in which the captives were placed with women and guards two or three days before the ceremony. In the other houses, feathers were prepared for a headdress or for body ornamentation, and inks were made for tattoos. Women and girls prepared fifty to one hundred vats of fermented manioc beer. Then, when all was ready, they painted the victim's face blue, mounted a headdress of wax covered with feathers on him, and wound a cotton cord around his waist. The guests began to drink in the afternoon and continued all through the night. At dawn, the one who was to do the killing came out with a long, painted wooden club and smashed the captive on the head, splitting it open. The attacker then withdrew for eight to fifteen days of abstinence while the others ate the cooked flesh of the captive and finished all of the drink made for the occasion.[10]

With insults ringing in his ears and cords cinched around his neck, Staden was forced into a canoe, and the war party quickly put out to sea before a general alarm could be sounded. Staden's comrades had no chance to save him. Neither their shooting at the canoes from the land, nor the firing of the guns of the stone fort, nor even their pursuit in canoes had any effect. The Tupinambá warriors paddled too fast; they knew how to stay out of range of the guns of Bertioga. As a final insult, they made Staden stand up in the canoe, naked, as the shots from the fort's guns splashed harmlessly in the water before him.

Heading north, the Tupi beached their canoes seven German miles out from Bertioga (approximately 53 kilometers), with the intent of spending the night on a small island. They carried Staden, bound, from the canoe to land. Staden describes his state of mind as he lay, barely able to see through his swollen eyes and wracked by pain from the arrow wounds in his leg, as "full of great fear and despair." Neither the two years spent near starvation in Santa Catarina nor the terrifying shipwreck outside São Vicente had prepared him for the desperation he felt as a captive. As his captors stood around him, boasting that they would eat him, he "dwelt on matters which I had never thought of before, and thought namely about how dark the valley of sorrows is in which we live." While tears streamed down his face, he sang out loud the chorale theme attributed to Martin Luther: "Out of the depths I cry to you, O LORD!" The Tupinambá mocked his attempt to comfort himself, saying, "See how he cries [like an infant]." Returning to the mainland to spend the night, his captors tied the cord around his neck to the tree on which they strung his hammock. From below, his captors insulted him all night long, calling up in their language, "Schere inbau ende" ("You are my bound animal [pet]").[11]

The Tupinambá took Staden to the village of "Uwattibi," in the vicinity of the fishing village and beach resort known today as Ubatuba. The Tupi were semi-sedentary peoples, and their villages were not permanent constructions, as in Staden's Hesse, but rather were agrarian communities that moved periodically. New villages formed to take advantage of fresh hunting grounds or virgin forest from which to clear new fields to plant or because of internal conflict. Old villages were abandoned when the game ran out, when plantings ceased to produce as well, or as a result of war. Staden's first sight of Ubatuba, as he made his way from the ca-noes, was of the women working in the gardens. In Tupi society, gender roles were clearly defined: men made war, hunted, and fished; they led villages as chiefs and elders. Women were the agriculturalists and tended small plots in clearings cut and burnt from the Atlantic forest where they grew corn, pumpkins, sweet potatoes, and manioc roots. Women prepared the manioc flour that was the staple of the diet and made the manioc beer that was consumed in vast quantities in the cannibalism ceremony. They were also potters (making vessels for drink and for cooking) and weavers (looming the cotton hammocks in which everyone slept). "I, your food, is coming," Staden says he was forced to call out to the women in Tupi.[12]

Ubatuba, as described by Staden, consisted of seven large communal longhouses, or lodges, with a central patio or plaza of beaten earth. It was surrounded by a palisade, or fence, for protection. Inside the tall, vaulted straw longhouses, nuclear families strung their hammocks together around a small fire. As they reached the village, the men retreated into one of the lodges, leaving Staden the captive of the women and children. It was the ultimate Tupi insult: to reduce a powerful male warrior to a plaything in the world of women and children. They surrounded him, dancing and singing, beating him and pulling at his red beard.

"With this blow I take revenge on you for my friend, the one who was killed by those among whom you have been!" the women and children cried out in Tupi, Staden says. The women took Staden to one of the longhouses and made him lie in a hammock and continued to beat him, mock him, and tell him that they would gladly eat him. The men, meanwhile, were drinking and singing in another longhouse.[13]

Soon the two Tupinambá brothers who had captured him, Nhaêpepô-oaçu and Alkindar Miri, came to tell Staden that they had given him to their uncle Ipiru-guaçu. Staden understood his fate: Ipiru-guaçu would keep him, then kill him, eat him, and thereby gain another name. Gaining a new name conferred honor among the Tupinambá, as Staden later explained to his readers, and those men with the most names (acquired by capturing enemies) were the most prominent in Tupinambá society. The brothers then informed Staden that the women would take him from

Figure 8. Staden Dances with Women and Children. From Hans
Staden, *Warhaftige Historia.* Marburg: 1557. Courtesy, Lilly
Library, Indiana University, Bloomington, Indiana.

the lodge to the place where the *poracé,* a dance, would be performed. The men
again withdrew, while the women held Staden by the arms or by the rope that was
pulled tight around his neck and dragged him out to dance in the center of the
village. After the *poracé,* the women led him to the chief's longhouse, where they
shaved his eyebrows and a woman attempted to cut off his beard. Certain that his
death was near, Staden looked around for the club with which he would be killed,
but he was told, "Not yet."[14]

Another dance followed; this time Staden was dressed with a string with rattles
around his leg and a feather headdress known as the *Araçoiá.* Again, the women
who danced around him sang, and they made Staden stamp his leg to keep time to the
rhythm of their songs. The dancing finished, and the women delivered Staden to
his new master, the brothers' uncle, Ipiru-guaçu, who guarded him but told him
that he still had some time to live (see fig. 8).

Staden knew firsthand the depth of the enmity between the Tupinambá and
the Tupinikin, but now, in the Tupinambá village, he heard how the Portuguese

regularly took advantage of the Tupinambá. Sometimes, the Tupinambá told him, Portuguese ships from São Vicente arrived, sounding their guns signaling that they wished to trade, but then, when their people had gone in friendship and boarded the ships, the Portuguese seized and bound them, carrying them away as captives. Staden further learned that his master's brother, the father of the two men who had captured him, had died from wounds that he had received from a Portuguese gunshot. Therefore, his two sons "wanted to take revenge on me for their father's death."[15]

How does the captive return? Escape is certainly the first strategy. For slaves, running away was the most common form of resistance to slavery, especially for those newly enslaved. Those captured by pirates often tried to flee by stealing a boat or by diving overboard and swimming for shore. Staden, too, hoped to escape and believed that he if he could run away, he could find his way back to Bertioga. However, the Tupinambá kept him bound tightly with the rope around his neck, and he was constantly guarded.[16]

A second strategy for escape might be rebellion—like slaves who mutinied on board ship, prisoners who plotted to overthrow a pirate ship's crew, or captive soldiers who overwhelmed their guards. Such resistance was difficult for Staden because there were few other captives in the villages he visited and because he was so closely guarded. He did hope that his companions would mount a raid to rescue him, but their first attempt to recapture him (as the Tupinambá carried him off in their canoes) had been unsuccessful. Staden had little choice but to accept his captivity and hope for the best.

Languishing as a captive, Staden stepped into a highly dangerous but powerful new role in order to survive: he became a transactional go-between. Typically persons of low status, transactional go-betweens were the brokers, the mediators, the translators. Leaders called on them when they could not manage contact and conflicts with those with whom they shared no common language or culture. The most important skills of transactional go-betweens were language and knowledge of culture: not only did they speak multiple languages, but they were skilled at understanding cultural differences and in using them to their advantage. They dealt in information, staged encounters, and managed expectations. Because such go-betweens often knew more than leaders on either side, they wielded great power in certain situations. But they were never fully trusted, even as they facilitated trade, interpreted at meetings, and gave valuable information on others. They were dangerous because they could so easily change sides.

While a captive of the Tupinambá, Staden adopted many of the characteristics common to other transactional go-betweens in sixteenth-century Brazil. The role was not completely unfamiliar to him. His best friends in São Vicente were the

Braga brothers, bi-lingual and bi-cultural men living on the edge of the colony, on the shifting frontier threshold between Portuguese and Tupi worlds. Staden knew firsthand another transactional go-between, whom he met soon after the ill-fated Spanish expedition arrived in southern Brazil. This Spaniard, Juan Fernando, had lived among the Guarani for three years to facilitate contact with Spanish ships heading to La Plata. When Staden went with his ship's captain to the Guarani village where Fernando lived, they were well received, thus proving the effectiveness of the transactional go-between.

The more familiar Staden became with his surroundings and the more he observed, the more he began to deal in information. He learned how to converse with the village elders and noticed the comings and goings of outsiders to the village. He began to use his ability to speak Tupi and his understanding of Tupinambá beliefs and customs as well as his experience in the larger Atlantic world to cultivate new identities. Before, Staden had been a seafarer and a soldier, a man who was valued for his ability to fire guns. Now he began to acquire information and manipulate it to his advantage. He began to lie, dissimulate, and play the sides against each other. He worked to create an image of himself that instilled fear in the hearts of his captors. He offered himself to the Tupinambá as a source of knowledge, as a mercenary, as a healer, and as a prophet. It was a dangerous game that might seal his fate as a captive or it might just lead to his release.[17]

Staden began to insist to his Tupinambá captors that their oracles, the gourds they called "Tamaraka" (*maracas,* or shakers) had no power and lied about him. The maracas were dried gourds that rattled when shook and were used by Tupi shaman in various rituals. Through the maracas, the shaman "spoke" and interpreted supernatural signs. There had been a prophecy, Ipiru-guaçu told Staden, that they would capture a Portuguese. Staden saw an opening. He writes: "Then I said: These things have no power and cannot speak. They lie about me being a Portuguese. Rather, I am a friend and relative of the French, and the land I come from is called Alemannia." The Tupinambá did not believe him and retorted, saying that "it was I [Staden] who lied, for if I were truly the Frenchmen's friend, what was I then doing among the Portuguese?"[18]

The Tupinambá had a point, and Staden knew it. After all, on his first voyage to Brazil, his Portuguese captain had explicit orders to attack any French ships trading in Brazil. Yet Staden persisted in his story because it planted a seed of doubt in the minds of the Tupinambá. Although the Tupinambá thought he lied, they would not kill him if there was a chance that he was indeed a friend of their French allies. Thus, Staden acquired his first taste of the power that came from his understanding of Tupinambá religious beliefs and his ability to speak their language well. He convinced the Tupinambá to wait until some of their French allies arrived. He had bought himself some time.

Was Staden lying? And if so, how do we, as modern readers, judge him? Within the context of the sixteenth-century western European culture from which Staden came, lying was a much discussed moral issue. A sixteenth-century maxim, *Nescit vivere qui nescit dissimulare*, which can be translated from the Latin as "He who does not know how to dissimulate does not know how to live," was one kind of lying. Dissimulation in this sense meant "feigning, concealing, or keeping secret." It was a behavior that came to be associated with courtiers in the sixteenth century, whose success at court came with "flexibility, posing, and role playing." In other words, it was through their flattery and lies that courtiers won the approval of their princes. Does this describe the dissimulation of Hans Staden while captive of the Tupinambá?[19]

Historian Perez Zagorin argues that there is another highly significant kind of dissimulation in early modern Europe related to "persecution by states and churches of heretical and minority religious bodies and heterodox and dangerous ideas." In such situations, dissimulation was required on the part of religious minorities in order to maintain their traditions and beliefs. Among many examples would be the Crypto-Jews of Spain (and later Portugal) who, after the expulsion of Jews in 1492, were no longer permitted to practice Judaism in public and subsequently practiced rituals in secret. Do Staden's lies fall into this kind of dissimulation?[20]

A third form of dissimulation is evident in yet another maxim of the sixteenth century: *Qui nescit dissimulare nescit regnare* (He who does not know how to dissimulate does not know how to rule). In this meaning, a ruler must dissimulate because it is necessary (and therefore excusable) in order to govern. From the hand of Machiavelli came the most influential text on this sort of dissimulation: the prince must know how to lie in order to maintain himself in power. Princes, according to Machiavelli, were not obligated to keep their promises, since most men are wicked and do not keep their word. A wise prince, therefore, Machiavelli writes, should not keep his word when it is not in his interest to do so; it is essential that a prince be "a great liar and dissembler." Is Staden similar to Machiavelli's prince?[21]

These are difficult questions, but there is no doubt that Staden lies repeatedly while a captive. His most strategic lie is rooted in his belief that if he can convince the Tupinambá that he is French, or a friend of the French, they will not kill him and will eventually ransom him. The lie would lead to his liberty, for in exchange for a ransom paid in trading goods, the Tupinambá would release Staden. This was a major lie, and Staden had trouble making it convincing to his Tupinambá captors.

This became evident almost immediately, for French merchants and sea captains from Normandy frequently visited the environs of the Guanabara Bay to trade, developing close alliances with the Tupinambá. The French had not yet tried to build any permanent settlements; instead, they had left ashore Tupi-speaking traders who established connections with local chiefs and collected peppers, feathers, exotic animal skins, monkeys, and parrots. These men were known as *truchements* in French, and they served primarily as interpreters.

One day, Staden reports, "the savages came running to me and said: 'A Frenchman has arrived and we want to see whether or not you are a Frenchman too.'"[22]

Staden's heart lifted. He was sure that the Frenchman would understand his plight out of a sense of shared values. "He [is in fact] a Christian," Staden writes, describing his state of mind before the meeting; "he is probably going to put in a good word for me."[23]

The Tupinambá took Staden, naked but for a piece of linen cloth covering his sunburned shoulders, to meet the Frenchman, "a young lad" in Staden's eyes. The Tupinambá gathered around to listen. The French youth had a Tupi name, Carautá-uára, and he was the adopted son of a prominent Tupinambá chief. He spoke to Staden in French. There was a problem. "I could not understand him well," Staden explains. "I could not answer him."[24]

Carautá-uára then took control of the exchange. He turned to the Tupinambá and said, "Kill and eat him, the good-for-nothing. He is a real Portuguese, your enemy and mine." Staden had not understood the French, but he clearly understood what Carautá-uára had just said in Tupi. Staden begged Carautá-uára in Tupi, because they had no European language in common, "in God's name," to tell the Tupinambá not to eat him. Then, Carautá-uára replied, according to Staden: "They want to eat you."[25]

What did it mean, this simple declarative sentence spoken in Tupi by a Frenchman to a German in Brazil in the middle of the sixteenth century? On the surface, Carautá-uára's words may have mocked Staden, but they also conveyed information about the Tupinambá. When the leader of the Jesuit mission to Brazil described the rationale of the cannibalism ceremony, he also linked it to the honor and to the desire of Tupi men; he wrote that it is in "killing their enemies that lies all of their honor, and this is their happiness and their desire."[26]

Staden failed to dominate this exchange with Carautá-uára, who was clearly the more powerful go-between. Staden tells his readers that at that moment he remembered a biblical verse: "Cursed are those who trust in mere mortals." He stripped off the linen that had covered his shoulders, throwing it at the Frenchman's feet (who, he noted, had given the Tupi the cloth in the first place), saying that there was no reason to protect his flesh any longer. Later he says that he wept and sang a hymn as he lay in his hammock. Yet he could not have failed to understand that Carautá-uára's words had more power than his own. Why?[27]

Carautá-uára was also a Tupi-speaking European in Brazil, yet the Tupinambá accepted his version of who Staden was, not Staden's. Carautá-uára's demeanor, his ties to a powerful Tupinambá chief, and the fact that he facilitated the exchanges with French sea captains who provided desirable trading goods gave him status and power, even though he was a young lad in Staden's eyes. Did Staden learn from this exchange with Carautá-uára the power of using language and situations skillfully? Did it teach him how to dissimulate more effectively?

Not long after this encounter, when taken to the village of Carautá-uára's adopted Tupinambá father, who was the powerful chief Cunhambebe, Staden showed a more sophisticated ability to manipulate his situation through language and dissimulation.

As Staden approached Cunhambebe's village, fear must have washed over him when he saw fifteen heads on pikes surrounding the village; these had been war captives seized from another tribe, the Maracaiás, also enemies of the Tupinambá.[28]

"I thought," Staden said, "that they would treat me in the same manner." When he entered the longhouse of the high chief, Staden writes that one of his guards proclaimed in a long, loud speech "in a harsh tone, so that the others could hear": "Here I bring the slave, the Portuguese." He also said, Staden noted, that it was a fine thing to have one's enemy in one's power.[29]

After the speech, the guard took Staden to Cunhambebe, who was drinking manioc beer with other men. The men, quite drunk, called out to Staden, with menacing looks, "Have you, our enemy, arrived?" Staden replied, "I have come to you, but I am not your enemy." The men invited Staden to drink with them. Emboldened, Staden then addressed a man with a large green lip plug in his lower lip and six cords of white shells around his neck. Using the information he possessed, his ability to speak Tupi, and taking advantage of the situation, he said: "Are you king Konyan Bebe [Cunhambebe]? Are you still alive?" and "I have heard much about you, that you are such a fierce man."[30]

Staden writes that Cunhambebe then stood up and strutted around arrogantly. Staden's flattery had worked. Cunhambebe then began to question Staden, and Staden supplied him with information about the Tupinikin, his former friends but Cunhambebe's enemies, as well as information about enemies of the Portuguese. In particular, Cunhambebe wanted to know why Staden had shot at the Tupinambá while he lived at Bertioga. Staden replied that he had to follow orders. Perhaps Cunhambebe accepted this answer, for he responded by changing the subject, at least as

Staden told the story. He declared that Staden was Portuguese, since Carautá-uára, the Frenchman who was his godson, had told him that Staden did not speak French.

Sensing the danger, Staden quickly answered that it was true, but that he had been gone for so long that he had forgotten the language. Staden's answer is ambiguous, for he does not say which language he had forgotten. He seems to be saying that he forgot the language that the Frenchman (and supposedly he) spoke. Cunhambebe did not believe his lie. His answer, as Staden reports it, caused him to lose all hope because Cunhambebe said that he had "already helped to catch and eat five Portuguese who had all said they were Frenchmen and had lied about this."[31]

Staden continued to talk to Cunhambebe, stroking his ego and providing more information. In answer to a question about whether or not his enemies thought about him, Staden replied that they (the Portuguese) knew a great deal about him. He told Cunhambebe that an attack by the Tupinikin was imminent, for he claimed to know that twenty-five canoes were being prepared for an onslaught into Tupinambá territory. Staden writes that "he asked me a lot and told me much," a statement that suggests that Staden—although still a captive who was mocked and tormented—was beginning to see the value of dealing in information.[32]

After returning to Ubatuba from visiting Cunhambebe, the village suffered an attack by the Tupinikin, as Staden had predicted. Staden took advantage of the situation to ingratiate himself with his captors and to prove that he was not Portuguese. He said, "You take me for a Portuguese, your enemy. Now, give me a bow and arrows, and let me go, and I will help you defend the huts." Staden proceeded to fight alongside his captors, not as a Hessian soldier trained to use the arquebus would have fought, but as a Tupinambá warrior, with a bow and arrows. Yet it was the pretext for yet another dissimulation, because Staden hoped to slip away in the heat of the battle and run for it. He was truly playing the middle, using the situation to his advantage. In fact, the Tupinambá held off the Tupinikin attack, and Staden was not able to escape. After the retreat of the Tupinikin, the Tupinambá still did not trust him, and they kept him closely guarded.[33]

One night, as Staden remembers it, the elders of the village gathered to smoke and to talk. They placed Staden in their midst and taunted him, bantering back and forth over when they would kill him. Staden noticed the bright full moon that had risen in the early evening above the village, and he later recalled praying silently. Asked why he was staring at the moon, Staden replied: "I can see that it is angry." Nhaêpepô-oaçú, one of his captors, then asked who the moon was angry at. "It is looking toward your hut," Staden replied.[34]

Registering Nhaêpepô-oaçú's violent rejection of such a thought, Staden quickly retracted and claimed instead that the moon's fury was directed not at his hut but at the Guarani, another traditional enemy of the Tupinambá. In the illustration that accompanies his account, Staden is naked as he gazes at the moon and stars, surrounded by his captors, who are squatting and smoking. Cut into the woodblock are the words "O my Lord and God, help me out of this misery to a bright [blessed] end."[35]

Soon after this exchange, Nhaêpepô-oaçú and the people of his longhouse left Ubatuba to help the village of Mambucabe recover after having been attacked and burned by the same Tupinikin war party that had besieged Ubatuba. While they were gone, a ship from São Vicente sounded its gun, announcing that it had arrived and wished to speak to the Tupinambá. Staden quickly invented a story that he had a brother, who lived among the Portuguese who was French. Staden hoped for a ransom—the payment of trading goods in exchange for his life. This was a common practice, and his Tupinambá captors even suggested that the Portuguese "might want to buy you." The Tupinambá had no intention of ransoming Staden, however, and in response to inquiries about Staden, they gave no information and sent the ship on its way. This encounter further convinced the Tupinambá that Staden was indeed Portuguese, for if the ship had been sent to look for him, then clearly they had the right man.[36]

When the families in Nhaêpepô-oaçú's hut began to return from Mambucabe, they came sobbing with terrible news. Disease had broken out during the two weeks when Nhaêpepô-oaçú and his people were there rebuilding the longhouses that had been burned down by the Tupinikin. Nhaêpepô-oaçú and his brother, mother, nieces, and nephews all became violently sick. Shocked at the impact of the disease that descended so suddenly and with such devastating results, the Tupinambá struggled to understand the meaning of the outbreak. Staden's prophecy of the anger of the moon was re-interpreted to foretell the sickness that befell them. Nhaêpepô-oaçú's brother came to Staden and said: "My brother suspects that your God must be angry."[37]

Staden immediately insisted that this in fact was the case: "I told him yes, my God was angry, because he wanted to eat me." Staden reiterated that he was not Portuguese, and yet Nhaêpepô-oaçú insisted on holding him as an enemy. Then Staden went even further, saying, "Go to your brother and tell him to come back to his huts. Then I would speak to my God and he would get well."[38]

When Nhaêpepô-oaçú and his people returned to Ubatuba, Staden played the role of healer, even though he recognized the danger in doing so. If those he "healed" recovered, they might kill him anyway; if he could not "heal" the sick, the others might call for his death. Nhaêpepô-oaçú begged Staden to cure them and promised to spare his life if he recovered. Staden began to walk among the sick, laying his hands on their heads. Death still struck. First a child died, then an old woman, then two adult men, another child, possibly three adult women, all from Nhaêpepô-oaçú's family; he too was still very sick. With eight people having died, others in the village feared death.

Two chiefs, probably also stricken with the illness, Guaratinga-açú and Carimã-cui, began to dream about Staden. In one dream Staden appeared and "told him he would die," while the other was so terrible that the chief thought he would certainly die. When he heard about these dreams, Staden cautiously took advantage of the opening and interpreted them to the chiefs, using the opportunity to insist that they would recover if they gave up the desire to kill him. Staden's status was definitely changing. The older women who had once tormented him now begged him to cure them, calling Staden "my son" (Chê-raira in Tupi). Moreover, the older women no longer believed him to be Portuguese, saying, Staden says, "We have already captured and eaten many Portuguese, but their God never got as angry as yours."[39]

Through clever manipulation of situations, words, and dissimulation, Staden had managed to prolong his existence. Yet he was aided too by outside events that he turned to his advantage. The outbreak of disease that gave him the chance to play the role of healer was a sickness unknown to his captors. This strange disease was likely one introduced by Europeans, and it attacked with shocking results. As contacts with indigenous populations increased along the coast of Brazil in the sixteenth century and as European settlements like São Vicente grew, diseases such as pneumonia, influenza, or malaria spread, resulting in high mortality for Tupi and Guarani peoples. Of course epidemic disease was also a fact of life for Europeans in the sixteenth century, but the millennia of isolation of the Americas meant that native populations had no built-up immunities. When epidemics broke out, most became sick and many died.[40]

When the French *truchement* Carautá-uára returned to Ubatuba, Staden describes him as surprised to find him still alive. Staden drew him aside and spoke to him in Tupi, urging him to tell the Tupinambá that Staden was a German and a friend to the French, and that Carautá-uára should take him to the anchorage where the French ships called so that Staden could return home. Carautá-uára promised to help Staden and told the Tupinambá that he wanted to take Staden to a French ship, but the Tupinambá would have nothing of it. Staden writes that they said that they "would not let me go, even if my own father or brothers came there and brought them a shipload of goods, because they had captured me in enemy territory, and I was theirs." In the minds of the Tupinambá, Staden was their captive because he had been captured in the country of their enemies. Moreover, they began to suspect Carautá-uára. "Why did he not give you a knife which you could have given to me?" Alkindar Miri asked when Staden insisted that Carautá-uára was indeed his countryman. The Tupinambá then began to mutter amongst themselves "that the Frenchmen were just as worthless as the Portuguese."[41]

When a second ship arrived from São Vicente five or six months into Staden's captivity, seeking to barter knives and sickles for manioc meal to feed the slaves on the sugar plantations, the crew inquired again about Staden. This time the Tupinambá revealed that Staden was still alive. The Portuguese crew attempted to ransom Staden, saying to the Tupinambá that they had a chest of trading goods to exchange for him. Staden assured his captors that his "brother" was on the ship and that he intended to ask him to ask his father to send a "ship full of goods" for his release. This dissimulation convinced the Tupinambá to allow Staden to come within speaking distance of the ship. In Portuguese, Staden cried out that only one of the crew should speak to him and that it must not be made known that he was not French.[42]

The man who spoke for the ship's crew, according to Staden, was a Spaniard by the name of Juan Sanchez. Apparently they spoke in Spanish, and Staden learned that the Portuguese captain of São Vicente had ordered the crew to try to ransom him or, failing that, to capture some Tupinambá to use in exchange for him. Staden asked only for some knives and fish hooks, saying that it would be impossible for the Portuguese to ransom him. When Staden delivered the knives and fish hooks to his captors, he claimed that they were from his French brother, who was going to escape from the Portuguese and return home and "bring a ship with many goods" as a reward for the Tupinambá treating him so well. Staden's deceit and lies worked, for afterwards the Tupinambá said, "He surely has to be a Frenchman. Let us treat him better from now on."[43]

Because Staden had neither money nor family in Brazil, he had to convince not only the Tupinambá to accept, but the French to offer, a ransom. When the French ship, the *Marie Bellotte,* appeared in the Guanabara Bay, Staden thought he would finally succeed. The ship's captain sent a boat, along with a few men and a sailor named Jacob, who was their interpreter, to the village where Staden was living. As Jacob negotiated the trade in peppers, monkeys, and parrots with the Tupinambá, Staden begged him to take him with him, but his master, Ipiru-guaçu, said that the ransom would have to be a good one. In other words, Staden's freedom would be expensive. Staden then suggested to the Tupinambá that if they took him to Niteroi, on the Guanabara Bay, his "friends" on the *Marie Bellotte* would offer plenty. The

Figure 9. French Sailors Refuse Staden. From Hans Staden, *Warhaftige Historia.*
Marburg: 1557. Courtesy, Lilly Library, Indiana University, Bloomington, Indiana.

Tupinambá men were not fooled, however, because they replied to Staden that these men were not his true friends, for they "would surely have given you a shirt, since you walk around naked, but they take no account of you." Staden begrudgingly recognized that what they said was true.[44]

Staden realized that the Tupinambá had caught him out, yet they still promised to deliver him to the *Marie Bellotte* before she left the Guanabara Bay. Having finished their trade, the French crew began to prepare the boat to return to Niteroi, where the *Marie Bellotte* lay at anchor. Staden panicked. He ran to the beach and swam out to the boat. He tried to climb aboard, but the French crew pushed him away (see fig. 9). It was clear to Staden that they did not want to take him, because if they had done so the Tupinambá would turn against them. Staden returned to the Tupinambá, who were pleased, and Staden recognized that he had to instantly tell another lie: "Do you think that I wanted to run away from you like that? I went to the boat and told my people that they should send for me again after your return from the wars, so that when you bring me to them they will have much to give you in exchange."[45]

The Tupinambá promised Staden that after they made war on the Tupinikin to the south they would allow him to board the *Marie Bellotte* and return. The eleven-day warring expedition occurred in August of 1554 and ventured into Tupinikin and Portuguese territory, very near to the place where Staden had been captured. The war party consisted of thirty-eight canoes, each with eighteen men, led by Cunhambebe, who insisted that Staden accompany the war party. On the way south, the men paddled and fished by day, and while camped at night, they listened to Cunhambebe preach, danced in preparation for war, and took note of their dreams each night. The men often asked Staden if he thought they would capture many enemies. The day when they spotted the enemy, Staden states, "I knew each of them."[46]

The Tupinambá chased the five canoes for four hours, and when their arrows and shot ran out, they stormed the canoes and captured the men. Among those were Staden's good friends from Bertioga, the Braga brothers. Captured also were several Tupinikin, including a woman, and other mamelucos whom Staden names as Jeronimo and Jorge Ferreira. Staden clearly understood that since all had been taken in war, all would be treated as captives and prepared for the cannibalism ceremony.

By this time in his captivity, Staden had observed several cannibalism ceremonies firsthand. In the most traditional ceremony, the captive was a member of a Tupi group known as the Maracaiás who, like the Tupinikin, were neighboring enemies of the Tupinambá. The ceremony took place in another village, a day's journey by canoe. Staden's captors had been invited to the feast, and the women had brewed drink from manioc roots. Staden spoke to the captive before the ceremony and was surprised by his countenance, remembering that "he spoke and acted as if he were going to the festival." Staden used the term *kermis,* which referred to the sacred and secular festivals commonly celebrated in Germany in the sixteenth century. These were popular peasant festivals that typically began on a summer or fall Sunday and continued for eight days. The festivals had a religious foundation, but they were accompanied by music, dancing, and drinking. The captive's greatest concern was with the woven cotton rope that would cinch his waist in the killing ceremony: it was too short. Among his own people, he told Staden, the ropes were much better done.[47]

Another cannibalism ceremony took place during the sixth month of his captivity, when the Tupinambá killed a Guarani who lived with them as a slave, performing such tasks as hunting for game. Staden feared this particular Guarani slave because he had given information against him to the Tupinambá many times. For example, the Guarani said that Staden had been the one who had killed one of their chiefs who was known to have been killed by the Portuguese. When the Guarani slave fell sick, Staden, who was still playing the role of healer, was asked to make him well. Staden attempted to bleed the man, but because the tooth he was using was too dull, he could not draw any blood. To the Tupinambá standing around watching, Staden replied that it was of no use. Since the Tupinambá man who owned the slave had already voiced his intention to give the slave away if there was no hope of his recovery so that his friend could kill him and obtain a new name, Staden had signed his death sentence. The Tupinambá said: "[H]e is going to die. We want to slay him before he dies."[48]

"No, don't do it, he might recover," Staden said, even though the Guarani had lost an eye due to his sickness and "looked terrible." The Tupinambá killed the man, and Staden's description of the event and subsequent cannibalism is gruesome. The man was killed and eaten without any of the ceremony that had accompanied the killing of the Maracaiá captive. The Guarani was not conscious when the blow descended on his head, and no preparations such as the brewing of vats of manioc beer had been made, nor were guests invited. The Guarani was not given the traditional feather headdress or cinched with a woven cotton rope; instead the women had to be called to make a fire alongside his body. Staden took advantage of this situation to insist that the Guarani had always lied about him, that he had become sick because God was angry at the lies he told, and that he had been killed as a punishment from God (see fig. 10).[49]

"My God will do the same to all evil persons," Staden proclaimed, "who have done or will do me evil." His words, spoken after a sick and ugly man had been killed and eaten, not in the usual ceremony that accorded honor and respect to the captive, he believed, struck a chord of terror in the minds of the Tupinambá.[50]

The capture of Staden's own friends, the Braga brothers, occurred following the successful Tupinambá attack against Bertioga, and before the war party had returned home, some rituals that involved or that would involve cannibalism were already being performed. When the Braga brothers asked if they were to be eaten, Staden told them "they had to trust in our Heavenly Father and in His dear Son Jesus Christ" and that "we have to be content with the things that Almighty God decides to do to us." When they asked about their cousin, Staden told them that Jeronimo "lay by the fire roasting" and that he had seen a piece of another mameluco, Jorge Ferreiro being "eaten." The Braga brothers began to weep, and according to Staden, he comforted them, saying that God would protect them if they trusted in Him. But Staden's words were not comforting, for he went on to say that since they had been born in São Vicente, they were used to cannibalism. Staden could not help adding that it was much harder for him, because he had come from

Figure 10. The Cannibalism of the Guarani Slave. From Hans Staden, *Warhaftige Historia*. Marburg: 1557. Courtesy, Lilly Library, Indiana University, Bloomington, Indiana.

afar and was not used to such customs. To which his friends replied that he had become so hardened that he had lost all sensitivity to their plight.[51]

Staden went to Cunhambebe and asked what he intended to do with the two mamelucos—the Braga brothers—and was told that "they were to be eaten." Staden told him to ransom them to their friends, but Cunhambebe refused. The chief was angry, Staden reported, saying the men should have stayed at home instead of fighting. This exchange, Staden claimed, took place as Cunhambebe was consuming human flesh. Staden writes that Cunhambebe held a leg to his mouth and asked him if he wanted to eat it. Staden refused, saying that even animals did not eat their own species. Cunhambebe replied in Tupi, according to Staden: "Jau war sehe [Jauára ichê]": "I am a tiger" (i.e., the American jaguar). Then he said, Staden writes, "it tastes good."[52]

Was Cunhambebe joking? Or was he speaking metaphorically (i.e., that he was transforming into a jaguar as he ate human flesh)? Which of these should we believe? We can't be sure. Staden's portrait of Cunhambebe at this moment is not flattering, but it is revealing. Staden's status had risen considerably among his captors by this time—"the savages were very favorably disposed towards me"—and he possessed a deeper understanding of the Tupinambá. Staden knew that he could not refuse to go on the war party, and even after the capture of his own friends and neighbors, he knew he could do little to free them from the rituals that awaited them. As he describes Cunhambebe and the other rituals that were taking place around him, he makes clear that the rituals had deep spiritual meaning for both the Tupinambá and the Tupinikin. In the evening, while the war party was camped near São Sebastião, Staden recounts that Cunhambebe ordered all of his warriors who had captured a prisoner to take his captive down to the beach where the captives danced with maracas. After the singing, the Tupinikin captives called out one after another: "Well, like brave people we set out to capture you, our enemies, and to eat you. Now you have gotten the upper hand and have captured us, but we do not care about that. Brave people who are fit to fight die in enemy territory. And our land is also big: our people will avenge our deaths on you." To which sentiments the Tupinambá replied: "Well, . . . you have already finished off many of our people. We want to take revenge on you for this."[53]

The dancing, singing, and shaking of the maracas all conveyed that this was a moment imbued with meaning for captive and captor alike. Perhaps some of those dancing were adolescent boys who had captured their first prisoner in battle; this would mark a moment in their transition to manhood. Others were certainly fierce warriors who would soon be able to add another name and thereby acquire more honor among the elders. Staden's recounting of the dialogue sung back and forth suggests that to be an enemy, to capture, to kill, to die were all central to how the Tupi peoples saw themselves and their world.[54]

When the Tupinambá returned home to their villages from this attack near Bertioga with the Braga brothers and other mamelucos as their captives, Staden hoped that he would finally be able to negotiate his freedom. The *Marie Bellotte* was still loading brazilwood farther north. Staden asked to be taken to the ship, and for the first time, his captors were willing to do so. However, they stalled, claiming that they must first finish the cannibalism ceremonies relating to Jeronimo and Jorge Ferreira. By the time they finished, the ship had left. Staden describes himself as much cast down, but in fact he was soon thereafter traded to a Tupinambá chief in the Guanabara Bay named Abati-poçanga. He told his new master—for he was still a slave—that a ship would be coming with goods for his ransom.

Hans Staden's freedom was finally secured by a ransom of five ducats and much dissimulation. The ransom was paid by another French captain, of the ship *Catherine*, to Staden's new master Abati-poçanga. The *Catherine* reached the port of

Niteroi in the Guanabara Bay in October 1554. Staden had learned of the *Catherine*'s arrival from two Tupinambá who came to the village known as Taquaraçu-tiba where he was being held. Staden had only recently come to live in this village; only two weeks before he had been given to the chief Abati-poçanga. Staden immediately asked to be taken to the ship, claiming that on it might be his brothers, who, he had told Abati-poçanga, would be coming for him. The Tupinambá promised to do so, but not immediately.[55]

Meanwhile, the *Catherine*'s captain, a Frenchman by the name of Guilhaume de Monet, began to trade with the Tupinambá. He heard from his trading partners, presumably chiefs living near Niteroi, that a European man had recently come to live in the village of Taquaraçu-tiba. Perhaps they said too that Abati-poçanga called him his "son" and that he had been hunting with his other sons. Intrigued, Monet sent two sailors with several Tupinambá chiefs friendly to him to investigate the case. Upon arrival at the village, they were received in the long-house of a chief named Coó-uara-açu, and Staden, who lived in Abati-poçanga's longhouse nearby, learned of their arrival. Because Staden was German and spoke no French, he greeted the French sailors in Tupi. The sailors gave Staden some clothes, and Staden learned from a sailor named Perrault, who spoke Tupi, that their captain intended to rescue him, using any means necessary. But rather than using force, Staden hoped to rely on guile instead. Staden persuaded Perrault to pretend that they were his brothers and that Monet's ship carried chests filled with trading goods for him. Staden further requested that Perrault tell Chief Abati-poçanga, Staden's master, that Staden must go to the ship and retrieve these chests. He must also tell Abati-poçanga that Staden would remain behind collecting peppers and other things for the *Catherine* when it returned the following year.[56]

Soon Abati-poçanga and Staden went down to where the *Catherine* lay at anchor. After spending five days on the ship, Abati-poçanga told Staden to take possession of the chests because it was time to return to the village. But Captain Monet suggested that Staden stall until all of the cargo had been loaded on board the *Catherine*. Then, when it was time for the *Catherine* to depart, and the sailors mustered, a drama of deception might begin.

It took place on the ship in full view of all. Abati-poçanga, Staden, and men and women from Taquaraçu-tiba were on the ship along with Captain Monet, Perrault, and the other sailors. Monet spoke to Abati-poçanga through Perrault or another interpreter, saying that he wanted to reward him for not killing Staden and that he intended for Staden to remain as his collector of commodities. Then ten of the crew, who had been selected because they looked somewhat similar to Staden, objected, saying that they would not allow their "brother" to remain behind, as their "father" was old and wanted to see his son before he died.

Captain Monet pretended to give in to the sailors and told Abati-poçanga that even though he was captain of the ship, he could not go against so many of his crew. Staden likewise said that although he wanted to return with Abati-poçanga to the village, he had to yield to the wishes of his brothers. Abati-poçanga began to cry out, saying that since the men would take Staden by any means, Staden must return on the first ship because he loved him as a son. One of his wives began to weep, and Staden joined her, lamenting in the Tupi way. Then Captain Monet gave five ducats worth of goods—knives, axes, mirrors, and combs—to Abati-poçanga, and he and his people disembarked and returned to their village expecting to see Staden again in a year.

On the surface, the five ducats paid by Captain Monet served as a ransom for Staden, but it was the drama of deception that secured Staden's release. Staden later described it as a hoax, the intent of which was to make sure that the *Catherine* left "the natives [or Wild Ones] in good spirits, ready to trade again in the future." It showed how well Staden and Captain Monet knew the Tupinambá and how unwilling each was to undermine the possibility of future commercial exchanges. Perhaps at that moment Staden did intend to return to Brazil, but by the time he wrote his account he had no intention of doing so. He wrote: "Thus the Almighty Lord, the God of Abraham, Isaac and Jacob saved me from the hands of tyrants."[57]

Five ducats was not a lot of money for a French sea captain such as Monet, although it may have been to Staden and the other sailors on the *Catherine*. A ducat was a Venetian gold coin equivalent to the Portuguese *cruzado*. Worth approximately 400 Portuguese *reis*, it purchased an *arroba* (32 pounds) of sugar in Brazil in 1550. Five ducats, or 2,000 reis, was one-tenth of the value of a female African slave purchased in Brazil before 1569. Indian slaves were worth far less than African slaves in Brazil in the middle of the sixteenth century; an Indian slave laboring on a sugar plantation was evaluated typically at 9,000 reis. As a slave, whom Abati-poçanga loved as his son, Staden was worth far more than five ducats. When the brazilwood trade began in the early sixteenth century, a hundred weight of brazilwood had the value of between two-and-a-half and three ducats, and a merchant could expect a half-ducat of profit on each hundredweight. Thus the value of Staden's ransom may have been on the order of one or two logs of brazilwood, which would have been nothing to Staden's master, Abati-poçanga. It was the drama that secured Staden's release, and the five ducats of trading goods symbolized only the good will of the French captain.[58]

The five ducats of trading goods also averted violence and war. Staden was well apprised of the military prowess of the Tupinambá. Staden's little drama of deception was dangerous, but it recognized not only the value of the Tupinambá as trading partners but the power of chiefs to make war against their enemies.

Monet did not intend to hold Staden as his slave, but he might well have been expecting Staden to grant him his loyalty and to offer services in repayment. Since Staden was an experienced gunner, one way to acknowledge the debt was to serve as Monet's gunner as the *Catherine* made her way home. Merchant ships were loaded with expensive cargoes, and pirates roamed the Atlantic. The Portuguese king had authorized any of his captains to attack French ships; hence, Captain Monet would certainly have welcomed Staden's expertise on board.

The first engagement came even before they left the Guanabara Bay, when the *Catherine* tried to take a smaller Portuguese vessel owned by Peter Rösel, a merchant with ties to Antwerp, who lived in São Vicente. Staden knew Rösel and many of those on board. His first test of loyalty to Monet therefore came when Monet sent him to persuade his former friends to surrender. In his role as go-between, Staden failed, for the Portuguese refused his overture and the French attacked in response. The Portuguese counterattacked, and soon several French sailors had died and Staden himself was so badly wounded that he later judged himself to have been near death. He recalls that he prayed for his life so that he "would return to Christian lands and proclaim to others the mercy He had shown to me."[59]

If the *Catherine* followed the typical French trading pattern, the captain would have stopped in West African ports on the outbound voyage before crossing the Atlantic for Brazil and the Caribbean. The financial backers of the voyage were interested in the large profits that the rich red dye extracted from the heavy brazilwood logs promised in the northern European textile markets. After loading cargo in Brazil, French captains usually selected the northern route across the Atlantic because this course took advantage of winds, currents, and additional trading opportunities. Heading north, they hugged the Brazilian coast to avoid the strong southern current, stopping in Paraíba, where they collected more brazilwood. Reaching Cabo de São Roque, the helmsman would then change course, following the coastline as it turned to the west toward the Amazon River delta. From charts and previous experience, he knew exactly where he was, even when sailing well out to sea to avoid the swift current of the Amazon River. On the quadrant and astrolabe, the latitude read nearly 0, which meant they were right on the Equator. Once in the northern hemisphere, navigating by the North Star led them to Caribbean ports known to be friendly to French ships.[60]

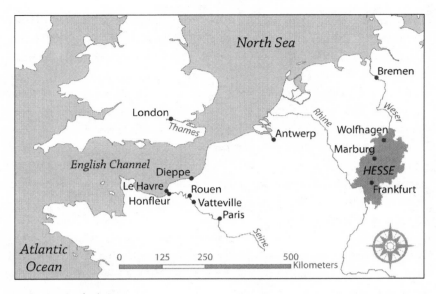

Figure 11. Staden's Return

It seems likely that the *Catherine* did take the northern route home. Staden would later claim to have sailed along more than 500 German miles (approximately 3,800 km.) of the Brazilian coast, which from where he first landed in Brazil, at 28 degrees south) would extend roughly to the coast of Ceará in northeastern Brazil. Once they left America, he writes, they were out of sight of land for four months, and good weather and schools of fish on Christmas Eve and on Three Kings' Day had blessed their return. As they approached the port of Honfleur in late winter, the hold of the *Catherine* would have been packed tightly with a variety of trading goods from many ports, such as brazilwood, ivory, and peppers, while parrots and monkeys lived up on deck with the crew. If all went well, and the *Catherine*'s voyage seems to have done so, high profits were in store for the merchants who had invested in this dangerous and unpredictable trade. Captain Monet would have made multiple stops to load and unload cargo for those who had invested in the *Catherine*'s voyage.[61]

Once anchored in the port of Honfleur and the cargo unloaded, Captain Monet continued up the Seine River, surely still in the *Catherine,* for the ship hailed from Vatteville, a small village upriver. The Seine was navigable by ocean-going ships all the way to Rouen, the largest and wealthiest city in the region, the hub of the French Atlantic trade and the seat of the provincial and royal government in Normandy (see fig. 11). Staden was still with him.[62]

In Rouen, the story of Staden's ransom was not particularly remarkable. Rouen was filled with families whose menfolk had been to sea or who had invested in the Atlantic trade, and Rouen had long been sending ships to Brazil. Staden's return in 1555 marked only an increase in the Brazil trade, for beginning in 1550 and extending until 1610, hundreds of ships sailed from Normandy to South America. Brazilian customs, even of the Tupinambá, were familiar to the people of Rouen.[63]

A famous "fête" had taken place in Rouen five years earlier, when King Henri II and his queen, Catherine de Médicis, were making their triumphant way through their kingdom following Henri's coronation. The fête prepared in Rouen to greet the royals had a Brazilian theme. It was an elaborately produced drama that sought to impress the new king and queen of the importance of Rouen's identity as a commercial town, tied to the Atlantic trade and especially to Brazil. An entire Tupi village had been reconstructed on the banks of the Seine outside the city for the fête. Two hundred and fifty sailors, all of whom had been to Brazil, as well as fifty Tupi Indians, were gathered together in a kind of mise-en-scène: the Indians lounged, naked and feathered, in hammocks, speaking Tupi; or they worked, pretending to cut, dress, and load the brazilwood logs in a pantomime that recreated the negotiations between a French sea captain, such as Monet, and a Tupi chief, such as Abatipoçanga. More exciting for the audience was the chief's passionate speech that preceded a mock battle between two archrival Tupi groups, such as the Tupinambá and their Tupinikin enemies. Following this fierce hand-to-hand combat, a mock naval battle between a French and Portuguese ship, such as that fought between the *Catherine* and Peter Rösel's ship, was staged on the Seine. Afterward, it was generally agreed that the drama was so near to life that "its effect was 'a certain simulacra of the truth.' "[64]

What did make Staden's arrival in Rouen unique in February of 1555 was that at that time word had certainly leaked out of an expedition preparing to sail for Brazil under the command of Nicolas Durand de Villegagnon. This would be no trading expedition, however. Villegagnon had a secret loan from King Henri II that was to fund the construction of a French colony in the Guanabara Bay. Captain Monet tried to persuade Staden to join another expedition, possibly even this one, but Staden claims to have wanted only a passport that would give him the right to travel freely in Normandy. Monet took the unusual step of introducing Staden to the lord admiral, Gaspard de Châtillon-Coligny, who personally granted Staden a passport. Coligny, with Villegagnon, was planning the French colony in Brazil to be known as France Antarctique. While many sailors in Normandy had made trips to Brazil, some even living among the Tupi peoples, Staden had worked for the Portuguese in the southern colony of São Vicente. As a result, he had expert, up-to-date knowledge about their forts and ships. Staden certainly would have been a man of interest to the admiral, and perhaps this meeting was another way in which he demonstrated his loyalty and repaid his debt to Captain Monet.[65]

Before leaving Rouen, Staden received some money from Captain Monet, which suggests that he not only repaid whatever debt he owed but provided additional services. We might speculate that it was the information that he provided to the Lord Admiral Coligny and to Villegagnon. With a little money in his pocket and papers that gave him permission to travel, Staden planned to stop first in the French seaport town of Dieppe before making his way to London, Antwerp, and then to Hesse. In Dieppe, Staden visited the house of the *Marie Bellotte*'s captain, where he unkindly declared that the crew of the French ship, who were long overdue, were despicable men. He does not tell us how he was able to communicate with the families, for while he was in Brazil, he was not able to speak French. Was he speaking through an interpreter, either German or Tupi-Guarani, while he was in France? Or could he have learned enough French on the four-month return voyage? Or was there a third common language, such as Spanish or Portuguese?[66]

Staden then departed for London, where he seems to have been a carrier of news. He stayed with merchants of the Dutch exchange, who had already had word of him from Captain Monet. At this time, when information about trade, investments, shipwrecks, and prices for commodities still traveled by word of mouth, Staden had much to convey. The Dutch merchants seem to have rewarded him, for they gave him money to travel to Germany. Staden then headed for Antwerp, where he stayed at the house of Jasper Schetz, who owned a sugar plantation in São Vicente. This plantation was managed by Peter Rösel, whom Staden knew; and it was Rösel's ship that Captain Monet had attacked in Brazil, after Staden, working as his go-between, failed to negotiate a surrender. Staden writes that he told Schetz that his factor's ship had been attacked by the French. Schetz gave Staden two imperial ducats (*Kaiserdukaten*). Did Staden tell him the truth about this sea battle, revealing his role on the attacking side?

Staden was a practiced liar, at least while trying to escape from the Tupinambá and return home. How might he have been judged in the sixteenth century? Lying, the nature of truth, and the art of dissimulation were, as we have seen, topics of reflection in sixteenth-century western Europe. In his famous essay "On Cannibals," Montaigne addresses the veracity of information delivered from those who claimed to have visited far-off lands. Montaigne's subject is also the cannibalism of the Tupinambá of Brazil, based on information he obtained from a Frenchman who had lived in Brazil for ten or twelve years in the middle of the sixteenth century. Montaigne was inclined to believe this man, for he was "a simple, crude fellow," and Montaigne believed that such a man was more likely to be truthful than a "clever" man, who was likely to embellish the truth. Montaigne writes that the clever "observe more things and more curiously, but they interpret them." In so doing, "they cannot help altering history a little" and "they never show you things as they are." Instead, they will "bend and disguise" things "according to the way they have seen them." Their tendency, in order to "give credence to their judgment and attract you to it," Montaigne observes, is "to add something to their matter, to stretch it out and amplify it." In the end, he concludes "the better to induce your faith," they "are willing to help out the business with something more than is really true, of their own invention." Because this is the case, Montaigne posits that one must have "a man either very honest, or so simple that he has not the stuff to build up false inventions and give them plausibility; and wedded to no theory." Such was his man, and moreover, he brought to Montaigne sailors and merchants who had been with him in Brazil and who confirmed his observations.[67]

In this famous essay, Montaigne asks the reader to question the source of information coming from newly discovered lands and peoples. His concern lies in the ways that a clever writer can slant information in order to disseminate a point of view. Montaigne prefers the description given by his simple and crude man over that of the educated cosmographer: "So I content myself with his information, without inquiring what the cosmographers say about it," he writes. Montaigne states his preference as: "I would like everyone to write what he knows, and as much as he knows, not only in this, but in all other subjects." His simple crude fellow tells only what he has seen, and therefore is superior in Montaigne's view, to the king's cosmographer.[68]

Should we believe Staden? On the surface, it would seem that Staden passes Montaigne's truthfulness test, for he is an ordinary man who claims only to humbly relate his story and as briefly as possible. He was not a clever cosmographer, and there is even some question as to whether he actually wrote his story down or simply dictated it to another. He was not a member of a religious order like André Thevet, or a Calvinist minister such as Jean de Léry, both of whom visited Brazil at around the same time and also published books about the Tupinambá in Brazil. Instead, Staden was a soldier who went to sea. Certainly this fact alone does not make him believable. Montaigne sets another, even higher standard for truth when he writes about dissimulation in the sixteenth century. In his essays on lying, Montaigne holds lying to be "an accursed vice" because he believes that human society is held together by words. "Mutual understanding," he writes, "is brought about solely by way of words"; thus, "he who breaks his word betrays human society." Montaigne laments that dissimulation is rampant in his time. "I do not know what people expect to gain by incessant feigning and dissimulating," he writes. For Montaigne, "what we say must be what we think; otherwise it is wickedness." Staden—the lying captive—would hardly have passed Montaigne's ideal of truthfulness.[69]

For the transactional go-between who dealt in words, in information, in subtle meanings, lying was part of the strategic arsenal, just as for Machiavelli's prince. Lies were dangerous but could be effective if delivered well. And if a greater good were served, then lies could be morally justifiable. Staden chose to lie to save his life, and later, having survived to tell his tale, he chose to let his readers see his lies to the Tupinambá. Was his hope that his readers would agree that the greater good was his life saved? Or was it that they would hail his transformation into a prophet of God's grace to those who sail the seas?

Perhaps these questions were on his mind while he was making his way home to Hesse. Signs of Brazil were around him still. While in Antwerp, Staden most certainly walked down the Twaalfmaandenstraat, where gates and a bell tower marked the entrance to the Antwerp Bourse, or Stock Exchange, just outside of the old city center. Brazilwood and Brazilian sugar were by 1555 important commodities on the bourse, and Staden may well have been there with his host and watched how this early stock exchange worked. Just outside the gates, booksellers hawked the new books, among them travel accounts and new publications on the Americas. Perhaps he also visited the stalls and showrooms opening around the bourse where painters, tapestry weavers, silversmiths, and jewelry makers were exhibiting and selling their work to merchants who marketed them all over Europe. Woodcut prints of all kinds would have been available for sale there. From Antwerp he made his way home to Hesse, perhaps telling his story all along the way.[70]

CHAPTER THREE

The Traveler Returns

I trust that your Highness may, whenever it pleases you, have read aloud to you at your leisure the story of my adventures by land and sea." So Staden wrote, and perhaps even said, to his prince, Landgrave Philipp of Hesse, sometime in the summer of 1556. But Staden's book, *True History,* was not a simple adventure story, nor was the publication of it a straightforward affair meant to entertain the prince. When Staden adds "if only as an account of the miracles that Almighty God granted to me in my distress," we have our first clue that his book, dedicated to his prince, was far more than a leisurely description of his New World travels.[1]

True History was the product of a representational go-between who related foreign experiences to people who had not made the journey themselves. As a representational go-between, Staden joined the ranks of the many who "through writings, drawings, mapmaking, and the oral tradition, shaped on a large scale how Europeans and Native Americans viewed one another." The book told of the strange and unfamiliar in familiar ways. One powerful framing device was the Protestant faith of Staden's prince and his native Hesse; another was the tradition of humanist inquiry spreading across Europe and represented in the figure of the doctor and scholar who wrote the introduction to the book, Johannes Dryander. Staden told his stories to his prince, and as he told his story, the tale took shape. With Dryander, the prince's advisor, Staden then wrote and illustrated a book that represented the New World. Once written, the book joined other words, images, and beliefs to shape European perceptions about peoples across the sea.[2]

True History appeared on a February day in the spring of 1557, on Shrove Tuesday, the day before Ash Wednesday. Traditionally, in Christian Europe, this last day before the beginning of Lent (the forty days of fasting and penitence before Easter) was a raucous, topsy-turvy time in which the existing order was turned upside down in riotous parades and drunken feasts, if only to further underscore that such excesses were meant to be the exception rather than the rule. But in Protestant Hesse, such drunken disorderliness was frowned upon because it was precisely that: unruly, unmannerly and disruptive—immoral, in fact.[3]

Like many other reformers and Protestant rulers, Landgrave Philipp (see fig. 12) believed that moral discipline was lax in the German lands and that it was the duty

Figure 12. Landgrave Philipp. From Helius Eobanus
Hessus, *De victoria Wirtembergensi.* Erfurt: 1534.
Courtesy Bayerische Staatsbibliothek, Munich.

of all responsible citizens to curb overindulgence, discourage avarice, and further
brotherly love. As Staden was growing up in the towns of Wetter, Homberg, and Korbach, he would have witnessed firsthand Philipp's public campaign against moral excesses. Edicts, decrees, and proclamations prohibited things such as public toasts (used
as an excuse to raise one's glass again and again), public drunkenness, cursing, guz-
zling, or quarrelling, all of which led to "evil and mischief." Although the frequency of
these edicts underscores how difficult it was to enforce such prohibitions from above,
it is clear that Philipp sought to clamp down on public activities that threatened the
moral order. The edict of 1543 had abolished all-night dancing and drinking, putting
an end in every Hessian town and village to festivities such as those once held on Shrove
Tuesday. Would Staden, although long familiar with these strictures, but perhaps
having experienced looser ways as a former soldier and traveler, have yearned for more
carefree days of drinking and gambling on the day his book appeared? Or was the
book's publication a sign that he had fully joined the community of true believers?[4]

When Staden left Hesse in 1547 to go to sea, his ruler's political and religious fortunes seemed to have hit a low point. Philipp's Schmalkaldic League had experienced setbacks; he was held by Charles V in prison in the Spanish Netherlands for five years. But as early as 1525, Philipp had instigated a number of far-reaching reforms that established a state church in Hesse: he created the new Hessian state on the basis of Protestant faith and practice. These efforts were part of the larger consolidation of Protestantism. The principle of secular sovereignty (that it was the prince and no one else who could determine belief and practice in his own realm) was formalized in the Peace of Augsburg (1555), which ended the Lutheran princes' war against the Holy Roman emperor. The famous expression *Cuius regio, eius religio* ("Whose the regime, his the religion") marks this moment in German history from which point on subjects were to practice the religion of their prince.[5]

When Staden returned home, Philipp's reforms had fundamentally restructured Hessian daily life, the social institutions of the land, and the expression of public morals. Released by Charles V in September 1552, Philipp returned to Hesse. An attempted escape had been unsuccessful and had only served to worsen the terms of his imprisonment (observers opined that the captivity had so aged him that his hair had turned gray). He spent the last fifteen years of his life consolidating his state and his church. Even before the Schmalkaldic War, Philipp had suppressed Catholic worship and established Lutheran doctrine in preaching and practice. In one of the earliest, fastest, and most thorough seizures of Church lands on the Continent, in late 1525 he dissolved convents and monasteries and converted their land and wealth for other purposes. Foremost among these new projects was an evangelical university in Marburg, the Philipps-Universität, founded in 1527. It was Philipp's goal that the university would replace the authority of the Catholic Church, educating Hessian scholars and serving as a new source of knowledge about the material world. Dryander oversaw the university's coffers and spearheaded the state's efforts to seize the wealth once held by the monasteries.[6]

Philipp used books as a means to spread his religious goals, and Dryander assisted him by serving as censor for all of Hesse. By the sixteenth century, states used censorship as a means of self-definition and protection. Printing and censorship in Marburg went hand in hand; books were printed in conjunction with the university, and most of the early books that appeared were meant to publicize religious reform in Hesse. Security could not be separated from religion. Books, therefore, could not challenge the ruler or ruling Protestant beliefs. The earliest proof we have of an existing censor in Marburg dates from 1538, when university chancellor Johannes Feige warned Landgrave Philipp of the danger of some texts that would be critical of the Schmalkaldic League. A ruling from 1548 laid out more clearly what such censorship entailed: before a printer could print something, the text had to be reviewed by the vice-chancellor, the rector, and someone on the faculty.[7]

All of these efforts to control morality, knowledge, and public behavior are part of a development that historians speak of as confessionalization. In this process, various religious confessions—Catholicism, Lutheranism, and Calvinism—began to take shape within the German territories. The pulpit would be the primary place from which people were to be instructed in the gospel. Morality and civil order were to be the result of this preaching, universities and schools would educate all the inhabitants within a principality, and religion would become the foundation for a new type of rule. This process also involved social discipline, whereby the state, in taking over the older functions of the church, took on a greater role in ensuring that subjects were obedient and virtuous.[8]

In a land ruled by moral stricture, the rules of community, censorship, and the power of authority, how could a man like Staden fit in? How could he return to a place he had left eight years before? Despite his time away, Staden was none the richer for all his travels. He had gone through numerous transformations: he was no longer a *Landsknecht,* a soldier for hire who might threaten the social order with his gambling, womanizing, and violent behavior. He was also no longer an experienced seafarer who had survived a shipwreck and who could live off the land in a remote area of interest to few but the Portuguese and Spanish crowns and their growing dreams of empire. Fortunately, he was also no longer a captive, alternately wheedling and threatening his tormentors, using all his knowledge of local customs and international rivalries—as well as proclaiming the power of his God—to escape his captors. Staden had returned, but he was not yet home, and all the power he possessed as a go-between would weigh in the balance at this moment when he stood between two worlds, using his knowledge of both to his advantage.

"Who are you?" "Where do you come from?" "What did you see?" Staden would have heard these questions and many others as he talked about his experiences. Like other travelers in the sixteenth century, Staden presumably told his story aloud to many—perhaps to anyone who would listen. We know that he shared his stories with interested merchants, sea captains, and entrepreneurs when he was in Rouen, London, and Antwerp.[9]

"What will you do now?" was a question that surely followed closely on the heels of the others, and we can only speculate about Staden's plans. One thing we know for sure: he would have had to find some honest work to occupy him, for idleness was equated with godlessness in Hesse, and those who lived from the charity of others were condemned as vagrant beggars who sapped the strength of the community. Only those truly incapable of work—the "feeble-minded, insane, blind, sick, lame, those burdened with the plague or sickness, the invalid, and those with syphilis"—were worthy of support and succor. These broken individuals could no longer seek assistance from the nuns or monks who lived nearby, but instead could be tended to in the new state-run institutions dedicated to their care: the *Landesspitale,* or territorial hospitals. As a part of his Protestant ethos of *caritas,* Philipp had established these to admit "the pious, Godly, and moral, and take care of them."[10]

"What do you have of value?" Staden's countrymen were likely to ask him. "Knowledge of strange, unknown places" could have been his answer. At least since the Middle Ages in Europe, the desire and demand for such information had fueled the trade in and production of travel accounts; and as a go-between, Staden could hope to benefit from his experiences. Some scholars, like Annerose Menninger, have argued that Staden, along with the publisher and others, cashed in on public expectations about gruesome customs in distant lands and created a book they knew would be a sensationalist bestseller. It is quite possible that Staden thought to win a final advantage from his journeys. Having set out on his first voyage with the intention of reaching India and on the second with the goal of finding gold in the Americas, Staden was clearly motivated by the promise of wealth. Yet he returned from Brazil largely destitute, with only the money given to him by Captain Monet and the imperial ducats given to him in Antwerp. What he brought back with him could not come close to resembling the tales of fortune that had led so many to take to the sea. Once back in Hesse, Staden could not even entertain the notion of collecting the reward he was promised for having extended his service to the Portuguese crown, defending the remote outpost at Bertioga. It was difficult for him to proclaim his value to anyone, for while he may have been traded for five ducats of trading goods, these were left in the hands of the Tupinambá. He was fortunate to return to German-speaking lands with his life. The only things of value that he possessed were his knowledge of guns (yet his familiarity with war at sea would not have served him well in landlocked Hesse), his knowledge of the New World, and the story of his adventures. If his adventures in Brazil were the only thing left to him that had any worth, Staden may have hoped to use his story to gain an advantage. He might have sought out his prince to tell him his tale in order to win his attention, prove his value as a gunner, or gain a position as a potential advisor. Just as he had used flattery to gain from Cunhambebe, so now he may have hoped to win a position at the court of Philipp or at the court of one of the lesser nobles of the land. Go-betweens shaped the truth to fit their audience, and Staden would have cast his story in the cadences of Protestantism to suit his listeners. Even if he were utterly sincere, Staden would have been influenced by the context in which he told his story back at home.[11]

"Why did you come back when others did not?" Staden's transformation into a pious Protestant witness began as soon as he set foot on European soil. His appearance in Dieppe in the house of the captain of the *Marie Bellotte,* in front of worried families who were anxiously hoping for news of their loved ones, long overdue from their voyage to Brazil, marked the first step. Staden announced to his listeners that he would be a prophet to them; he then condemned the crew, who had failed to assist him in Brazil, as "godless." His last words to the families in Dieppe emphasized his belief in God's special providence: he had already made it safely back home, while the others had not. Indeed, he told them, they might never return.[12]

"How do we know what you say is true?" In Protestant Hesse, it would be up to the authorities to determine this. "Hans Staden was questioned closely a long time ago," Dryander noted in the introduction to the *True History.* Landgrave Philipp himself, as well as "many others," subjected Staden to intense questioning "in all matters relating to his voyage and his captivity." Perhaps Staden had sought an audience with Philipp directly, or perhaps he had been called to court to give a report after news of his adventures had reached his ruler.[13]

If he made an appearance in the landgrave's castle, Staden would surely have been impressed by its setting, situated as it was atop a steep hill, towering over the timbered houses that lined the Lahn valley (see fig. 13). Depicted in Münster's *Cosmographia,* the castle had served as an important site of religious disputation during the Marburg Colloquy, a famous debate in 1529 between Martin Luther and Huldrych Zwingli about the presence of Christ in the Lord's Supper.

Perhaps Staden had an audience in the beautiful Renaissance hall, with its dramatic arched Gothic ceilings, in the presence of Philipp's court. Dressed in the somber fashion set by the Spanish kings and Emperor Charles V, Philipp's advisors would have surely been struck by the colorful, gripping images Staden conjured up before them, perhaps even projecting their own forbidden desires onto the Americas.

Part testimony, part theater, Staden's questioning and the story that emerged from it likely resonated with Landgrave Philipp. Did Philipp recall his own imprisonment at the hands of his Dutch and Spanish captors when Staden spoke of his tribulations? Did Staden's descriptions of his attempts to flee remind Philipp of his own failed attempt at escape? And did Philipp, upon listening to Staden speak of how the Tupinambá had mocked him, recall how his captors had tormented him, jumping up at odd hours in the night to rip the curtains away from his bed? Did Philipp ask Staden if he prayed to God for his safety, and did Staden reply in the affirmative because he knew his answer would be well received? Staden's questioning was a stage in his journey from a transactional to a representational go-between, and he would, like any go-between, shape his story to fit his audience. Just as he had to

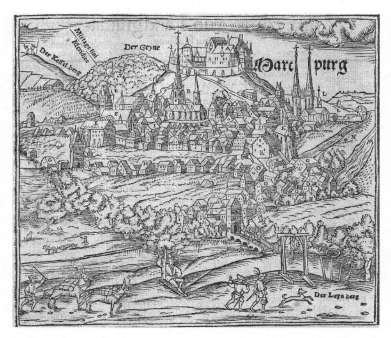

Figure 13. The City of Marburg in Hesse. From Sebastian Münster, *Cosmographia universalis.* Basel: 1550. Courtesy, Lilly Library, Indiana University, Bloomington, Indiana.

argue to the Tupinambá that he was not their enemy, not a Portuguese but a Frenchman or a German, so Staden had to prove to his lord and ruler that he was a loyal and trustworthy son of Hesse, not a duplicitous servant of Spanish, French, or Portuguese rulers or an unreliable vagabond who may have "gone native" during his residence on the other side of the Atlantic world. His appearance could even be seen, as the Brazilian scholar Luciana Villas-Bôas has argued, as a kind of public profession of faith necessary for Staden's reacceptance into the community of believers.[14]

Once questioned, Staden could be accepted back into the community, and as a consummate go-between, he knew how to search for allies and to use available resources to get value from his knowledge and experience. Johannes Dryander became a powerful ally. Having served as an official interrogator and censor, and in all likelihood arranging for Staden to work with the Kolbe printing house, Dryander shaped the *True History.* As he himself reports in an introduction to the text, he was asked by Staden to "look over" and "correct" "and where necessary, improve" his work.[15]

In dry and rather stilted language (much different from the simple German Staden employs), Dryander addresses the reader directly in the preface, demonstrating the honesty of the storyteller and the truthfulness of his tale. Dryander seeks to establish both through a number of arguments. First, he claims Staden must be telling the truth because he comes from a good family, a family that Dryander knew. Furthermore, Staden's simple manner, and the straightforward way in which he tells his story, is additional proof that what he writes really happened to him. We have seen Montaigne make a similar argument. Liars, says Dryander, would use "decorative or fancy words and arguments." So too, Montaigne held that truthfulness could best be established via simple, unadorned words rather than elaborate and embellished tales. Here we also find evidence of the idea that the noble court could be a place of elaborate ritual and therefore deceit: simplicity equaled honesty in Dryander's eyes. To account for the fact that the reader would expect Staden to be spinning tales (because travel narratives are generally not to be trusted), Dryander says that he can see no possible gain for Staden in not telling the truth. In a move becoming familiar to readers of newspapers (*Neue Zeitungen*), Dryander argues that, like facts, travel accounts can be measured and verified. Then Dryander refers to a witness: because Staden says he met a fellow Hessian (and can even name the time and place of the encounter), his story must be true. Moreover, since Staden chose to return to Hesse, he cannot belong to the group of vagabonds and liars who would spread untruths. Dryander quotes the old saying, "He who wishes to lie should do it from afar and out of reach." As a native son returned home, Staden had to be honest and upright.[16]

Dryander concedes that on the face of it, Staden's story might appear preposterous, but he argues that it can still be true nonetheless. He uses as an example the fact that even though classical authorities believed that the globe was unpopulated in the "Torrid Zone" (a band of lands thought to lie above and below the Equator), observation and discovery had shown that this was not the case. And finally, in keeping with his role as censor and advisor to his Protestant prince, Dryander places Staden's tale in the context of a profession of faith: his story must be true because he is not desirous of fame or earthly possessions, but instead he writes to praise and thank God, who saved him from his captivity.

"He comes from this country," says Dryander in the introduction to *True History*, "as do his parents," attesting to the honesty of the man and his tale. Hans Staden should be believed, wrote Dryander, because "he does not wander from place to place like the gypsies, vagabonds, or liars." Dryander places Staden within a setting of like-minded, settled, truthful citizens. Yet he does not say that Staden is an honest citizen of any one town, a dues-paying, rule-abiding Protestant, Dryander's neighbor or friend. What about Dryander's life would have brought him into contact with and made him so interested in Staden's story?[17]

Johannes Dryander (1500–1560) and Hans Staden may have come from the same country, but their lives could not have been more different; Dryander's travels took him as far as Paris to study but no further. While Staden took to the sea to find wealth, Dryander found power, influence, and material stability all within Hesse's borders. Dryander's real name was Johann Eichmann. Like many other humanists of the age, Eichmann wrote under a Hellenized version of his name (*Eiche* [German] = oak; *dry* [Greek] = large tree or oak; *Mann* [German] man; *ander* [Greek] = man; thus Eich-Mann = Dry-ander). His likeness, later engraved by Thomas de Bry (1645), shows him holding a small oak leaf by way of identification (fig. 14). For humanist scholars, choosing to write one's name in a Latinized or Hellenized manner signaled respect for the ancients (as well as an ability to read classic texts in the original language) and membership in an international community of learning and inquiry.[18]

Humanists were unlike seafarers in that most were what we would think of as armchair adventurers, but they shared with men of action like Staden an appreciation of the physical world and an interest in measuring, cataloging, and understanding it. Humanists joined other educated men—natural philosophers, scientists, cartographers, artists, and poets—in reconsidering humanity's place and role in the cosmos. Humanists took a different view toward knowledge, nature, and the past than had their medieval predecessors. Just as cartographers charted new maps based on the stars, humanists reconfigured the place of humanity in the cosmos. Rather than relying on ancient authorities to prove truths, humanists recognized that truth itself was historical, a product of a certain time and place. This meant that humanists focused on the texts themselves, seeking to remove the weight of the centuries—the editing mistakes of medieval copiers—to reveal the original text in its unaltered and unadorned form. Their motto of *ad fontes*, or "[back] to the sources," indicates their interest in carefully examining original texts. They embraced the idea of identifying themselves by Greek or Latin versions of their names to underscore their respect for the knowledge contained within such texts.

After attending the famous humanistic school in Wetter in the small city of his birth (home to Staden's father as well), Dryander went on at the age of eighteen to study at Erfurt University, where Martin Luther had also studied. From there he moved to Paris, where he studied mathematics, astronomy, and anatomy. He followed the nomadic practice of other early modern scholars, returning to Mainz, where he received his doctorate in 1533. Upon completion of his studies, he served as the personal physician of Johann von Metzenhausen, the archbishop of Trier in Ko-

Figure 14. Johannes Dryander. Engraving by Thomas de Bry from Jean Jacques Boissard, *Bibliotheca chalcographica.* Heidelberg: 1669. The text above reads, "Johannes Dryander, Doctor, Anatomist and Mathematician," and below, "Dryander lays bare the human form and [the secrets of] the stars Whence his name bears renown and upon which he bestows his fame." Courtesy, University of Chicago Library.

blenz. In 1535 he was called to Landgrave Philipp's new Protestant university in Marburg. There he served as dean and chancellor.[19]

Dryander would have been keenly interested in a man like Staden, since the former had such novel and intense experiences about a world unknown to the scholar. Dryander's interests were wide-ranging. He wrote for scholars as well as for a broader public, and the underlying thread of all of his work, as we can see from the epigram translated next to the engraving of Dryander (fig. 14), was his desire to "lay bare," or make visible, legible, and knowable, everything that could be captured concerning the physical world, from the stars above to the human form below. The body was, after all, as Dryander argued in his book *Mirror of Medicine (Artzenei Spiegel,*

1541), a smaller world that imitated and replicated the larger world beyond. A study of any object would thus reveal the patterns behind all creation. In keeping with this desire to observe and know, Dryander was interested in maps, astronomy, and astronomical instruments. As a doctor and teacher, he also performed public dissections at the university in an attempt to spread knowledge about the human body. These are regarded as the first ever performed in Germany. Might Staden or a member of his family have attended one of the four dissections carried out on corpses at Marburg's university—two per year in 1535 and 1536?[20]

These dissections served as the foundation for Dryander's famous book, *Anatomiae* (1537), which was accompanied with graphic depictions drawn from Dryander's own work on human anatomy. Yet the publication of the great German humanist's work was not without controversy. In his pathbreaking book *On the Fabric of the Human Body* (*De humani corporis fabrica*, 1543, 1555), published a few years later, the French physician Andreas Vesalius accused Dryander of plagiarism. In the preface, Vesalius complains about a scholar—unnamed but certainly Dryander—who was "indiscriminately compiling pictures from other people's books everywhere and publishing books of that kind at Marburg and Frankfurt." He furthermore castigates those, like Walter Ryff, a well-known plagiarist, who had taken images from Vesalius's earlier work *Tabulae anatomicae,* used them out of context, and mis-colored and mislabeled them. Vesalius calls the "German doctors" who would do such things the "lackeys of unscrupulous printers," implying that such men were making money in a most dishonest fashion.[21]

Dryander's own experiences with questions of credibility and publishing linked him with Staden's attempts to establish that his story was true. Dryander's woodcut illustrations do bear a remarkable similarity to Vesalius's far more beautiful woodcuts (see fig. 15), which served as the basis for a new understanding of human anatomy. Dryander, like Vesalius, had studied under Sylvius in Paris, and so was in any case a proponent of learning anatomy firsthand from dissections. We might speculate that for Dryander the higher truth lay in understanding the actual biological nature of the body rather than knowing who "drew" or "owned" the images. Vesalius had a much different perception of his images—he was extremely protective of them, almost obsessively concerned with piracy. Vesalius wanted the *Fabrica* to make a reputation for him, so he chose to have the wood blocks for his images cut in Venice. Thereafter, he sent them over the Alps to a printer in Basel that, because of its central location, could reach Italian, French, and German markets where the plagiarism of Vesalius's earlier work had been most widespread. Vesalius, unlike Dryander, attached a great deal to the idea of individual authorship and inventiveness.[22]

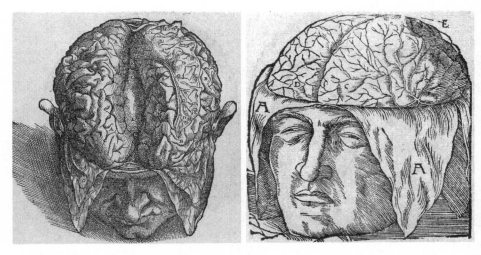

Figure 15. Vesalius's Brain (left) and Dryander's Brain (right). From Andreas Vesalius, *De humani corporis fabrica*, 2nd ed. Basel: 1555; and from Johannes Dryander, *Artzenei Spiegel*. Frankfurt: 1547. Courtesy, Lilly Library, Indiana University, Bloomington, Indiana.

Defenders of Dryander have argued that it was Vesalius who relied on Dryander's work, not the other way around. They believe that Vesalius attacked Dryander because the German had accused him of being ungrateful toward his teacher, Guinther von Anernach. In this version, hurt pride lay behind Vesalius's actions. Whatever the truth of the matter, we can see that in the production of knowledge, originality, prestige, and standing were of great importance to humanists, scientists, and scholars alike.[23]

Vesalius's criticism raises another point, one that was to be of great import for Staden's book, and that was Dryander's close ties to publishing houses in Frankfurt and Marburg. Dryander had published numerous books for specialists as well as for the general public with the printer Christian Egenolff in Frankfurt am Main. In 1538, Landgrave Philipp asked Egenolff to open a branch of his printing house in Marburg because he was convinced that the printing press would serve as an important agent of change in the spread of Protestantism. Egenolff did so with his colleague Andreas Kolbe, who later took over the business himself. Even though the printing house mainly printed commissioned pieces from university scholars and government officials (half of the books printed in the Kolbe shop were published in Latin), profitability was a major concern, and Kolbe, like other printers in early modern Europe, sought to print titles that would make money. As historian Rudolf Hirsch has argued, printers chose to print those books for which they assumed there would be a demand so that they could recover their initial investment and make a profit.[24]

Dryander published on a wide variety of subjects, but the most by far were concerned with mathematics and astronomical and other measuring instruments, the means by which one could grasp the world. Dryander's book the *Annulorum* (1537) was an illustrated treatise on astronomical instruments that showed how such instruments worked. His interest in cartography explains his involvement in the publication of Johannes Stöffler's *Cosmographicae aliquot descriptiones* (1537) as well as his role as editor of the Marburg edition of Sebastian Münster's work (1544 and 1545). Dryander also worked at mapping, for manuscripts in his hand, such as a map of Hesse, served as models for printed maps of Hesse used by Sebastian Münster and later Abraham Ortelius. Most broadly, Dryander's interest in mapping, measuring, and travel can all be seen as part of the subject of *navigatio,* which belonged to the mechanical arts or *artes mechanicae.* This area of study united under a common subject the acts of measuring, revealing, and exploring the natural world in all of its manifestations. Here the world of the scholar met that of the traveler. The two men came together, perhaps at the court of their prince, or in the streets of Marburg, or when Staden sought to publish a story.[25]

Staden had proven himself a skilled go-between in extremely perilous contexts. But like any go-between, he had to draw upon local sources of knowledge and expertise. Staden was a soldier, a gunner, and a traveler; he could read, possibly even write and draw, and yet he was no author. Like many other travelers who became authors, Staden needed the assistance of a man like Dryander to write, illustrate, and publish his story.

The result of their meeting was a shared work, a book filled with observations about the natural world of a land far across the sea, a book inflected by the tones of Protestantism, a book that soon became known popularly throughout Germany and the Low Countries as "The Men-Eater Book" (*Menschenfresserbuch*). Appearing quickly in a second printing in Marburg that same year (1557) and then again in Frankfurt, *True History* was followed by translations into Dutch and Latin. Its message of personal strength and salvation spoke, it seems, to mostly Protestant audiences.[26]

Printed and bound before the Marburg spring market that opened the last weekend in April, the *True History* was ready in time for the annual book fair held in Frankfurt am Main. As early as the year 1480, the Frankfurt fair had attracted as many as 120 different merchants and publishers from within and without Germany; they transported their "books"—sheaves of unbound papers stored in wooden barrels—via boats along the river or in heavy wagons across land routes.

Under tents lining the square where the fair was held, scholars, booksellers, and authors learned of the newest developments in any number of fields, looked for new books and ideas, or searched for publishers for their unpublished works. Once these sheaves were bound and sold, Staden's story entered into the larger world of print culture, and the meaning of his travels became something that was no longer his alone to control.[27]

Even before he left for Brazil, Staden had to have been well aware of the power of the book to persuade, inform, and captivate. Living as he did in the middle of Germany, he was witness to the dramatic revolution and amazing transformation of print culture that began with Johann Gutenberg's invention of the moveable type in his Mainz workshop during the middle of the fifteenth century. Gutenberg's technological innovation accelerated a longer process that had moved the production of books beyond the confines of the monasteries and had expanded the number of books in circulation. Books were no longer just the possessions of the clergy, the powerful, the learned, or the wealthy. More people were reading more and more books in the sixteenth century, thanks to the spread of the printing technique and to the growth of a new reading public. In addition to turning out editions of the Bible, books of prayer, and reformation tracts, printers were producing books about European travels to the New World.

Although books were still expensive in sixteenth-century Europe, people from all walks of life, not just the wealthy, were buying and reading them. In particular, people like Staden's parents—artisans who lived in cities and towns: cobblers, cloth cutters, and leatherworkers—bought books written in German about the natural world, healing plants, and the New World discoveries. Even laborers possessed books, generally excerpts from the Bible with images (like the illustrated Bible known as the *Biblisher Auszug oder Historien mit Bildern* by the Frankfurt pastor Bartmann Beyer).[28]

We can point to several places and times when Staden would have been introduced to books as important tools in spreading knowledge. He was likely aware of the growing body of travel literature and captivity narratives that were filling up booksellers' stalls even before he made his way out of Hesse. With deep roots in Western culture, the travel narrative gained a new popularity in early modern Europe, in part as an offshoot of European expansion overseas. Accompanying the boom in book production and the growth of a reading public, the news brought back from voyages of discovery, such as stories of encounters with unknown lands and peoples, made for exciting reading. Historian Peter Mancall has shown how the sixteenth century marked a radical change in the production and sale of travel accounts. The expansion of European trade in the sixteenth century was accompanied by a similar spread of stories about travels to distant lands written by Europeans who had made the journey and who had come back home again, eager to share tales of their exploits and the marvels they had encountered with European audiences. New discoveries or developments were trumpeted not only by those who had made the journeys themselves, such as Christopher Columbus or Amerigo Vespucci, but also by collectors of tales such as Peter Martyr d'Anghiera (1457–1526) or Giovanni Battista Ramusio (1485–1557), whose books eagerly shared the news with others.[29]

When he arrived in Lisbon and before he set sail for the New World, Staden would have encountered the German printers in the city who (like gunners) enjoyed special privileges granted by the Portuguese crown. Valentim Fernandes is considered the best known of these men. A translator, publisher, and printer in Portugal at the turn of the century, this German from Moravia had made his way via Seville to Lisbon around 1493. He printed books such as the *Vita Christi* on the king's orders, and he translated and printed Marco Polo's travel narrative, dedicating it to King Manuel I with a line from the New Testament (Luke 5:26: "We have seen marvelous things today"). Fernandes's lively interest in the Portuguese discoveries and his desire to publicize the marvels and wealth associated with these journeys in Africa, India, and the Atlantic made him a key source of information in Germany and one of the more important early publicists of these efforts. Fernandes wrote, collected, and collated information and travel accounts, sending them to his colleague Konrad Peutinger in Augsburg. It was through Fernandes that news reached Germany of Cabral's discovery of Brazil in April of 1500; it was his drawing of a rhinoceros sent to Nuremburg in 1515 that served as the model for Albrecht Dürer's famous woodcut of the marvelous beast.[30]

Staden certainly saw the role that books played in spreading information about the New World before he left for it, and when he returned, his time in Antwerp would have underscored the role that books played in transferring information in the emerging global world. Staden may have stopped in at the booksellers' stalls before entering the exchange, for they were located right before the main entrance. There he could not have failed to notice the numerous books, pamphlets, broadsides, woodcuts, and even the first business newspapers for sale. There were also a variety of books on the Americas known to have been published in the early 1550s in Antwerp that might have been for sale while Staden was in the city. These books include the *Cosmographia* of German mathematician Peter Apian (Petrus Apianus) that had an Antwerp edition of 1553, as did the chronicle of Peru by Pedro Cieza de León (1554) and Francisco López de Gómara's history of Mexico (1554), which had a fold-out map of the Americas appended to the text.[31]

Staden lived in a world increasingly defined by the printed word. A few fellow Germans had penned accounts of their travels beyond the borders of the empire. We know of only a handful of other firsthand travel narratives written by Germans and in German (rather than in Latin, Spanish, or Portuguese) about travels in the New World before the publication of Staden's story. Initially, news about the Portuguese and Spanish discoveries was published in "news-papers" (*Neue Zeitungen*) with a large readership in the Holy Roman Empire. These had their origins in the letters written by individuals back home. Columbus's letters and Vespucci's reports are examples of these types of documents which were collected, printed, and distributed in German-speaking lands. Vespucci's letters were printed in German in Augsburg, Nuremberg, and Strasbourg. The Fuggers and Welser, large German family firms in southern Germany, were particularly interested in news of the new world, and this interest fueled production of such prints.[32]

The most popular books about the New World did not stem from the pens of single authors but were collections of both old and new travel pieces, mixing accounts of the fantastic with commercial reports or letters from sailors, merchants, and kings. Such accounts bore the imprint of printers and editors who compiled the materials into a complete whole. Later in the sixteenth century, perhaps the most popular of such works was the *Cosmographia* of Sebastian Münster, which "included hundreds of pages on the history and geography of European and Mediterranean regions and dozens of pages on the newly discovered territories of Africa, Asia, and America." At the bottom of the title page, a woodcut shows the traveler encountering the wondrous things of the world, as will the reader on turning the page.[33]

At the time of Staden's return, only a few Germans had written firsthand accounts of their travel experiences. Balthasar Sprenger (?–ca. 1510), who went to sea on behalf of the Augsburg trading family of the Welser, published his diaries. These detailed his trip along the coast of Africa to India in 1509 in search of spices. Soon after the publication of Staden's *True History,* two other Germans published travel accounts: Nicholas Federmann wrote about his activities on behalf of the Welser family in present-day Venezuela in 1557; and Ulrich Schmidel from Straubing in southern Germany published an account of his travels in the La Plata region (the same area that had tempted Staden to take to the sea for a second time) in 1567. But Staden's book became such a sensation not only because of its vivid account of cannibalism but because the way Staden told his story highlighted his own personal perspectives and insights—indeed, they were woven into the story to show how God's saving grace had protected him and brought him back home to safety. His contemporaries who wrote about their travels could not match the power of Staden's story.[34]

The lens of the Protestant faith is a key framing device of *True History,* one sure to resonate with listeners. Staden crafts a story about his travels that is a testament to God's mercy. He sets the stage for the first part of his book, about his two journeys to the New World, in his dedication to Prince Philipp. Writers had long seen the wisdom in soliciting the aid of powerful and wealthy patrons to assist them in the publication of their works, and Staden was certainly no different. But the bulk of his two-page letter is devoted not so much to Philipp as to Philipp's (and Staden's) God. The first paragraph is almost a complete recitation of Psalm 107. Staden invokes it as a prayer, and its structure shapes the tale that he will tell. "Some go down to the sea in ships," he proclaims, "doing business on the mighty waters." In this vision of the world, God commands the waters and raises the stormy depths. In their distress, men cry out to God, who is merciful. Once saved, they must "thank the LORD for his steadfast love, for his wonderful works to mankind!" Psalm 107 evokes the image of the sea and all its dangers. In the narrative of his travels and captivity, Staden suffers great danger, only to be saved by divine grace, and it is his duty to report on his salvation as evidence of God's divine intervention. Thus, Staden ends his dedication with a justification for the book itself.[35]

Staden divides his story into two parts: the first, the *Historia,* consists of 53 chapters and tells the tale of his travels from Hesse to the New World; the second, the *Beschreibung,* or Description, consists of 38 chapters, which are shorter ethnographic excurses on the land, animals, and plants of Brazil and the customs of the Tupinambá. The first section recounts Staden's sea journeys, shipwreck, and his establishment at Bertioga and then spends 34 chapters detailing his captivity, his attempts at escape, his encounters with cannibalism, and his eventual return to Germany via Dieppe, Antwerp, and London. In the first part of the book, Staden figures as a central character in the narrative, and the story is devoted to his captivity. In the second, Staden is largely absent, present only as an afterthought, as a recording eyewitness.

The two parts of the *True History*—the *Historia* and the *Beschreibung*—cannot be seen separately from each other, as some scholars have chosen to view them. Rather, they need to be seen as a whole (and indeed, the two parts were consistently reproduced together, although it was certainly possible to publish one half without the other). A result of the collaboration between Dryander and Staden, the story highlights Staden's actions as go-between. Together, the two parts enable Staden to establish his eyewitness authority while also emphasizing his suffering and ultimate salvation by an all-forgiving God. The *Historia* and the *Beschreibung* allow him to be simultaneously a captive victim and a knowledgeable insider; together they also enable him to prove his trustworthiness and reliability by recording his familiarity with Tupinambá culture and customs.

Part I of the book, the *Historia,* bears a striking resemblance to the stories of saints' lives, or hagiographic accounts. These stories belonged to some of the most popular reading in medieval and early modern Europe. Literary scholar Dwight E. Raak TenHuisen has explored the similarities between Staden's description of his travails and the sufferings of saints. He argues that "hagiographic language is the principal lens through which Staden both frames and interprets his experience, and the discourse of martyrdom also determines his view of the indigenous peoples that he encounters." Even with a Protestant upbringing, Staden would have been familiar with the stories of the saints and martyrs, and the structure of such stories— suffering, steadfastness, and salvation—would fit easily into the logic of Protestant understandings of the power of divine grace.[36]

The logic of captivity and martyrdom shapes the *Historia,* in which Staden draws spiritual lessons from his captivity. From the first moment that he hears the cries of the warriors while he is out collecting game, he marks his trials with prayers and hymns. Like the martyrs and saints, Staden is mocked and tormented by his captors. He is ridiculed for his beliefs, and in his deepest despair he cries out to his God, who ultimately saves and avenges him. He recounts that when he is captured at Bertioga, he stands there praying, waiting for the blow to fell him, but the Tupinambá take him captive instead. Later, when he is bound and captive, unable to see because of his swollen face, wounded in the leg, and surrounded by the "savages" who threaten to eat him (fig. 16), he begins to sing Psalm 130, with tears streaming from his eyes and from the depths of his soul: "Out of the depths I cry to you, O LORD." Martin Luther wrote a hymn based on this psalm in 1523. It was widely used in Lutheran services, and having taken on aspects of a burial hymn, it was sung at the funeral of Duke Frederick the Wise in 1525 and upon Luther's own death in 1546.[37]

When the Frenchman Carautá-uára told Staden's captors that they should kill and eat him because he was evidently Portuguese, both his enemy and theirs, Staden tells the reader that he thought of Jeremiah, who said, "Cursed are those who trust in mere mortals" (Jer. 17:5). Tearing from his shoulders the linen cloth that had been given to him because his skin was badly sunburned, he threw it in disgust at the feet of Carautá-uára. After Staden was led back to his hut, he reports, he lay there crying out in anguish the verse "We now implore the Holy Ghost."[38]

In keeping with the narrative tradition of saints' tales, Staden recounts many miracles that serve to set him apart from his captors and establish his Protestant faith. Literary theorist Stephen Greenblatt, in his path-breaking work on European responses to the New World discoveries, *Marvelous Possessions* (1991), has explored how "wonder" served as an entryway into European appropriations of the New World and the marvels it contained. For Staden, wonders are not acts of possession or a

Figure 16. Staden Prays. From Hans Staden, *Warhaftige Historia.* Marburg: 1557.
Courtesy, Lilly Library, Indiana University, Bloomington, Indiana.

means to create distance between himself and the Other, but rather they are direct
signs of God's grace and proof of divine intercession on his behalf. The *Historia* is
marked by a series of wonders that protect Staden, set him apart, prove his value,
and accompany him on his return to Hesse.[39]

The first miracle occurs shortly after his capture, when the Tupinambá are returning to their village with Staden in tow. The canoes cut through the waves, and
two miles away from the place where the Indians intend to spend the night, "a
large, black cloud" rises from the sea behind them. The Tupinambá paddle swiftly,
hoping to make land ahead of the cloud and the winds. When they see that they
cannot get ahead of the storm, they call out to Staden, "Speak to your God so that
we aren't harmed by the great rain and the wind." Staden reports that he lay silent
and prayed to God because his captors had asked him to: "Oh Almighty God, Lord
of Heaven and Earth, who from the beginning has helped those who call your
name among the heathen. Show me your mercy so that I may know that you are
with me, and show the savages who do not recognize you that you, my God, have
heard my prayer." Although unable to see well because of his bonds, Staden can
raise himself somewhat to observe that the great clouds would pass by. He gives
thanks to God, but he knows that he is not yet saved. Although his God had protected

Figure 17. Staden's Cross. From Hans Staden, *Warhaftige Historia.* Marburg: 1557.
Courtesy, Lilly Library, Indiana University, Bloomington, Indiana.

him, this intercession only hurries Staden on his way, ever closer to the home of his
captors. Yet God has sent a sign, and Staden is filled with wonder in the face of his
powerful God. Staden knows that if he keeps his faith, he will be saved in the end.[40]

There are no more miracles for some time, but as Staden seeks to lie, cajole, and
use his knowledge of the ways of the Indians to his advantage, he interprets signs
granted by God to prove his value to his captors. We have seen how Staden played
a dangerous game in claiming that the illness that befell the families in Nhaêpepô-
oaçú's hut was a sign of God's displeasure. When Staden seeks to comfort the Maracaiás captive who is to be killed in the traditional cannibalism ceremony, his captors
accuse him of causing a great wind to rise and blow off the roofs on the huts.

In chapter 46, entitled "How Almighty God Sent a Sign," Staden recounts how a
woman removes a cross he had erected outside of his hut and gives her husband the
boards to use as tools. Staden recalls that he "had warned the savages not to remove it
or some misfortune would befall them." In the woodcut accompanying the original
text, we can see Staden praying in front of the cross in the bottom right corner, while
the women work the fields and clouds threaten from the left side of the image (fig. 17).[41]

Shortly after the removal of the cross, it begins to rain heavily, a rain that lasts for several days. Staden recounts, "They came into my hut and told me that I should talk to my God and make him stop the rain, because if it didn't stop it would hinder their planting, since it was planting season." "It's your own fault," Staden tells them— "you made my God angry, because I would speak to my God near the piece of wood." With their help, Staden erects another cross, and as soon as they do so, the weather improves.[42]

Staden reports another wonder, one in which God once again intercedes on his behalf to improve the weather. Out fishing with two other men, Staden prevents a storm from arriving and ruining their catch. By praying to his God, Staden performs a miracle of the fish, and further increases his standing in the eyes of those who held him captive.[43]

In all of these examples, Staden shares with his readers an image of a man tested but true to his faith, a man protected by his God, despite the dangers he faces. It also shows a Staden able and willing to interpret signs and wonders as expressions of his own abilities as a shaman and prophet. By comparing himself to Christ, Staden draws on earlier literary forms and traditions, placing his experiences within a liturgy of the saints, and explaining his salvation and return.

Staden directly compares his mockery at the hands of the Tupinambá women, when he is bound and made to dance, to the persecution of Christ. He writes: "I had to think about our Savior Jesus Christ who suffered at the hands of the miserable Jews for our sins." He portrays himself as a martyr giving himself over to God's power when he pretends to pray to the moon, "Oh my Lord and my God, help me to put a happy end to this misery." Staden accounts for his power within the village (he was even given as a gift to another chief) by explaining that in becoming a kind of shaman to the Tupinambá, he was in fact an instrument of Divine Providence, a kind of spiritual go-between—a story that would easily echo with the beliefs of his audience.[44]

Staden suffers as a martyr or a saint, but he does not always forgive his enemies. His sense of aggrieved righteousness is at its fullest when he condemns those who have wronged him. We have already seen how he rails against the French sailors who "abandoned" him in Brazil, and how he taunts the families of their loved ones with the prospect that the sailors may never return to their homes. He claims that it is God's punishment that caused the death of the Guarani slave, saying that the man had "always lied about me" and that his God was angry with him "because of the lies he fabricated about me." The woodcut image of this scene reinforces this idea of righteous punishment. In the front and center of the image, Staden is standing, pointing down with one hand at the dismembered body of the captive slave while pointing with his other up to the heavens (see fig. 10). "I ask the reader to pay attention to what I write," says Staden, "for I do not take the trouble to write because I want to write something new, but only to bring the blessings that God gave me to the light of day."[45]

By having suffered such travails and yet being saved by God's grace, Staden argues that God protects the believer who had lived with "wild, naked, savage, man-eating people." Since God had so clearly favored him, surely Landgrave Philipp and his fellow Hessians could do the same? Staden ends this section of his book with "My prayer to God, our Lord, while I was in the hands of the savages, who wanted to eat me." Thus, he acknowledges his hopeless powerlessness in the face of the saving grace of his Lord, who alone could release him.[46]

If one narrative strand of the *Historia* is the martyr's tale, the go-between is also explicitly part of the story Staden tells. Readers would have been excited by the scenes of drama and deception that made up a main part of this story. In this counter, or competing narrative, Staden reveals himself to be a shrewd manipulator of situations, sometimes for fun, and other times for survival. In two dramatic performances, Staden relates how he is able to dissimulate. These are exciting scenes that compete with the religious message of his story. The first occurs shortly after Staden arrives in Brazil on his second voyage. Staden goes out on a boat in the bay to make contact with the Indians and meets there a European who has lived among the Guarani for three years. Staden returns to the ship with this man, accompanied by numerous Indians. As they approach the ship, the sailors whom Staden had left behind on board look uneasily to Staden, who sits silent in the canoe and gives no answer when they call to him. It is only when shots are about to fall that Staden laughs and cries out, "Do not fear, [I bring] good news! Let me come nearer and I will give you a report." The approach is a joke carried out on orders of the captain, who orders Staden to "look sad" so as to see what his comrades will do at the sight of Europeans who appear to be wholly in the power of the Guarani.[47]

In the second performance, Staden is on the deck of the *Catherine,* the French ship that will return him safely to Europe, and there he plays out the part of a son, surrounded by his brothers, who demand that he accompany them home across the sea to visit his sick father. While the crew playact and embrace him in a sign of kinship, the Tupinambá who had adopted him cry, and Staden cries with them. They leave the ship with a number of goods in return for finally letting him go.[48]

Literary scholar Christian Kiening has argued that these two stagings mark the borders of Staden's Brazilian captivity. The first story, in which Staden appears to be in the power of the Indians, is meant for the Europeans and reveals the German among his "friends," captive in their power. This serves as an emblem and a precursor to the story to follow. But it also makes sure to set out in advance the fact that Staden has not gone native, but is only playacting to test his comrades. The second performance on the ship deck, Kiening argues, is meant for the Indians, whom he hopes to leave behind, and involves Staden playing at being a relative back in the arms of his family, among his brothers.[49]

Both charades reveal a Staden who can cross borders with ease and even with a sense of bravado. Playacting in this manner is essential for the survival of the go-between, and it is clear that Staden takes some pleasure in conveying the power he enjoyed in the two situations. It is the humility of the Christian that takes away some of the hubris, and it is the story of suffering and captivity that tempers the playfulness of both acts. The tension between the two ways of being and reporting is never fully resolved in the book.[50]

Part 2 of the book, the *Beschreibung,* or description, does not have a narrative, although there are stories to be found among the matter-of-fact descriptions of the fauna, flora, and peoples of Brazil. Dryander makes clear his own interest in the scientific and ethnographic aspects of Staden's observations in Brazil. He writes in his introduction that "the people on the island all walk around naked; they have no domesticated animals for food, and none of the things which are common for us to the sustenance of the body, such as clothes, beds, horses, pigs or cows; not even wine or beer, etc." We can see here the outlines of what was to be a more systematic approach in the second half of the book, which describes lives and customs of the Tupinambá. Literary scholar Wolfgang Neuber has argued that the schemata of this section corresponds to an emerging rhetorical strategy called *apodemia,* a literary form that sought to order the act, experience, and recounting of travel.[51]

The "apodemic method" was developed by humanists in Germany during the course of the sixteenth century. As Neuber has shown, two traditions feed into this method. The first is topography, or the systematic description of a place. The second is medical travel advice, which originally sought to direct travelers how to avoid chills, fevers, or thirst. These texts also prescribed a "proper" way to travel. Rather than wandering aimlessly, travelers should be purposeful, using their senses to understand their surroundings and the "life and ways" of the people they encounter. Thomas Zwinger, a physician from the Swiss city of Basel, published the foundational text of this method in 1577. Entitled the *Methodus Apodemica,* the work laid out a grid for describing foreign lands and peoples, starting with the name and location of those encountered and ending with descriptions of plants and animals.[52]

This model was close to the large compilations such as the *Cosmographia* by Münster, but it was also more systematic; it was one being developed by humanists and scientists such as Dryander, and it would have been unfamiliar to Staden. We can imagine Dryander asking Staden such questions as "What do they look like?" or "How do they sleep?" "What do they believe in?" and "Why do enemies eat each other?" Such are the titles of the descriptive chapters in the book's second half.

Staden does not draw on classical texts or iconography when talking about his experiences, something that humanists like Dryander would have done as a matter of course. When describing the New World, Staden abstains from quoting classical texts and very rarely even makes comparisons to Europe. Staden has no use for the strategy that historian Anthony Pagden has described as the process of attachment in European encounters with the New World. In this process, European observers, according to Pagden, sought to comprehend utterly foreign sights and practices by taking them out of context, placing them within known (and often utterly inappropriate) contexts, practices, and landscapes. Once armed with a classification system, the Europeans could chart, observe, and possess the New World.[53]

Staden's frame of reference, as we have seen from his quoting of hymns, psalms, and prayers in book 1, is not other classical authors or texts but his religion. It is therefore likely that Dryander set out the 38 chapters of book 2 and questioned Staden about the details, which he then set out to answer. Dryander's collaboration took the form of providing a learned framework for the second half of the book that consisted of a series of questions he would have asked Staden. Once Staden had been subjected to the questioning, the ethnographic detail of his answers would have convinced Dryander of the truthfulness of his tales. Book 2 clearly reveals the "learned shadow" of Dryander, who proved to be so instrumental in writing and producing the *True History*. Dryander even suggests in his introduction that he intends to write a more systematic and scientific account of Staden's travels at a later date. "I have dedicated my introduction or preface to Your Highness," Dryander assures his prince, "begging that it may suffice until such time as I am able to publish something more worthy in Your Highness's name." That time never came, and the representation that Staden created was the one that shaped European understandings of those who lived in Brazil.[54]

The *Beschreibung* also inadvertently shows Staden to have been even more fully integrated into life with the Tupinambá. Again, we see Staden as the go-between: this time as the one who has adapted to life in the Tupinambá villages where he is held captive. In the *Historia*, Staden qualifies statements that suggest that he has "gone native." For example, Staden explains how he, armed with bow and arrow, "yelled and shot [my arrows] and did things their way, *as best I could*." Yet in the accompanying illustration (see fig. 18), it is impossible to discern which is Staden; if present, he is indistinguishable from the Tupinambá.[55]

Figure 18. An Unidentifiable Staden Fights with the Tupinambá.
From Hans Staden, *Warhaftige Historia*. Marburg: 1557. Courtesy,
Lilly Library, Indiana University, Bloomington, Indiana.

But having just revealed that he fought alongside the Tupinambá against their
enemies as if he were a Tupinambá warrior (not a German *Landsknecht*), Staden
then explains that he did so only because he "wanted to get through the stockade
that surrounded the huts and to run to the others [i.e., his friends from Bertioga]
because they knew me well." Staden must convince his readers (and his interroga-
tors) that he was never fully an insider of Tupinambá life, but an outsider posing
as an insider in order to bring about his escape, return, and reintegration.[56]

The *Beschreibung,* as a "brief account of the manners and customs of the
Tupinambá, whose captive I was," belies this fact. The descriptions of daily life (which
also include a detailed account of the cannibalistic rites Staden witnessed) reveal a
Staden who took part in the daily lives of his captors. He inadvertently reveals that
he must have had a wife while in captivity—he reports that a captive, after he is
decorated, bound, and mocked, is given a woman "who waits upon and who has
truck with him." His authority in the village is so established that he can name a
child. And in a chapter concerning the "bees of the country," he tells us that he,

like the savages who kept him, took "honey when I was naked, but the first time I had to run to a stream in great pain and wash them [the bees] off, to get them off my body." In the *Beschreibung,* as in the *Historia,* Staden moves beyond the narrative—the martyr's tale or the apodemica—and reveals his role as the go-between. The relative ease with which Staden seems to have lived in both worlds—with the Christians on the ships and the natives on the shore—is remarkable.[57]

What does the *True History* tell us about Staden's adventures "by land and by sea," and what does the book's narrative structure say about Staden's intention and about the circumstances in which he wrote his book? The book shows us a Staden who tells his story as a moral tale, which helps to explain his suffering and his return. In the *Historia,* Staden writes a story in which he could cross over to the other side and yet emerge unscathed. He performs a difficult rhetorical task: he must describe his own lies and deceptions told in captivity while also proclaiming to give a faithful accounting of his experiences. The framework of a martyr's tale allows him to do this. In the *Beschreibung,* he provides details about the landscape, animals, customs, and traditions that prove his reliability as an honest traveler by underscoring his familiarity with the place he had visited.

Written in a state permeated by Protestant faith from the top down, the story could not have been written any other way. Both sections of the book were necessary; both went hand in hand in allowing Staden to tell his story in the Protestant Hesse which he had left and to which he had returned. Yet neither section of the book completely followed the formula of the martyr's tale or the apodemica. In each, Staden as the unreliable, lying, gone-native go-between emerges to fascinate, entertain, and puzzle the reader.

Upon returning to Hesse, Staden put into print the things that he had experienced. The text that bore his name and that told his story circulated far beyond his native lands, resonating with readers who were hungry for news of the discoveries of the New World, ready to believe tales of gruesome and barbaric behavior, and schooled in a literature that focused on the sufferings of martyrs and saints. Staden had become a representational go-between whose representation of Brazil would now take off and circulate as an explanation of Brazil and the peoples who lived there. And, as had been key to the success of many a traveler's tale, it was told in more than words. Staden's book was accompanied by images that allowed his readers to return to Brazil with him. Through the images, readers stepped into scenes where they too might know the otherness of the Tupinambá and the gift of God's grace.

CHAPTER FOUR

Staden's Images

$\mathfrak{F}$irst seen hanging from market stalls in Marburg and fluttering in the cold spring breezes at the book fair in Frankfurt, the title page of *True History* begins with an elaborate capital *W* (for *Warhaftige*, or "true"), printed in brilliant red, with its loose ends or *schnörkels* intertwined like elephant trunks. The gothic type used for the first word was known as Fraktur, and it had become popular in a major center of German printing and woodcut production, Nuremberg, the home of Albrecht Dürer. After the first line in Fraktur, the font changes to Schwabacher, a more elegant German gothic typeface with curved strokes, to finish Staden's long title and his dedication of the book to Landgrave Philipp. The font changes yet again to italic to signal to the reader that the prominent humanist Johann Dryander, professor of medicine at Marburg, has written an introduction. Finally, a black-and-white illustration, depicting a naked man reclining in a hammock suspended over a kindled fire, finishes the title page. The man holds a severed human foot to his mouth, while at his side, on a wooden grate, human legs and arms are roasting over a fire (fig. 19).

Would this title page have looked inviting to German readers in 1557? The vivid red, the vertical strokes, the curves and angles, and the ornamental flourishes of the typeset words are striking. Fraktur was popular as a heading type, the exaggerated use of *schnörkels* was a decorative feature often found on title pages on upper case letters, and Schwabacher was a familiar German gothic font. The italic type used to introduce Dryander was the preferred typeface of the Renaissance humanists, who generally found the heavy black gothic "barbarous." Printing in red added an extra expense, but it was not new: printers had used red ink for a hundred years. We may find the use of type on this title page remarkable, but to readers of books in the middle of sixteenth-century Germany, it was familiar. What would have caught their attention, because it was profoundly unfamiliar, was the woodcut image. The only textual clue explaining its meaning, moreover, was undecipherable: the undulating scroll over the top of the hammock is inscribed with the phrase "Sete katii" (*sete katu*). Virtually no one in Germany would recognize the Tupi-Guarani words, written in phonetic German, but the meaning of the image was clear: it depicted cannibalism.[1]

Figure 19. Title Page of Staden's *True History*. From Hans Staden, *Warhaftige Historia*. Marburg: 1557. Courtesy, Lilly Library, Indiana University, Bloomington, Indiana.

Why was this woodcut on the title page? By Staden's day, title pages were standard in the book trade, and printers knew that an attractive title page would help to sell the book. When posted as flyers, as historian Eleanor Shevlin writes, "on booksellers' stalls, mounted in cleft-sticks, hung over shop doors, tacked on public posts, and even pasted on church doors," they served as advance publicity for books.

As a result, title pages were carefully designed to introduce a book's contents through layout, style, ornamentation, and words; when a woodcut appeared, it pointed to the subject of the book. By this definition, the title page of *True History* proclaims that the book contains the "true" account of a Hessian who had traveled to distant shores and a description of the man-eating peoples encountered there. The story was approved by a prominent humanist, and it promised to unfold through both words and pictures.[2]

The woodcut on the title page establishes a pattern that repeats through Staden's *True History,* for the book is full of woodcut images that accompany the text and that create a second, visual narrative to the text. While illustrated books were common in sixteenth-century Germany, the pattern of Staden's images are not. Like the woodcut on the title page, Staden's images are not immediately familiar to his readers. If we study Staden's images carefully, it becomes apparent that they match the text and provide further information on Brazil. That *True History* was illustrated with woodcuts created specifically for this particular book makes it highly unusual for its genre, whether we label it a religious book or a travel account. The distinctiveness of the images, moreover, is integral to the success of the book. The images extended Staden's representation of Brazil and its peoples far beyond his printed words. A representational go-between usually characterizes and explains through words, but just as words can convey an understanding of peoples and cultures, so too can images. If the images in *True History* derive from Staden's own hand, they double his power as a representational go-between.

There was nothing unusual about an illustrated book, and it was logical to assume that a book published in sixteenth-century Germany, even an inexpensive one such as Staden's, would contain images. Images had long been used in Medieval and Renaissance Europe for spiritual instruction and reflection. They were incorporated into the architecture of churches and appeared as illuminations to manuscripts such that virtually every scene in the Bible had been depicted by artists. With the advent of print, illustrated Bibles became common, first appearing in Germany as early as in 1475. Books printed in the vernacular, that is, in everyday languages rather than Latin, were often illustrated, since these books were intended for a large popular readership. Illustrated "block books," the forerunners to typeset books with woodcut images, were mass produced and marketed to the semiliterate, who followed the (usually religious) story through the pictures. By Staden's time, illustrated books were part of the mass appeal of reading.[3]

Nor was the kind of image in Staden's book at all unusual. The pictures were woodcuts, printed in black ink on white paper, which was the least expensive way of illustrating books in the sixteenth century. Typically, the designs for the woodcuts were made by an artist or draughtsman and then cut by the *Formschneider,* or wood-cutter. The design was either drawn directly onto the woodblock (backward) or on paper that was oiled to make it transparent, then turned over and glued onto the block. While the technique of making a woodcut was not difficult, a trained crafts-man was needed to cut the drawing that was transferred onto the block of wood with special tools. The cutting had to be done in reverse so that the gouged-out grooves would appear as white in the finished print, while the black ink adhered to the raised ridges. The woodcutters had specialized tools—flat knives with sharp beveled cutting edges and a long steel rod with a sharp point known as a graver—to cut the gouges in the wood block.[4]

In assessing the images in *True History,* the nineteenth-century historian of printing in Marburg, Arey von Dommer, describes the woodcutting as "fleeting and rough," suggesting that they are not the work of a skilled, accomplished wood-cutter. Cutting blocks of wood was the least expensive way of illustrating a book, far less costly than other processes, such as engraving copper plates. But while practical and inexpensive, woodcuts had become an art form, whether printed in-dividually for sale or inserted into books. Albrecht Dürer's woodcut of the rhinoc-eros can hardly be described as "fleeting and rough," even though Dürer does get some key features of the animal's anatomy wrong (the hooves, for example).[5]

The *Nuremberg Chronicle (Liber chronicarum)* had popularized the use of woodcut images in German books. Originally written in Latin but subsequently published in a German language edition, the *Nuremberg Chronicle* included hundreds of original woodcuts of biblical scenes, vistas of walled towns, and a world map that extends onto two facing pages. In addition to large woodcuts, small illustrations of kings, crowns and scepters, and natural phenomena (the sun, moon, rain, comets) were inserted alongside or within the text. These woodcuts were designed and cut under the guidance of Michael Wolgemut, the teacher of Albrecht Dürer, who most likely worked on the book. Printed in 1493, the book circulated widely, and its images were well known and extensively copied.[6]

A generation later, another very popular illustrated book was Sebastian Mün-ster's *Cosmographia,* which had a first edition in 1544 and an expanded second edition in 1550. A cosmography invited readers to wonder and marvel at the history of the world and all of its peoples by bringing together a mass of geographical, historical, ethnographic, and scientific data. Münster's survey of the world in his *Cosmographia* was enlivened with stories, travel accounts, and anecdotes, and it was heavily illustrated with woodcuts and maps. Münster also deliberately published in German (as well as Latin) so that he could capture the attention of the ordinary German reader. In his *Cosmographia,* the German states and cities—their histories,

royal genealogies, peoples, and local customs—were featured prominently. Münster's *Cosmographia* went through thirty-five editions in less than a hundred years,
and eventually tens of thousands of copies were in circulation, making it a hugely
influential book, especially in Germany.[7]

Whether in the *Nuremberg Chronicle* or in Münster's *Cosmographia,* the re-use
of images in books was a standard practice. Once cut, printers often recycled the
blocks throughout the text, creating a richly illustrated book. Readers were used to
"reading" images as stock or generic images—meant to gesture toward a broader
subject rather than to reproduce an individual moment, event, or person. For example,
in the *Cosmographia,* standard heads were used over and over again such that, as
historian Gerald Strauss notes, "the reader is soon reconciled to recognizing in
'Gutenberg' the same face he studied a while back as 'Albertus Magnus' and before
that as 'Ptolemaeus.' "[8]

Illustrated travel accounts were also popular in Germany. Yet, while illustrations ideally supplemented the reading and understanding of the text, this did not
mean that original illustrations were necessarily used. Printers often illustrated
travel accounts with stock images—the generic cut blocks that they already had
on hand in the shop. Only occasionally did printers of travel accounts specifically
commission artists who worked from peoples, animals, and artifacts brought back
from overseas journeys. Even when an artist had been commissioned, the artist and
the writer typically worked independently, and the effect of this was that illustrations did not necessarily complement the text.[9]

Often publishers merely used images they had on hand from one book to illustrate another. Sometimes the images used only broadly matched the content of the
book. Such is the case for the second, pirated edition of Staden's book, printed by
the publisher Wiegand Hans in Frankfurt in 1557. Instead of using the images from
the first Marburg edition or commissioning new ones, Hans reprinted woodcuts that
had first appeared in a German edition of the famous travel account by the Italian
Lodovico de Varthema some forty years earlier. A scene from Varthema's book of
travels to Asia, published in Augsburg in 1515, adorns the title page of this second
edition of Staden's account (1557)! Originally, it appeared to illustrate a description of
euthanasia and ritual cannibalism in Java, as purportedly witnessed by Varthema;
however, readers of the Frankfurt edition of Staden's *True History* would assume that
the naked bearded man in the foreground represented Staden (see fig. 20).[10]

Historians have identified the artist who illustrated the German edition of Varthema's travels as Jörg Breu. Breu created the images by drawing on a variety of influ-
ences. He did not limit himself to depicting the places where Varthema traveled as
he created the drawings for the woodcuts; indeed, he even used characteristics

Figure 20. Title Page Woodcut of the Second, Frankfurt Edition. From Hans Staden, *Warhaftige Historia.* Frankfurt: 1557. Courtesy of the John Carter Brown Library at Brown University.

associated with the Tupinambá—such as feathered skirts—in some of the images. In the European imagination, and by the hand of the artist, the Tupinambá were becoming interchangeable with Muslims. Breu's illustrations show that whereas the author of the text was the traveler (Varthema), the artist created images from his own imagination, freely combining images that had been stimulated by his understanding of the text. According to literary scholar Wolfgang Neuber, an artist was required only to do justice to the text and to create illustrations that met the scientific and aesthetic expectations of the reader.[11]

For most illustrated books, printers normally took charge of the illustrations, and it was the printer who hired artists to design the images and woodcutters to cut the blocks. In the case of the second edition of Staden's book, it might have been cheaper (or quicker) for the Frankfurt printer to purchase and reuse the woodcuts from the Varthema book than to employ an artist to copy Staden's original illustrations or to create new ones. In any event, it was the printer, Wiegand Hans, who decided how to illustrate his edition of Staden's tale.

According to Neuber, it was rare for the author of a travel account to influence the production of the illustrations. How then did Staden's *True History* come to have images that were so clearly influenced by the author? Was it the printer, Kolbe, or Dryander, or Staden himself who played the key role in deciding to use original illustrations?[12]

We may assume that Andreas Kolbe, Staden's printer in Marburg, would not have found an illustrated book at all out of the ordinary. Certainly by the 1550s, German printers and authors generally were well aware of the power of the wood-cut illustration. It emphasized the text, it provided a breathing space in the heavy gothic typeface, and it energized the reader. Readers had come to expect illustrated books, and publishers competed to provide them. Kolbe's partner was none other than Dryander's printer, Christian Egenolff, a well-known German printer of Frank-furt who had, during Staden's youth and maturity, printed hundreds of books on many different topics. As a printer resident in Frankfurt, the site of the famous book fair, Egenolff well understood the popularity of illustrated books.[13]

Kolbe could have found stock images to illustrate the first edition of Staden's book. Certainly there was precedent for doing so, and it probably would have been cheaper for him. Instead, new images were created for this particular book, and it is clear that the woodcuts were meant to accompany specific passages. By the mid-dle of the sixteenth century, some illustrated books did insist on matching up il-lustrations with the text. Dryander's medical text, *The Mirror of Medicine,* which Egenolff published, used woodcuts to complement the text (some the very illustra-tions that Vesalius accused Dryander of plagiarizing; see fig. 15). Dryander's wood-cuts are labeled and further explicated with text, suggesting that it would have been contrary to his belief in the centrality of direct observation in medical training to use images that did not correspond to the text.[14]

Similarly, despite the presence of generic stock images that appeared over and over again in Münster's huge *Cosmographia,* both in the first edition of 1544 and in the second edition of 1550, Münster did insist that many of the images—the larger and more important ones—correspond to the text. The original *Cosmographia* (1544) had 520 woodcuts and 24 large double-page maps, while the second edition (1550) had 910 woodcuts and 54 new maps. These woodcuts were produced in Basel, where Münster and his printer (his stepson Heinrich Petri) lived, but they were made from drawings not necessarily created by artists. Instead, Münster collected the infor-mation for his *Cosmographia* from a vast network of scholars who were asked for drawings that were later fashioned into woodcuts by artists in Basel. These drawings were to be carefully done, because it was central to Münster's method to learn by experiment, to observe with the eye, to take surveys, and to meticulously record observations.[15]

If Kolbe had been influenced by Dryander and Egenolff and accepted that a text with matching illustrations was desirable, why not contract an artist to create them?

Here is where Staden, and possibly Dryander, may have intervened. For if an artist had been so contracted, he would have "illustrated" Staden's story using visual metaphors familiar to European audiences and an artistic style that echoed the visual imagery in other German woodcuts of the middle of the sixteenth century. Just as Breu used his artistic imagination to illustrate Varthema's travels for a German audience, so too would a contracted artist have illustrated Staden's tale.

Moreover, we may assume that all of the woodcuts would not only resemble each other but would employ the artistic conventions used in woodcuts in the middle of the sixteenth century. Since woodcutting flourished independently of the book trade and attracted even esteemed artists such as Dürer (who sold his prints at fairs for small sums of money to ordinary people), the language of the woodcut was widely disseminated among German artists. This language included themes, stylized ways of representation, references to earlier woodcuts, and techniques. A contracted artist would have used such conventions in his or her work.

The woodcut images in *True History* do not, as a corpus of work, suggest the hand of an artist. There is a significant variation in quality and execution, which suggests that an artist had not been contracted to "illustrate" the book. Some scholars have assumed that Staden drew sketches for the woodcutter. Because they are positioned to follow the text closely, they reveal, as anthropologist Neil Whitehead notes, "an intimate familiarity with the contents of the narrative [which] would have been required to compose and design the woodcuts." Who else but Staden could have had such familiarity? Moreover, as Whitehead concludes, "Staden's text is exceptional for the wealth, and probable accuracy, of its visual materials," again implying that only Staden could have supplied such accurate details. Whitehead does not assign authorship of the images directly to Staden; however, he does posit that the images could be the "more authentically personal expression of Staden's own viewpoint" as opposed to the written text. Similarly, German historian Franz Obermeier believes that the images are most likely based on Staden's own sketches, while French historian Frank Lestringant refers to woodcuts in the *True History* as if Staden had drawn them.[16]

The crude nature of many of the images implies that they were simple woodcuts of Staden's own sketches. Sketches, argues historian Peter Burke, "are more trustworthy as testimonies than are paintings worked up later in the artist's studio" because the sketch is drawn from life and is free from the conventions of style that artists are expected to employ. If Staden had made sketches, they were drawn not from life but from memory. Extrapolating backward from the woodcuts, it seems that they were simple drawings with a little shading. It was certainly possible that Staden could draw; there are amateur artists, after all, and in the sixteenth century,

Figure 21. Woodcuts of the Sky in the *Nuremberg Chronicle.* From Hartmann Schedel, *Liber chronicarum.* Nuremberg: 1493. Courtesy, Lilly Library, Indiana University, Bloomington, Indiana.

artists who worked as soldiers and sailors were contracted to go to sea and to battle in order to document what they saw.[17]

Yet the hand of an artist or a professional designer is clearly visible in many of the images, showing artistic conventions that Staden would have been unlikely to know or to reproduce well, such as the icons for waves and clouds or trees and hills. Some of these stylized images derived from the *Nuremberg Chronicle,* which had not only popularized woodcuts but had, through its popularity, created stylized shorthand visual icons. The small images of clouds, rain, the sun, or the moon that adorned the text of the *Nuremberg Chronicle* (see fig. 21) became part of a visual vocabulary, easily available to artists who designed woodcuts in sixteenth-century Germany.

Similarly, woodcut maps, such as those in Münster's *Geographia* of 1540 or his later editions of the *Cosmographia,* abound with stylized icons for wind heads, towns, bodies of water, hills, mountain ranges, cliffs, and so on. Since there was no standardization of these map signs, artists were free to create their own, subject to the limitations placed on them by printers. Despite the lack of standardization, there are many similarities in the signs used on printed maps because artists and woodcutters were influenced by what they had seen. Waldseemüller's magnificent giant world map of 1507, for example, uses closely cut lines to represent open water and curling white froth to suggest waves. Land masses appear in white, and hills and mountains are suggested by curved overlapping lines with judicious shading. On the elaborate border of the map, wind heads mark the directions of the winds. Waldseemüller's map, which apparently had a print run in Strasbourg of a thousand copies, was not particularly unique in the use of these icons, but its large print run and excellent reception did mean that these icons were seen by many and influenced later mapmakers such as Münster (see fig. 22).[18]

Figure 22. Mountains and Ocean (left), Wind Head (center), and Waves and Ocean (right). Details from the Waldseemüller World Map, 1507. Courtesy, Library of Congress.

Rather than simple woodcuts of Staden's crude sketches, the images in *True History* most likely emerged from an unusual collaboration between Staden, an artist, and a woodcutter. We hypothesize that the artist who collaborated with Staden would have used familiar visual vocabulary to depict the sun, the moon, rain, waves, settlements, trees, coastlines, and wind heads, while Staden would not. We also hypothesize that mistakes in the content of the images were likely to have been made either when the artist attempted to depict Brazil or when Staden attempted to draw for the woodcutter.

Two views of São Vicente are strikingly different and suggest the tension in the collaboration between Staden and the artist. In one view, which depicts Staden's arrival at São Vicente, the sinking ship takes up nearly half the image; it is carefully executed, and the rough sea is energetically rendered by frothy waves (fig. 23). The depiction of the foundering ship echoes a magnificent woodcut of a wrecking ship with a sailor floating ashore on a paddle on a map of Mediterranean Africa in Münster's *Geographia* of 1540. The waves, along with the trees on the land and the box-like houses with towers, are all stylized. The landscape displays several mistakes that suggest that the image was drawn by an artist and cut by a woodcutter, neither of whom had any familiarity with the setting. The woodcutter has inserted type or cut elegant letters to mark São Vicente (S. Vin) and Santo Amaro (S. Maro), while the artist has transformed the small frontier settlement of Bertioga, located across from the fort where Staden served, into a large fortified town. Bertioga is

Figure 23. Two Views of São Vicente. From Hans Staden, *Warhaftige Historia.* Marburg: 1557. Courtesy, Lilly Library, Indiana University, Bloomington, Indiana.

misspelled, and the artist has depicted it as a stylized Muslim town with a crescent moon rising above it, as would appear on a sixteenth-century woodcut map. The woodcut seems unfinished, with much empty space remaining. It is as if Staden has intervened, reining in the artist and not allowing him to let his imagination fill in the mainland.

In another image of São Vicente, there is less evidence of artistry, and the woodcut seems to be more of a sketch. There are fewer artistic conventions such as the frothing waves, and Bertioga is depicted (more accurately) as a small settlement surrounded by a palisade fence (fig. 23). The lay of the land and the island of São Vicente are less stylized and more precisely drawn. There is a mistake that most woodcutters would not have made: the S that begins S Maro (Santo Amaro) is backward. With the exception of the canoes filled with warriors and the thick, overlapping fighting force on the island, which must have been drawn by the artist, the entire image could have been produced by Staden.

The erratum (list of errors) appended to the book suggests that there were problems in the creation of the images. These errors make clear the collaboration between Staden, the artist, and the woodcutter. The erratum states that five woodcuts were accidentally turned around during the production of the blocks. One of the two images of São Vicente discussed above was reversed, for Bertioga appears on the right in one image and on the left in the other. The error would be visible to someone who could read the geographic information and see that Bertioga appears inconsistently. Presumably, Staden caught the error and wanted to correct it by way of the erratum. The error must have been made in the communication of information; Staden's inexperience and desire to intervene could have resulted in a drawing that was not properly reversed for the woodcutter.[19]

Is the title page, then, the exception, compared to the other images, because of its importance? In other words, could it have been primarily the work of the artist working with the printer? In this scenario, the mystifying violence of the title page woodcut image made sense since German woodcuts of the sixteenth century often depicted gruesome and violent images of werewolves, deformed animals, and monstrous births. The aim was to produce an exciting visual combination of text and image to encourage readers to buy the book. Certainly the title page, with its use of multiple typefaces, was designed by the printer, and the ornamental capital *W* that begins the book was a special block in the shop's collection of type. The woodcut of the Tupinambá man in the hammock was surely a new image designed for this particular book. Might a German artist who had seen other images of the Americas have created the woodcut?[20]

It is certainly possible that an artist living in Marburg was already familiar with the idea that cannibalism was believed to exist in the newly found lands across the Atlantic. By the middle of the sixteenth century, descriptions of cannibalism had appeared in a variety of printed texts, beginning with the widely published letters of Christopher Columbus and Amerigo Vespucci. In his letter written to Luis de Santángel (1493), Columbus briefly referred to the existence of cannibalism in the Caribbean even though he had not actually seen it. Vespucci offered a more vivid, eyewitness description of cannibalism in his *Mundus Novus* letter, claiming that "human flesh is common fare among them" and that he had seen "salted human flesh hanging from house-beams, much as we hang up bacon and pork."[21]

After the publication of Columbus's and Vespucci's letters, cannibalism became a recurring theme in the descriptions of America, especially descriptions of the peoples of Brazil and the Caribbean. The vibrant print culture in Germany included books of travel accounts, letters, and histories, and Germans read substantially the same reports of the Americas as did other literate Europeans. The chronicles of the Spanish court historian Peter Martyr d'Anghiera, who knew many of the early conquistadores and wrote vivid accounts from their point of view, were widely published in Germany. Anghiera described violent wars, enslavement of Indians, human sacrifice, and cannibalism. Anghiera's "Decades" were often repackaged and republished with other accounts of the Americas, including those of Brazil.[22]

Although printed texts described purportedly "true" witnessing of cannibalism, for an artist, visual icons of cannibalism would have been more memorable than printed descriptions. Typical images of cannibalism that circulated in Europe included severed limbs, hanging body parts, bodies being chopped up, or bodies or body parts being roasted on spits. Some of these images derived from mythological or imaginary beings imagined to be real. Of the monstrous races that medieval Europeans believed inhabited the edges of the earth, for example, the dog-headed man resurfaced as a cannibal. In other images, artists envisioned cannibalism to be similar to the way Europeans butchered and cooked their domestic animals, such as cows, pigs, or sheep.[23]

The image of cannibalism on the title page woodcut of *True History* is gruesome and shows severed limbs, yet it is not similar to the way cannibalism was depicted in sixteenth-century Germany. It resembles neither the images of cannibalism that first appeared in early German editions of Vespucci's letters, nor those on printed German maps. Maps did popularize images of cannibalism and associated the act with the Americas. One early map of the world, a painted map by an unknown cartographer dated ca. 1506, is the first to include a graphic representation of cannibalism over Brazil—a man's body is impaled on a long spit and roasting over a fire. But this map, which was most likely commissioned by Cardinal Bernardino Lopez de Carvajal, was privately held and therefore not well known. Printed maps, on the other hand, were widely seen and explicitly connected cannibalism with the Americas.[24]

On Martin Waldseemüller's *Carta Marina,* a printed map of 1516, cannibalism is depicted off the coast of northern Brazil. Human body parts and limbs hang from a tree, while limbs are roasted on a long spit (fig. 24). Whether this map by Waldseemüller sold well is uncertain, but a revised German edition by Lorenz Fries, which was printed after Waldseemüller's death by his Strasbourg publisher, did. Fries's world map appeared with a similar image of cannibalism over Brazil in 1525, and it sold well to its intended German audience, being reprinted in 1527 and 1530. Sebastian Münster's map of the world, first published as a supplement to a collection of travel accounts in Basel in 1532, contains an elaborate depiction of cannibalism on the lower left border, below South America. The artist who created the woodcut images for the map's border is thought to be Hans Holbein; his rendering of the continent—replete with a teepee festooned with hanging heads and limbs, bodies being cut up with cleavers, and an entire body roasting on a spit—forcefully projects the message that cannibalism is real. Because of the placement of the images, the viewer of the map cannot help but associate the location of these horrendous deeds with the Americas. When Münster redesigned his world map for his own publications, *Geographia* (1540) and *Cosmographia* (1550), he moved one of these visual icons depicting cannibalism—the teepee—and placed it directly over Brazil, thus eliminating any doubt about where cannibalism took place (see fig. 24). The

Figure 24. Cannibalism Associated with America on Two German Maps. Münster's World Map (left); Waldseemüller's Carta Marina (right). Münster's Map detail courtesy the Lilly Library, Indiana University, Bloomington, Indiana. Waldseemüller's Carta Marina detail reproduced with permission from the Jay Kislak Foundation.

other images of cannibalism created by Holbein appear in simplified form in his *Cosmographia* as illustrations alongside text describing the peoples of the Americas.[25]

All of these images of cannibalism are quite different from the image of cannibalism on the title page of *True History*. The woodcut image on the title page presents details of life in the Americas that had appeared in written accounts and that were known to those who had been to Brazil, but these details had not yet joined the growing stock of visual imagery available to artists in Germany. In Staden's image, a fire burns underneath the hammock, and next to the man is the grate known as the *boucan*. These details had appeared in published texts on the Americas (such as Vespucci's letters), and they were visually depicted on the highly illustrated French manuscript maps of the Dieppe, or Norman school of cartography. Most of the surviving examples of these maps created in Normandy are lavishly done by hand and are collected into ornamental atlases that were owned by wealthy merchants, nobles, and kings; they were not published nor widely disseminated. Staden may well have seen such maps while he was in France. In Marburg in 1556, however, it is not likely that artists would have been familiar with them. It seems clear that only Staden could have supplied the ethnographic information contained in the woodcut, including the Tupi Guarani phrase, "Sete katii" (*sete katu*).[26]

Indeed, all of the images in the book argue for a collaboration between Staden, an artist, and a woodcutter. Did Staden produce the drawings that served as the basis for the woodcuts? Or did he hover over an artist and intervene orally as the drawings took shape on the page? Whichever it was, Staden remained very near to the production of the woodcuts and limited the artistic expression and imagination. Perhaps because he was a gunner and thus close in social status to a craftsman, it might have been somewhat more natural for Staden to have worked directly with the artist and woodcutter. Or because it was of the utmost importance to Staden (and to Dryander) to produce compelling images to complement the text, Staden may have insisted on a close collaboration. In his introduction, Dryander even states that Staden was bearing the expense of printing and cutting the woodblocks, which would give Staden reason to work directly with the woodcutter and artist.[27]

The captions written inside some of the images hint at Staden's direct intervention, for they use the first person voice and seek to clarify the images for the reader. For example, on one image "The fort where I was" is written over the building on Santo Amaro Island where Staden served as gunner for the Portuguese king (see fig. 23, right). We also know that Staden must have seen the woodcuts before the book's text was finished, since he makes reference to the images in his text. "It is shaped like this," he writes in chapter 23 of book 2, referring to the shakers or rattles (maracas) that, he writes, were believed to hold prophetic powers. An image of them follows immediately thereafter.[28]

Other images in *True History* show that the collaboration between Staden and the artist was capable of producing a visually stunning image. The depiction of two Tupinambá men that begins book 2, for example, is so artistically done that it seems unlikely that Staden could have produced it. The positioning of the two men at the front plane of the image, with stylized clouds, trees, and other vegetation comprising the background, and the use of shading and contrapposto all suggest the hand of an artist. And yet the image contains ethnographic details—such as the feather work, body paint, ornamentation, and especially the feathered and carved war club—that could only have come from Staden himself (fig. 25).

The many images of ships that appear throughout Staden's book all suggest the hand of the artist and reinforce an implicit metaphor of the story: life's journey is analogous to the ship's voyage. This was familiar territory for sixteenth-century German artists. Images of ships and metaphors using ships were well known because of Sebastian Brant's *The Ship of Fools* (*Das Narrenschiff*), which was originally published in Basel in 1495 and was the most successful book written in German in the sixteenth century (except for Luther's translation of the Bible). Quickly going through numerous reprints and translations, the book became a standard

Figure 25. Tupinambá Warriors. From Hans Staden, *Warhaftige Historia.* Marburg: 1557. Courtesy, Lilly Library, Indiana University, Bloomington, Indiana.

in booksellers' inventories. Brant describes more than a hundred different types of fools. The world is full of fools, he says—in fact, it is a regular ship of fools. In pointing out the discrepancies between how people were expected to act and how they did act, Brandt hoped to reform them by satirizing them. In the woodcut illustrations that appeared in the various editions of Brant's book, a ship is typically shown at sea with silly fools on board. These images, as well as the book itself, further popularized the idea of the ship as a symbol of society, fraternity, and fragility.[29]

The ships in *True History* are not ships of fools, however; rather, they are ships of knowledge. These ships cross the north and south Atlantic, not with fools on board but with trained men of the sea who use the scientific instruments of the day to navigate their course. The first image in the book is an almost full-page image of a ship under full sail. It is a polished and artistic image of the sort that trained professional designers or artists might produce. It may even be signed by the artist and the woodcutter—the DH and the AII that appear on the main mast flag may well be their initials. Sea creatures frolic in the waves around the craft, while the sun and moon shine down benevolently. With its four masts and six sails unfurled,

Figure 26. A Ship of Knowledge. From Hans Staden, *Warhaftige Historia.* Marburg: 1557. Courtesy, Lilly Library, Indiana University, Bloomington, Indiana.

the vessel is staffed by a skilled crew: two sailors climb the rigging to trim the sails, while two navigators take readings with the nautical instruments of the day. The cross staff was used to take readings of Polaris (the North Star), while the astrolabe was used to measure the altitude of the sun (note the rays of the sun extending down into the instrument in fig. 26). The ship is therefore prepared to sail both in the northern Atlantic, using Polaris as its guide, and in the south Atlantic where, because the North Star is not visible, latitude would be reckoned by measuring the height of the sun at midday. The five circles in the ship's foremost flag identify it as Portuguese, who were known to be on the cutting edge of nautical science.[30]

If the goal of the image was realism (and after all, the first word of Staden's title page is "True"), the ship falls short, for there is a striking error: the flags on top of the masts extend in the wrong direction. At sea, the flags would fly away from the wind, whereas in the woodcut, they are pointing into the wind. This first image could not have been drawn by an artist who regularly studied and drew ships under

Figure 27. Ships at Sea. From Hans Staden, *Warhaftige Historia.* Marburg: 1557. Courtesy, Lilly Library, Indiana University, Bloomington, Indiana.

sail. Perhaps it was drawn by Staden, who accidently reversed the direction of the flags. Or possibly for the artist who drew it, realism was not as important as the artistic balance between the moon, clouds, flags, and sun at the top of the image.[31]

The other woodcuts of ships in *True History,* it seems clear, were drawn by artists. The images contain familiar elements in sixteenth-century German woodcuts such as the wind heads in the top corners, the billowing clouds, the shading of the sky, the elaborate ship, the waves, a sun, and the sea creatures. These ships are carefully drawn and cut, and their flags fly in the correct direction (see fig. 27). But they are stylized, for they are not accurate representations of known designs of sixteenth-century ships.[32]

Together with the scientific emphasis of the first woodcut of a ship (fig. 26), these images of ships project the idea of exploration, travel, and contact with distant lands. They were not the first woodcut images to do so, for images of ships had appeared in early woodcut illustrations accompanying the letters of Columbus, travel accounts, and histories. Yet the sheer number of ships as well as their prominent placement is noteworthy. Similarly, images of ships appear frequently on sixteenth-century maps. On maps, according to historian Richard Unger, artistically drawn ships reflect not only artistic traditions but also the importance of emerging technology, the conquest of the sea, and pride in accomplishments of overseas exploration.[33]

The ship symbolized the theme of travel, peril, and ultimate homecoming, which would have resonated deeply with Christians. The presence of so many ships serves to reinforce Staden's central narrative. Even a ship of knowledge required the grace of God to reach its destination, a message made abundantly clear in the text above the first ship that introduces Staden's story: "What does it help the watchman in the city / [or] the course of the mighty ship in the sea / If God does not preserve both?" As seen in the images of the ships, when the sailors are not working, they fold their hands in prayer; see figure 27 (left). Going to sea was a dangerous undertaking, and it required God's grace in order to survive storms, battles, and shipwrecks and to return home with new knowledge of the world.[34]

The ships in *True History* travel to real, not imaginary, places—a point underscored by the geographical information that accompanies many of the woodcut images. These geographic images double as simple maps that mark important locations in the story and make the point over and over again that Staden's trials happened in specific places. The maps in *True History* are influenced by German woodcut maps, not in their geographical information but in their visual composition and style. Just as the revolution in print had made books more accessible, so too had woodcut maps and landscapes become available to mass audiences in Germany. By the sixteenth century, map printing flourished in German cities such as Nuremberg, Cologne, and Ingolstadt; and when printed, maps could be consulted by a wide variety of people. Elaborate, expensive Latin editions of Ptolemy's *Geographia* were treasured by humanist scholars such as Dryander, but Münster's *Cosmographia,* with its many maps, was intended for a mass audience. Single-sheet printed maps were also readily available in Germany and were collected by merchants, lawyers, scholars, and even tradesmen.[35]

While the geographical content of Staden's maps had to have been supplied by Staden himself, the artist provided the visual imagery that made these images more attractive and more comprehensible to the reader. An artist would have understood that certain signs, icons, and symbols were easily read on maps as representations of towns, cities, mountain ranges, rivers, and coastlines, because although they were not standardized, they had been so widely reproduced on printed maps. Similar visual icons and signs can be seen in the woodcut maps of the *True History;* they mark coastlines, bodies of water, hills, villages, settlements, and fortifications. This content would have been provided by the artist.[36]

The image of the battle to contain the slave uprising in Iguarassu in Pernambuco is a case in point (see fig. 28). Staden's image is quite specific, suggesting that it is meant to be read as a map. The coastline is represented by one or two black lines, and the water is recreated by parallel lines to suggest the ocean. Stylized hills, mountains, and settlements recall those of other printed German maps, such as in Münster's *Cosmographia*. The Cape of St. Augustine, a major geographical feature

Figure 28. Map and Battle Scene in Pernambuco. From Hans
Staden, *Warhaftige Historia.* Marburg: 1557. Courtesy, Lilly Library,
Indiana University, Bloomington, Indiana.

(and landmark for sailors), is labeled; palisaded Indian villages appear on shore
amid the forest; and the Portuguese settlement of Marin (Olinda) rises from the hills.
Staden's map/image is complex, and the many sequential events depicted on the
map allow the reader to follow the action described in the text. The reader can see
the trees chopped down to hinder passage along the waterway, the sugar plantation
fortified by cannons, and the attacks by Indian men armed with bows and arrows.
The geography serves as a tableau for the events narrated in the text. The reader can
read the geography in the image because it uses familiar conventions of sixteenth-
century printed maps.

Staden's book includes a strikingly original fold-out map of Brazil. Using maps
to accompany travel accounts was not unusual; in 1486, when Bernard von Breydenbach published an account of his pilgrimage to Jerusalem, it was illustrated
with fine, fold-out woodcut landscape maps created by Erhart Reuwich (who was
also the printer). The map in *True History* is unusual, however, in that it goes beyond
the landscape-like woodcut maps such as that of Pernambuco (fig. 28), and attempts
to represent all of Brazil much as in a sea chart. It was not drawn by a cartographer,

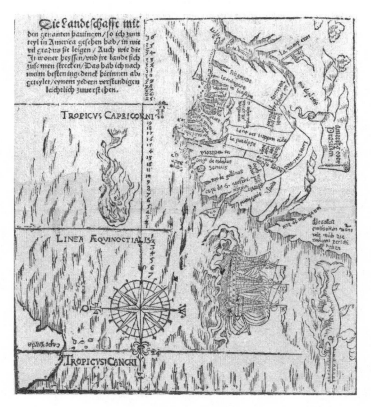

Figure 29. Staden's Map of Brazil and Representation of the South Atlantic. From Hans Staden, *Warhaftige Historia.* Marburg: 1557. Courtesy of the John Carter Brown Library at Brown University.

nor does it imitate any recognizable school; rather, it appears to have been drawn by Staden. In Germany, woodcut topographical maps would have been known to him, especially given his mercenary profession. While on board ship or in the ports of Lisbon, Seville, Rouen, and Dieppe, he would have seen the sea charts drawn in the Portuguese, Spanish, and French traditions.[37]

Staden's map (fig. 29) contains elements characteristic of both woodcut maps and navigational charts. The map is oriented with south at the top, as was characteristic in the French atlases drawn in Dieppe and on some German topographical maps of the sixteenth century. Signs used on the map—curving lines to suggest waves in the ocean, black lines to represent coastlines, or inverted, shaded V's to signify mountains—are similar to printed woodcut maps of the sixteenth century. The large compass rose was more commonly found on nautical charts because of its importance in navigation. Combined with rhumb lines that radiated out from the points of the compass roses that adorned the chart, pilots could set their course. Staden's map could not be used for navigation because it lacked rhumb lines, a scale, and accurate measurements, but the prominent placement of the compass rose underscored Staden's claim to readers that he knew the ways of the sea.[38]

The text at the top left of the map is written in the first person and proclaims that Staden is indeed the maker of the map:

> The landscape with the named ports / as I partially have seen them in America / in the gradients in which they lie / also as the inhabitants call them / and how their lands are put together / this I have tried to show to the best of my abilities / something that each can easily understand.[39]

Staden's map displays the clearest indication of how he must have worked with the artist and the woodcutter. Staden drew the coastline of Brazil, labeled the ports, marked the Equator and the Tropics, and drew in the territorial boundaries of indigenous groups in Brazil. Then the artist drew the ship, the sea creatures, the scroll, and the signs common to woodcut maps—the waves and parallel lines to signify water or, on the mainland, the hills to represent mountain ranges, and the clouds. The woodcutter cut the block and inserted the type for the legend.[40]

How does such a map relate to sensationalist tales of cannibals, the ethnographic description of the new world, or the religious message of salvation central to Staden's text? The first reason is obvious: the fold-out map, as well as the other map-like images, proclaim that the places that Staden describes can be found on maps and visited by ships. His cannot be an invented tale. But there is more. The ships make possible travel to a new world, a world only recently unveiled where new knowledge was becoming known with every ship's voyage. In the Protestant world view, Wolfgang Neuber suggests, the discovery of the Americas was seen as a renewed revelation of God in the world, and through scientific study of the New World, the workings of God would be understood.[41]

Similar collaborations between artists and eyewitness travelers are visible in the woodcuts that appeared in *Les singularités de la France Antarctique,* another major book that described the Tupinambá of Brazil. This book was published later in the same year, in December 1557, in Paris. Its author was the Franciscan André Thevet, who later became cosmographer to the French king and who had accompanied Villegagnon on the French expedition to establish a colony in the Guanabara Bay in 1556. It is unknown whether Thevet and the artist who drew the images for *Les singularités* had seen Staden's book. The original woodcuts for *Les singularités* are more artistic than those in Staden's book, but they also reveal that the artist must

Figure 30. Tupinambá Smoking and Making Fire. André Thevet, *Les singularités de la France Antarctique.* Paris: 1558. Courtesy of the John Carter Brown Library at Brown University.

have worked together with either Thevet or another who had been to Brazil. Perhaps the artist had seen Tupi men and women in France or had examples of Tupi featherwork, war clubs, fire sticks, and flora and fauna to work from. In his images, the naked Tupinambá adopt statuesque poses and are placed in scenes with foregrounds and stylized backgrounds—these suggest the influence of the artist. Yet the Tupinambá bodies are infused with ethnographic details, such as featherwork, tools, and body ornaments that came from information unique to Brazil (see fig. 30).[42]

The classical-looking Tupinambá who appear in the woodcuts of Thevet's *Les singularités* offer some clues that help us to understand the rhetorical meanings of Staden's images. In Thevet's text, the images play two roles: they reinforce the classical allusions made in the text, and they display the ethnographic signatures of the Tupinambá. In a typical example of Thevet's method, he describes Tupinambá warfare, complete with woodcut, and then segues to a description of the Romans and the Gauls at war. Why? According to French scholar Frank Lestringant, he does this to show the reader that the Tupinambá, although portrayed as barbaric and different, are nevertheless considered by Thevet to be part of human history.

The images work with the text to persuade the reader that the Tupinambá lifeways can be compared to the cultures of antiquity and that Christianity is superior to them.[43]

Staden's woodcuts serve a different purpose. They are not there to reinforce classical references, of which there are few if any in Staden's text. Rather, in Staden's book the images provide a second, pictorial narrative with its own voice, metaphors, scenes, and geographic descriptions. The visual narrative reinforces the main points of the story: that it is through God's grace that one is saved, that Staden's story is true, and that the Americas are populated by very different peoples, who may be observed and studied.

The images reproduce the dual nature of Staden's text, in which book 1 conveys Staden's story to demonstrate the power of God's grace and book 2 serves as an ethnographic description of the Tupinambá. Some images invite the reader into the story to feel Staden's suffering and in so doing to reinforce Staden's rhetorical strategy in book 1: to create a martyr's tale. For just as saints' (or martyrs') tales were illustrated so that readers (or viewers) could more deeply contemplate the spiritual lesson, so too Staden's images engage the reader emotionally.

The narrative images feature Staden in scenes from his captivity. Not all of these images, however, are particularly striking or even easy for the viewer to decipher. Staden is not always recognizable: one must search for the man with the beard, or the bound captive, or the figure marked with a cross or with "H.S.," Staden's initials. Despite the drama of the written story, some of the narrative images are much less dramatic than an artist might have envisioned. For example, although the single action taking place at one moment in time makes for good drama and a good scene for an artist to depict, many of the illustrations are multi-scenic, that is, several events are portrayed in a single illustration as Staden might have remembered them. For example, in one image, after he arrives in the village of Ubatuba (Uwattibi), with its four large *ocas,* or longhouses, Staden appears naked with feathers around his waist and led by the women. An event that happened before, when a woman shaved off his eyebrows, is depicted in the same image. Staden is recognizable but seems lost among the women and children (see fig. 31, left).[44]

Another image that is much more powerful suggests collaboration between Staden and an artist. Staden is posed carefully in the center of the image praying; he is standing and unbound, while the Tupinambá men smoke. Smoking was not a European custom, and the depiction of the adult men holding the long canes and exhaling bursts of smoke was profoundly unfamiliar to Europeans. The men are naked and smoke while squatting on the ground, which portrays them as inferior in comparison to the fully upright Staden, standing in contrapposto. The scene is also

Figure 31. Staden among Women (left) and Making a Prophecy among Men (right). From Hans Staden, *Warhaftige Historia.* Marburg: 1557. Courtesy, Lilly Library, Indiana University, Bloomington, Indiana.

marked as barbarous: the village is surrounded by a large palisade that imprisons Staden, and its entrance is marked with two heads (or skulls) on top of two posts. Stylized trees appear outside the palisade, and judicious shading focuses the viewer's eye on Staden. The sky is peaceful, studded with stars and the moon. Staden's prayer is his own intervention to make clear to the reader the significance of what is taking place. Carved into the woodcut are the words: "O my Lord and God, help me out of this misery to a bright [blessed] end" (fig. 31, right).[45]

In book 2 the ethnographic images dominate, and on the surface they seem to have nothing to do with Staden or his religious message. In these illustrations the viewer looks directly into the lives of the Tupinambá, who are shown fishing, making fire, dancing with shaman, and committing acts of cannibalism. Their villages, their lifeways, and their rituals are emphasized to the viewer. The illustration of fishing (fig. 32) is emblematic of this style. It shows fishing in an undisclosed place that has no direct impact on Staden's narrative. The men use bows and arrows, wade into the water, and swim to catch fish.

In combination with his map and map-like images, the scientific descriptions contained in the ethnographic images of book 2 convince the reader of Staden's truthfulness. Geographic and ethnographic images show the reader that it was possible to return to the lands of the Tupinambá to verify his story. The crux of Staden's story, after all, is that it was not fantasy, but real, and that he had experienced God's

Figure 32. Tupinambá Men Fishing. From Hans Staden, *Warhaftige Historia.*
Marburg: 1557. Courtesy, Lilly Library, Indiana University, Bloomington, Indiana.

grace in the Americas. This new world could be reached via any ocean-going ship
with a competent navigator.

Why do the images of the Tupinambá not include the popular stock images of
monstrous peoples assumed to inhabit the edges of the earth? Why are there no
dog-headed people, or one-eyed men, or men with their heads encased in their
chest cavity, with long ears or huge feet to shield their heads from the sun as recorded and popularized by the *Nuremberg Chronicle?* What is the reason for the
realistic and somewhat sympathetic portrayal of the Tupinambá?

Possibly influenced by Dryander, Staden follows the descriptive style used by
Münster in his *Cosmographia,* which has been called an "implicit" ethnography or
the "tentative beginnings" of comparative anthropology by scholars. Münster had
few new sources with which to describe the peoples of the New World—he repeats
information from Columbus's and Vespucci's letters, for example—and therefore
his ethnographic approach to the Americas is weak and out of date. For the images,
he simplifies the gruesome images from Holbein's illustrations on the borders of
Fries's republication of Waldseemüller's *Carta Marina.* But his comparative ethnographic approach is quite successful when he can describe Germans and other

Europeans of whom he has information supplied by humanists, or to some extent even of peoples outside of Europe but somewhat familiar to Europeans, such as Turks. In his book on Brazil, Thevet, who, like Münster, considered himself a cosmographer, also applied the successful part of Münster's approach in his description of the Tupinambá. Not only did Thevet have the advantage of having traveled to Brazil, but he had access to information collected by others. As a result, the images created for his *Les singularités* were original and sought to reproduce the lifeways of the Tupinambá; they were not the stock images one finds illustrating Münster's description of America in his *Cosmographia*. So, too, do Staden's images in book 2 seek to use the cosmographical approach to describe who the Tupinambá were and how they lived in Brazil.[46]

Among the ethnographic images of book 2, appearing near the end, are eight images that depict the cannibalism ceremony. These images do not repeat earlier visual depictions of cannibalism in German books and maps, and they are not elaborately staged to project a drama of gruesomeness. Rather, they reinforce what Staden conveys in his text: that cannibalism is part of a larger and far more elaborate ritual connected to the treatment of enemies that are usually, but not always, acquired through warfare.

As anthropologist Neil Whitehead and others have argued, Staden's text, as well as his images, provides details about Tupinambá culture and lifeways that are not found in any other printed sixteenth-century accounts. The image that depicts the preparations for the festival, for example, shows the separate hut that had been constructed (with the killing club suspended inside) and men and women, their bodies feathered and painted, dancing with maracas. Another image is devoted to dancing; it shows a feathered shaman leading the dancing with the maracas and the serving of the manioc beer by the women. The killing of the captive, cinched with rope, is the subject of one image, while the cannibalism of the victim is shown in three different images.

These ethnographic depictions of cannibalism, with one exception, exclude Staden. Only in the last one does he appear as an eyewitness observer. This image is more dramatic than the others, and it displays more of the vocabulary of an artist in the use of stylized trees, the sun, and the sense of a vanishing horizon. The image is grotesque, having at its center a severed head in a cooking pot. Staden is shown standing, his hands folded in prayer, his pose one of modesty and piety. Over his head, his initials are incised, with a cross between the H and the S, reinforcing his distance from the barbarism occurring beside him (fig. 33). The reader cannot fail to grasp his status as an eyewitness who does not participate in the ritual but who prays to God instead.

Figure 33. Staden Observing Cannibalism. From Hans Staden, *Warhaftige Historia.* Marburg: 1557. Courtesy, Lilly Library, Indiana University, Bloomington, Indiana.

Why would Staden permit the depiction of himself naked in this image? On the surface, it would seem that Staden is naked because he was stripped naked as a captive and because the Tupinambá did not themselves wear clothes. On a deeper level, Staden's nakedness taps into meanings familiar to Christian Europeans. Male nakedness appeared in Christian art associated with Adam and with Christ nailed to the cross. Nakedness symbolizes God's creation of man, as in Michelangelo's Sistine Chapel or Dürer's representation of the innocence of Adam (and Eve) in the Garden of Eden before the fall. In sixteenth-century German art, male nakedness also appeared as a form of self-introspection and as a way to link oneself to Christ's suffering, as can be seen in Dürer's nude self-portraits. In his writings, as in his artistic work, Dürer makes references to the artist and Christ; similarly, in his written story and in the images, Staden compares his tribulations to the sufferings of Jesus. Staden's nakedness underscores the religious message of the text, wherein nakedness marks both closeness to God (Adam at creation) and empathy for Jesus' suffering on the cross. Staden's nakedness was not demeaning, nor was it a sign of his helplessness, but it was reflective of his spiritual journey.[47]

It seems clear, then, that Staden both insisted on the creation of original images and intervened in the making of them to ensure that his eyewitness gaze was faithfully reported by the artist and woodcutter. By doing so, he underscored the spiritual message of his text—that he had received God's grace—and he reinforced his claim that everything he wrote about was true and could be verified. By including the images, especially those that depicted cannibalism or that showed ships crossing the ocean or that doubled as maps, he made his printed text all the more powerful. Perhaps this was not his intention, but it certainly was the result.

Once the book with its images was printed and sold, it took on a life of its own. Staden could not intervene as his book was read nor as his images were viewed. Readers pondered his words and studied his images and used their own imaginations, associations, prior knowledge, and interests to understand and interpret his text. Two themes of his book that likely disturbed his readers were cannibalism and women.

Staden's portrait of women, in words and images, is complex because of both what he says and what he does not say. In book 1, women taunt Staden. They beat him, tear at his beard, drag him by the cord around his neck, scrape off his eyebrows, and dress him in the ritual garb worn by captives. They often appear with a hand at their mouths, as if they are biting their hands to suggest what they will do to Staden's body or laughing, making only a small attempt to hide their mockery of him. In their actions, they invert normal gender relations and treat him as their pet. Staden does not immediately reveal a central ritual aspect of his captivity: that he would have been given a woman who would have slept with him and provided his food—in essence have been a wife over whom he had no control.[48]

The images reveal that Staden was quite familiar with the lives of women and with the gender roles of the Tupinambá. For example, several woodcuts depict women at work, often with babies strapped to their backs. They show how women wore their hair in one long braid, how they scraped in the sand for shellfish, how they weeded the garden plots, and how they carried heavy loads (see figs. 9 and 17).

In book 2, Staden devotes a short chapter to describing how a Tupinambá woman could become a shaman, and he notes that a female shaman could offer prophecies. Staden's longest treatment of women occurs when he describes the cannibalism ceremony, in which he presents women as playing central roles. It is they who prepare the drink, paint the captive, weave the long binding cord, and decorate the war club. It is they who sing, dance, and shriek with joy before the ritual killing. After the captive has been killed (by a man), it is the women who place the body on the wooden grate, scrape off the skin, place wood in the rectum, run screaming with severed limbs, and cook the intestines, serving them to children.

Claiming to be an eyewitness and delivering this description both textually and visually, Staden presents a portrait of women who are at one moment calmly doing the work that makes life go on, such as preparing food, weaving cotton hammocks, making clay pots, or caring for babies, and at another shouting with happiness as they run around the longhouses carrying the arms and legs of a recently killed captive. Staden's women are passive domestics and yet are powerful in the cannibalism rituals, when they reduce men (such as he) to their bound pets. Some women become shamans, and even if Staden does not think much of their prophesies, it is clear that they are listened to at certain moments in Tupinambá society.

To Germans reading the words and seeing the pictures in Staden's book, the juxtaposition between women's domestic duties and their ability to become shamans, or the association between women and cannibalism, recalled something deeply familiar and frightening: the perceived power of witches. According to Charles Zika, a fundamental characteristic of the witch is her cannibalism. This association between witchcraft, women, and cannibalism emerged in Europe from the fifteenth to the seventeenth century. Part of this association was created by images of New World cannibalism, including, possibly, Staden's own images. New World imagery that was published in Europe and that linked women with cannibalism may have helped to spark or to stimulate the outbreak of witch-hunting in the middle of the sixteenth century.[49]

Staden's images were redrawn in later editions, and in the process, the association between women and cannibalism became even more laden with outrage and fear. The engraver, Theodor de Bry, published Staden's tale in volume 3 of his Great Voyages series, where he combined it with Jean de Léry's account. (Léry was the Calvinist minister who published, in 1578, a highly detailed ethnographic account of his residence in Brazil with some woodcut images.) Under de Bry's skilled artistic hand, the images of the original *True History* become more dramatic and more condemning of the Tupinambá. Staden becomes a helpless eyewitness of the orgiastic gluttony of the Tupinambá (see fig. 34).[50]

While these images do derive from Staden, de Bry makes them both artistically more accomplished and more violent. De Bry stages the scenes dramatically and fills them with action. His human bodies are muscled, posed, and full of depth. De Bry's engravings are significantly larger than Staden's woodcuts, to the extent that, according to literary scholar Darlene Sadlier, they overtake the text, which serves as a backdrop to them. These large and striking images illustrate Staden's own account but also Léry's, though the images in Léry's original French edition had also sought ethnographic accuracy. By using the new images for both accounts, de Bry transformed Staden's story into a more general portrait of the hopeless wicked-

Figure 34. De Bry's Recreation of Cannibalism. From Theodor de Bry, *Americae tertia pars.* Frankfurt: 1592. Courtesy, Lilly Library, Indiana University, Bloomington, Indiana.

ness of Tupinambá life in Brazil. In them, women play a prominent and demonic role. Although Staden's images formed the basis of these later reworkings, we should be careful to distinguish between the original woodcuts that accompanied Staden's texts and these that came later.[51]

Neither an author nor an artist by profession, but a soldier who had gone to sea and returned home, Hans Staden produced an illustrated book. In doing so, he became a sophisticated representational go-between who explained to a German audience, in words and pictures, who the Tupinambá were. The woodcuts dramatically enhanced the power of Staden's printed text, for the narrative images invited readers to identify with him, while the ethnographic details took the reader to the specific places where God's grace had saved him. As the title page suggests, cannibalism was indeed intended to be a major theme of Staden's narrative. Staden's brush with the cannibalism of the Tupinambá was meant to serve as a stage on which he could proclaim the infinite mercy and grace of God to those of true faith, while the detailed descriptions of cannibalism fit into the model of scientific description advocated by cosmographers such as Münster. Yet at the time his book

appeared, cannibalism had already become a powerful justification for the European colonization of the Americas. Was this apparent to Staden, who was a gunner
and not a colonial official or a missionary? Did he know that his account of cannibalism among the Tupinambá would serve to define them further as barbaric and
savage? Did he apprehend that by the seventeenth century such attitudes toward
native Americans would lead settlers to believe that it was their duty to "bring the
savage within the orbit of civilized values" and that, when that failed, "extermina-
tion is justified"?[52]

What should we make of Staden's association between women and cannibalism
and witchcraft? Was it apparent to him that his stories of Tupinambá women might
strengthen the belief in the existence of witchcraft in his own homeland? Whatever
he thought, whatever he intended, his images and text would take on new meanings as his book was read and understood by others. Such was the power of the
printed word and image in the early modern world.

Staden's book is not illustrated as an artist would have liked, nor does it read as a
humanist would have preferred; his text is unique both in its voice and in its imagery.
Together, the words and images bring us closer to the sailors, soldiers, and ordinary
people who crossed the Atlantic in the sixteenth century. Montaigne understood how
the mindset of the humanists might cloud their descriptions of native peoples, and
he thought that a purer description could be had from ordinary men. We know that
Staden was not in any sense a "better" man merely because he was a gunner. Of course,
having listened to Staden's voice, we know that even the "ordinary man's voice" has its
own biases, is judgmental, and is shaped by its own moral code.

Despite the formula of the martyr's tale that served as the framework for
Staden's story and the grid imposed by the humanist Dryander to recreate the
lifeways of the Tupinambá, we can hear in the text and see in the images the voice
and precarious position of one who lived among the Tupinambá, not as a martyr
or as a humanist, but as a go-between. Staden recognized the power of the Tupinambá chiefs, and he understood the strength of Tupinambá beliefs, rituals,
customs, and traditions. He also knew that to survive he had to manipulate the
intersection between the Tupinambá's cultural universe and the opportunities presented by the fact that the Tupinambá had become engaged with a rapidly changing Atlantic world, a world that he knew better than they. Because go-betweens
were individuals cut loose from their homelands and making their way through
unknown and unfamiliar terrain, they understood that to survive they must adapt,
be cunning, trade in information, tell lies—in short, to simulate and dissimulate.
If they were able to do so, they could exert a measure of control over their situation
and even, for a time, become powerful as cultural brokers. Their power endured

only as long as they were needed; once other brokers appeared or situations changed, their services were no longer needed, and go-betweens lost their influence. Most never returned, and most never became representational go-betweens.

Staden's collaboration with Dryander and with an artist and woodcutter changed the way he told his story and designed his images. Nevertheless, his voice and his eyewitness gaze were not lost, and together they made him a highly influential representational go-between. Because his depiction of Brazil was both textual and visual, it made his representation of the Tupinambá doubly powerful. Staden's *True History* is evidence of the power of the illustrated book in sixteenth-century Europe. Among the hundreds of books with woodcut or engraved images, *True History* conserves a unique voice and a distinctive vision. Its printed images, maps, and text combined to create a portrait of the Tupinambá and of Brazil that would endure for centuries.

Epilogue

L ittle is known about many of the individuals who have appeared in this history beyond what was captured in the text and images of the *True History*. Of Hans Staden himself, there are few remaining hints about how he spent his days after returning to Hesse. It is likely that he tried his hand at making gunpowder, running a small mill in the town of Wolfhagen. Powered by water, the mill would have been used to crush, grind, and then mix charcoal, sulfur, and saltpeter. Possibly he also produced soap, making a mixture out of charcoal, oils, and soda. Staden may have spent some time in the town of Korbach with relatives, learning how to make saltpeter; we think there is evidence linking him there to a loan of ten *taler* that he had failed to repay. It is probable that he married, sharing his work and his life with his wife. Perhaps of an evening one could visit him and find him at home, answering questions about his travels or telling one too many stories about foreign lands and foreign customs to his neighbors, people who, like him, would have been artisans and craftspeople.[1]

An image exists of Staden, supposedly from the days after his return to Hesse, but we do not know if this is what Staden actually looked like. He is represented as a respectable burgher; his long beard (familiar to readers from the *True History*'s original woodcuts) is framed by the large, starched ruff of his collar. He holds a small, slim book, likely his own, and thus he is posed as an author. His features are refined, and he stares off into the middle distance, looking more like a successful citizen than a soldier for hire (see fig. 35).

The image was published by Johann Justus Winckelmann in 1664 in a new, modified German edition of the *True History*. Winckelmann claimed that he had discovered this image of Staden in Kassel, among the original woodblocks. Possibly produced a hundred years after Staden's voyages, the image tells us about how respectable Staden must have appeared in the years following the publication of his book. Winckelmann was born in Homberg, studied at Marburg, and served as court historian to the count of Kassel. This "true portrait" of Staden has become iconographic, even if it may be inaccurate.[2]

We know more about the final days of Landgrave Philipp, the Protestant leader to whom Staden had dedicated his book and the ruler who had so carefully ques-

Figure 35. Seventeenth-Century Portrait of Staden. From Johann Justus Winckelmann, *Der Americanischen Neuen Welt Beschreibung.* Oldenburg: 1664. The Library Company of Philadelphia.

tioned Staden in the presence of other lords and advisors of his court. The captivity he endured at the hands of his emperor, Charles V, had taken a toll on his health, but he lived for many years thereafter, focusing in these last fifteen years on consolidating his rule and with it the authority of the Protestant Church in his lands. He took to his bed on the Thursday before Easter in 1567 with, as he told his sons, "an extraordinarily heavenly feeling," and he died on Monday evening. Attended by his deacon, Bartholomew Meyer, Philipp is said to have uttered the words, "Father, into thy hands I commend my spirit," before closing his eyes for the last time.[3]

The bubonic plague had ravaged European populations in the fourteenth century, and it continued to hit northern Europe in the sixteenth century, recurring in irregular intervals. The old and the young were more susceptible to illness, and the spread of the disease seemed to coincide with warm weather. This so-called second wave of the plague flared up and died down again intermittently and fitfully, spread by trade, warfare, and travel. Wolfhagen was hit hard by the plague in the year 1576, during which 673 people died. In a town of some four hundred families, this was a serious epidemic, striking rich and poor alike. Among the dead was a "soapmaker," who succumbed to the disease and was buried on September 7, 1576. He was preceded in death by his wife, who died a few weeks earlier and was buried on August 20, 1576. Whether this soapmaker is the man Hans Staden who traveled to Brazil, surviving treacherous seas, shipwreck, and captivity only to return again and to write about his experience, remains unclear.[4]

Andreas Kolbe, the man whose Marburg publishing house was responsible for printing the *True History,* also died of the plague; the university noted his death at some point between September and November 1568 of a "pestilent fever." His sons Zachary and Augustine had already taken over their father's business, which they kept afloat only until the end of 1570.[5]

Johann Eichmann, known as Johannes Dryander, died in 1560, a mere three years after the first publication of the *True History.* He had married well, and, with his wife from the Breul family (who, like Dryander and Staden's father, was from the town of Wetter), he had three sons and one daughter. Two of his sons became, like their father, physicians, and another took the degree of doctor of philosophy in the year 1558. The same year that his son began to lecture at the university, Dryander's health began to deteriorate, and he asked his prince for an assistant to help him with his duties. He died two years later, in December, without having written the book about Brazil that he had hoped to compile from the material gathered in the *True History.*[6]

And the many others, both named and unnamed, in Staden's story? What became of them? We do not know if the French ship, the *Marie Bellotte,* returned to Dieppe with Carautá-uára and the other French soldiers who refused to ransom Staden from the Tupinambá. The French, however, did ramp up their efforts to colonize Brazil, and we know that as a result the world of the Tupinambá was about to change forever just as the *True History* was published. In August of 1555, two ships left Dieppe bound for the Guanabara Bay. Under the leadership of Nicolas Durand de Villegagnon, the French were attempting to establish a colony that, in addition to protecting the French trade in Brazil, would harbor French Protestants, known as Huguenots. Accompanying Villegagnon on the voyage out was the Franciscan André Thevet, who remained in Brazil for ten weeks.

One of Villegagnon's two ships arrived in Brazil in the summer of 1555, carrying disease. The ships were provisioned in the Cape Verde Islands before sailing south along the coast of Africa to São Tomé, from whence they set course across the south Atlantic. On the crossing, a deadly fever broke out on one of the ships and "of the ninety who became sick five died." When Villegagnon's two ships reached the coast of Brazil in November 1555, some men were still ill, and André Thevet could not celebrate the Christmas mass one month later.[7]

After Villegagnon's arrival, reports of disease breaking out among the Tupinambá allies of the French living around the Guanabara Bay increased. Thevet describes meeting chief Pindahousou, whom he found "sick in his bed with a continual fever." Nicholas Barré, Villegagnon's pilot, referred to a "pestilential fever since we arrived here, from which more than 800 [of the Tupinambá] have died." It is likely that the arrival of settlers with Villegagnon as well as the construction of a colony greatly increased the spread of disease among the native Tupi peoples living in the Guanabara Bay. This introduction of diseases to which the native peoples had built up no immunities decimated the coastal villages.[8]

In 1556, three ships left France with three hundred soldiers, sailors, and the first Protestant missionaries to the New World, all with an eye to increase the size of the French Huguenot colony in the Guanabara Bay. Among them was Jean de Léry, a French Calvinist who intended to be a missionary. After an initial welcome, Villegagnon turned on the Calvinist missionaries, and Léry and several others fled from the French fort on the island and spent two months living with the Tupinambá on the mainland before they returned on a merchant ship, arriving in France in 1558. Léry would later write passionately about the problems of the French colony, which he said was deeply divided over religious issues, and acutely undermined by Villegagnon's cruelty, vanity, and treachery. Villegagnon returned to France in 1559, apparently to recruit more colonists, and he left his nephew in charge of the French colony in the Guanabara Bay.[9]

Meanwhile, in the Portuguese colonies in Brazil, the Jesuits, the first governors, and the colonists sought to establish their own presence in the Guanabara Bay and its adjacent regions, where the French continued to trade. The Jesuits wanted to open a new "door" of conversion and in the process unseat any influence left by French Protestants, while the Portuguese governors had long recognized the strategic value of a Portuguese settlement in the Guanabara Bay, which they called Rio de Janeiro. In 1560, Brazil's third governor, Mem de Sá, attacked the island where the French fort built by Villegagnon was located. The Portuguese troops defeated the French garrison, and the French survivors fled to the mainland, where they took residence among the Tupinambá. Without sufficient men to occupy the fort, Mem de Sá razed it and withdrew from the Guanabara Bay. The Tupinambá villages around the Guanabara Bay and south along the coast toward São Vicente, where Staden had once been held, continued to resist the Portuguese. Bras Cubas, a man Staden knew in São Vicente, wrote the king of Portugal asking for *bombadeiros* (men like Staden) who could defend the colony against such attacks.[10]

United as the so-called band of the Tamoio under the leadership of Cunhambebe, the great chief Staden had encountered in his captivity, the Tupinambá attacked Portuguese sugar plantations. Seeking peace, the Jesuits José de Anchieta
and Manoel da Nóbrega traveled to Iperoig, the very same or near the same village
where Staden had been held captive ten years earlier, and remained as hostages as
the peace was discussed. Both men feared for their lives, yet they avoided what
appeared to them to be certain death. Anchieta attributes their safety to Divine
Providence, but it is clear that their ability to speak Tupi and the protection of powerful chiefs, one of whom was Cuñambebe, saved them. Nóbrega decided to return to
São Vicente in June of 1563, while Anchieta remained a hostage until September,
when Cuñambebe and twenty others brought him by canoe to the fortress of Bertioga in São Vicente, where Staden had once been the gunner in residence. This
marked the conclusion of what became known as the Peace of Iperoig.[11]

This peace did not hold for long. Mem de Sá sent his nephew, Estácio de Sá, to
re-secure the Portuguese foothold in the Guanabara Bay. Anchieta accompanied
Estácio de Sá with his approximately three hundred men, and leaving São Vicente
and Bertioga in January of 1565, the expedition reached São Sebastião Island,
some forty miles south of Ubatuba, another location that Staden knew well. There,
Anchieta reported, the men, famished, torched a Tupinambá village, killed a man,
and took a boy prisoner. The rest of the village having fled, Estácio de Sá's men
then moved into the site, where there was plenty of fish and game. Continuing
north, Estácio de Sá entered the Guanabara Bay and founded the first Portuguese
settlement there, at the base of the Sugar Loaf Mountain. French ships were still
trading in the bay, and Anchieta noted the persisting presence of Lutherans and
Calvinists among the Tupinambá. Two years later, in 1567, Mem de Sá returned,
and with his nephew Estácio, they systematically attacked the remaining Indian
villages around the bay. Estácio lost his life, and Mem de Sá decided to abandon
the settlement in favor of a site on the mainland farther inside the bay. This became
known as São Sebastião do Rio de Janeiro, the site of the present day city of Rio.[12]

Just as the independent Tupinambá villages were being destroyed in Brazil, the
Tupinambá were becoming known in Europe as ferocious cannibals. Thevet's
book, *Les singularités de la France Antarctique,* appeared in 1557, the same year as
Staden's *True History.* Thevet's illustrated text with descriptions of the Tupinambá
depicts them as inhabiting a world that seems timeless. Yet in fact, the world as the
Tupinambá knew it was being forever altered by disease, colonization, and war.
Staden's book, as we have seen, lived on in the pirated edition of 1557 and in numerous reprints and translations, carrying forth the idea of the Tupinambá as a still
powerful and living people. Léry's *History of a Voyage to the Land of Brazil* was

published twenty years after his return, in 1578, and his book also proved to be very influential. Léry harbored much anger at Thevet and was, in fact, spurred to publish his own account of Brazil after Thevet released his *Cosmographie universelle,* which not only repeated what Thevet had written earlier about Brazil in *Les singularités* but also blamed the Calvinists for the loss of the French colony in Brazil.

Through Léry and encounters with Tupinambá in France, Montaigne became fascinated with the meaning of cannibalism; his essay "On Cannibalism" was published in 1580. Léry learned of Staden's book only in 1586, when it was translated for him to read. Léry believed that Staden not only "spoke the truth" but that their two accounts were fundamentally similar. Staden and Léry's accounts were joined by Theodor de Bry in his *America tertia pars,* to which he added the more dramatic engravings that are frequently, even today, attributed to Hans Staden. Samuel Purchas, the influential compiler of travel literature in seventeenth-century England, was little impressed with Staden's *True History,* however. Having translated the text into English from de Bry's volume, he decided against including it in his own collection of travel accounts on Brazil because it related, in his eyes, "onely his [Staden's] owne Tragedies, in his taking by the Savages, and often perils of being eaten by them, as some of his friends were before his face, with other like Savage arguments wherewith wee have glutted you already: I being alreadie too voluminous, have omitted the same and hasten to other Relations."[13]

By Purchas's time, then, the English-speaking reader had been "glutted" with accounts of cannibalism, all of which shaped their view of native peoples. Although many historians and anthropologists blame Staden for contributing to this glut and for its role in reduction of indigenous people to faceless, barbaric cannibals, Staden's text contains much more than mere "Savage arguments," for if we read it carefully, it leads us back into the early modern world of the sixteenth century and to the complex choices brought about by the cultural contacts initiated by European exploration, the expansion of trade, and the creation of settlements in the Americas.

The image of the cannibal that served to label, caricature, inspire fear and loathing, and justify war and colonization was recast in the twentieth century by Brazilian artists. This occurred in São Paulo (the modern city that was founded on the Piratininga Plateau of São Vicente at the time when Staden was there). Following the extraordinary Modern Art Week of 1922 in São Paulo, Brazilian poet Oswald de Andrade published his *Manifesto Antropófago* (Cannibalist Manifesto), in which he urged artists, indeed all Brazilians, to cannibalize from European culture in order to find the essence of what was Brazilian. "Tupi or not Tupi," he famously argued, "is the question." By turning the cannibalism metaphor on its head, Andrade at once embraced the indigenous past and looked forward to a new, uniquely

Brazilian identity. Yet, at the time when Andrade presented his manifesto, there were no longer any cannibalism ceremonies taking place along the coast of Brazil, nor were there any remaining independent Tupinambá villages along the coast.[14]

For Andrade, and for us, Staden's account remains one of the few detailed reconstructions of the Tupinambá way of life as understood by an ordinary European man, a mercenary from Hesse. Although Staden's tone can be faulted as too preachy, his woodcuts as crude and self-serving, his cultural bias as overpowering, his book nevertheless preserves a memory of a people, of a place, and of a moment in time. Staden's story is compelling today, not for the reasons that he set out to write, but for new reasons. He has left us closer to the Tupinambá and to the ordinary Europeans who crossed the oceans in the sixteenth century.

Staden's book opens up for the modern reader the shifting and uncertain place of the go-between, whose roles were nevertheless hugely significant in the opening of the Atlantic world. Most go-betweens were never able to return home or to write books, draw maps, and oversee the creation of images. As a result, the history of the go-betweens—who they were, what they did, how they were influential—has often been lost to historians. Not so with Staden. Not only can we reconstruct his story, but through him we begin to understand who go-betweens were, how they became powerful, and what their impact was. Moreover, Staden has now become our go-between. For not only did he traverse oceans, manipulate situations, and recreate what he had seen and lived through words and images, but his book still takes us back, 450 years later, to encounters that still disturb us today.

Was Staden despicable or odious, as some of our colleagues have suggested? Was his book part of a larger project that consciously cast the native peoples of the New World as horrid man-eating savages, making their subjugation morally and culturally just? Was he simply a blatant liar? Or did he slyly repeat and lavishly embellish what he had heard? And might all of this have been what others had imagined about peoples and places they had never seen?

In the course of writing this book, we have found these questions helpful for approaching the encounters that took place in the New World and the representations of the New World made by Europeans eager to learn about strange lands. However, they do not take us very far in understanding the complexities of Staden's experiences. Staden's is a story written by someone who was always on the margins or altogether an outsider. When he writes of his encounters, we know that he is aware of the power of individuals on both sides of the Atlantic to determine his fate. It is the people of the New World who take center stage in his book, standing next to him in his story and his images. These peoples are very real to him, and they are not imagined. Staden was well aware of the power that the Tupinambá women had over him, and he grasped the supremacy the Tupinambá chiefs exercised in their own world. The figures of the powerful back in Germany—Dryander, Landgrave Philipp, and unnamed others—have a more ghostly aspect in the text and are absent in the images, but they clearly leave their mark in the framing of the story and in its acceptance, by giving it their formal approval.

If Staden's book is filled with real descriptions of, even insight into, the lives of the Tupinambá, what in the end do we make of the lies that he told to the Tupinambá? Why does he repeat his lies in his story? Do they not undermine his credibility? If, as it seems, he understands the importance of his lying to be central to his survival among the Tupinambá, does this strategic agency on his part not diminish the role he assigns to God? Which in the end saved him: his lies or God's grace?

Even the writing of his story and the creating of the woodcuts, which on the surface seemed to be a witnessing of the truth, were a form of lying. In seeking to make intelligible who he was and where he had been to those to whom he had returned, Staden shaped his story to fit his audience. Selectively remembered, told, written, and illustrated, Staden's story was created in a form that was comprehensible to "his" people of sixteenth-century Germany.

If Hans Staden is our go-between, who takes us back into the sixteenth century, allowing us to understand it better, what can we learn from his travels and his tale? On the one hand, Hans Staden's *True History* offers us a window of understanding onto other worlds. As we have argued in this book, we can take his story as a starting point to see new worlds slowly coming into focus on both sides of the Atlantic. Staden's voice speaks to us across the centuries, and the Tupinambá who come alive in his pages are living, breathing men and women. Staden's descriptions of them allow us to take in many details of their daily lives with a vivid intensity that would otherwise be lost.

But while the *True History* may open a window or shed light on worlds lost to us, it also threatens to slam a door shut—a door that would allow us to comprehend the world in which Staden lived and moved as well as the peoples and things he encountered in the New World. Even after a careful reading of the *True History*, we may never be sure of anything Staden writes about; his entire story could be a lie, a twisted tale told for reasons that we can only surmise. As historian Michel de Certeau has so insightfully observed, travel texts like Staden's structure knowledge in ways that mirror the voyage itself.[15]

Staden describes his journey as a trial and tribulation, a martyr's tale of ultimate salvation. At the end of his story, he returns to the safety of his homeland, effectively ending the chapter of his life when he had been held captive. His return to Hesse and the act of his storytelling put a final seal on things seen and experienced.

With the narrowing of experience comes the creation of a story that confines the past safely within the pages of a book. The living peoples Staden had encountered became things to be read about and consumed by a public hungry for sensational tales that purported to be true.

For most of Staden's sixteenth- and seventeenth-century readers, the *True History* firmly shut off any possibility of truly entering into another world, although it offered a glimpse into heretofore unknown cultures and practices. For Staden's readers, the cannibalism he described—especially when represented in the shocking engravings by de Bry—could easily be understood as worse than anything known to exist. This reading of Staden's book marked the Tupinambá as not only violent but cruel beyond anything known. Therefore, readers could conclude that the Tupinambá deserved whatever they got, whether it was Staden's dissimulation, Villegagnon's conquest, epidemic disease, colonization, or being lost to history altogether.

Can we move beyond the ways in which Staden's early modern readers reacted to his text? With hindsight, Hans Staden helps us to see the myth-making that occurred in encounters between different peoples in the past. Many encounters in the Atlantic world were shocking and violent, even when go-betweens were present to facilitate communication. Human cruelty, for example, existed on both sides of the Atlantic, and some European observers, such as Jean de Léry, did not think the Tupinambá were any more cruel than Europeans of the sixteenth century. But because of the way Staden told his story, the Tupinambá were transformed into strange and remote man-eating demons. In this way, what were to the Tupinambá honorable rituals associated with warfare became to Staden's readers atrocities deserving of any kind of punishment. That this is more evident to us than it was to early modern readers is an insight that we should take from Staden. This insight enables us to see how the moral issues that his text and images raise are not unique but are universal questions that emerge when cultures come into contact.

Staden has indeed unlocked a massive door into the past for us. But the door is heavy, weighted down by nearly five hundred years of history. As we come to the end of this book, we hope that we have propped open the door of understanding. By reconstructing Staden's life and revisiting his text, we step onto the threshold and gaze into the sixteenth century. We recognize that Staden is a complicated character who challenges us to understand an emerging Atlantic world that was never one-sided in its encounters and that was populated by people who often, set adrift, sought to make sense of it. In so doing, these wandering, roaming beings—our go-betweens—created situations and produced texts and images that would long define the Atlantic world.

Introduction

1. See Legassie, "Differently centered."

2. "some godless people": es sein eyn teyl Gottloser leut im schiff, *Warhaftige Historia* (hereafter *WH*), bk. 1, ch. 53, paragraph 2 (hereafter given as 1.53.2). "I escaped": vnd ich were den Wilden entlauffen vnd zů jnen bei das bott geschwummen / aber sie mich nicht hetten woellen einnemen / hette derhalben wider muessen an Landt schwimmen vnter die Wilden / welches mir das mal eyn groß hertzwehe war, *WH* 1.53.2. "gave a Portuguese": Auch hetten sie den Wilden eynen Portugaleser geben / welchen sie gessen, *WH* 1.53.2.

3. Mit solchem allem sehs ich nun wol / das es der liebe Gott so gut mit mir gemeynet hette / Das ich / Gott sei lob / vor jnen hie bin / euch die newe zeitung zubringen. Sie moegen auch kommen wann sie kommen sollen. Aber ich wil euch eyn prophet sein / das von Got solche vnbarmhertzigkeyt vnd tyrannei / so sie da im Land bei mir gethon haben/Gott vergebs jnen / nicht wuerde vngestrafft bleiben / es were gleich kurtz oder lang / dann es augenscheinlich were / das mein seufftzen den herrn Gott im hymel erbarmet hette, *WH* 1.53.2.

4. Weigand Hans published a pirated version in Frankfurt in 1557; a Dutch edition by Christopher Plantin appeared in 1558; for further information about editions and reprints, see Neuber, "Die Drucke der im Original deutschen Amerikareiseberichte," 12–34. See further, Obermeier, "Hans Stadens Brasilienbuch," 5–51. The most recent English-language translation of Staden's work is Whitehead and Harbsmeier, *Hans Staden's True History*.

5. On Marco Polo, see Larner, *Marco Polo and the Discovery of the World;* Larner refutes earlier claims that Marco Polo never traveled to India. For John de Mandeville, see Mandeville, *Travels of Sir John Mandeville;* on the popularity of John de Mandeville's book, see Tzanaki, *Mandeville's Medieval Audiences.* For Varthema, see *Itinerary of Ludovico di Varthema.* A new German translation is Reichart, *Ludovico de Varthema.* For a consideration of his and other accounts, see Maxwell, "Journeys of faith and fortune." For Vespucci's letters, see Formisano, ed., *Letters from a New World.* The name America derives from Vespucci's first name, Amerigo, and was coined by Martin Waldseemüller and others in St. Dié, Alsace-Lorraine. The name first appears on Martin Waldseemüller's world map of 1507 and in the accompanying small volume, *Cosmographiae introductio,* published in the same year in St. Dié. See Waldseemüller, *Cosmographiae introductio,* trans. John Hessler

(London: Giles, 2008). Waldseemüller's magnificent world map is on permanent display at the Library of Congress, and its story is ably told by Lester in *The Fourth Part of the World*, and Schwartz in *Putting "America" on the Map*. Vespucci's truthfulness has long been questioned by historians; see Fernández-Armesto, *Amerigo*.

6. Arens, *Man-Eating Myth;* Neuber, *Fremde Welt;* Menninger, *Die Macht der Augenzeugen;* Lestringant, *Cannibals;* Forsyth, "Three Cheers for Hans Staden."

7. Campbell, *Witness and the Other World* and *Wonder and Science;* Said, *Orientalism;* Aune, "Early Modern Travel Writing."

8. TenHuisen, "Providence and Passio," 249.

9. Arens, *Man-Eating Myth*. Arens's work caused a storm among anthropologists, many of whom argued that he was wrong. See, for example, the review by James J. Springer in *Anthropological Quarterly* 53 (1980): 148. Arens reflects on the controversy unleashed by his book in "Rethinking Anthropophagy," 39–62.

10. For accounts of cannibalism in early Spanish encounters in the Caribbean, see Palencia-Roth, "Cannibal Law of 1503," 28. For a facsimile of Columbus's letter to Santángel with an English translation, see *The Spanish Letter of Columbus*. For the woodcut broadside thought to accompany Vespucci's *Mundus Novus* letter, see "Anonymous: Illustration of Indians, Broadsheet, 1505," in Wolff, *America: Early Maps of the New World*, 29. The *Mundus Novus* letter first appeared in print in Florence in 1502 or 1503, while the *Lettera,* was first printed in Florence in 1504 or 1505; both letters were widely published, especially the *Mundus Novus,* see Formisano, *Letters from a New World*, xix–xxv.

11. For the law of 1503, see Palencia-Roth, "Cannibal Law of 1503," 22–26. For images on cannibals on early maps, see Colin, "Woodcutters and Cannibals."

12. Lestringant, *Cannibals*, 1–5.

13. For claims about sensationalism, see Menninger, *Die Macht der Augenzuegen,* and Neuber, *Fremde Welt;* see also Schmölz-Häberlein and Häberlein, "Hans Staden, Neil L. Whitehead, and the Cultural Politics of Scholarly Publishing."

14. Eisenstein, *Printing Press*.

15. The literature on Luther is vast; for a thorough and insightful overview of recent publications on Luther and the Reformation, see Boettcher, "Review Essay."

16. Obeyesekere, *Cannibal Talk*, 252–53, 260, 266.

17. Forsyth counters Arens's presentation of Staden's account point by point and argues that Arens's dismissal of Staden is unwarranted in "Three Cheers," 17–36. For Lestringant on Thevet and Léry's descriptions of cannibalism, see *Cannibals*, 51–80. For sociologist Florestan Fernandes's work on the Tupinambá, see his *Organização social dos Tupinambá* and *A função social da guerra na sociedade Tupinambá*. For a critique of Fernandes's functionalist interpretation that does not question his reliance on Thevet, see Castro, *From the Enemy's Point of View*, 274–80. For Whitehead and Harbsmeier's argument on Staden as an ethnographer, see *Hans Staden's True History*, xvi–xvii and lxxxiv–lxxxix; for Whitehead's argument on violence, see Whitehead, "Hans Staden and the Cultural Politics of Cannibalism."

18. Martel, "Hans Staden's Captive Soul," 58.

19. geschickt vnd erfaren / beyde in der Christen vnd auch in der Wilden leut anschlegen vnd spraachen, *WH* 1.15.1. Villas-Bôas, "Wild Stories of a Pious Travel Writer," 207.

20. Daston and Park, *Wonders and the Order of Nature*, 62–63.

21. Here we follow Metcalf, *Go-betweens and the Colonization of Brazil.*

22. Ich Hans Staden vonn Homberg in Hessen / name mir vor / wens Gott gefellig were / Jndiam zubesehen, *WH* 1.1.1.

Chapter 1 · Staden Goes to Sea

1. Ich / wer aus meinem Vaterland gezogen. And: wann es mir gelingen möcht in Indiam zu siegeln, *WH* 1.1.1.

2. There are few traces of Hans Staden linking him to his native land of Hesse other than the book he wrote after returning from Brazil. This lack of information about individuals is not unusual for the early modern period. Until the emergence of the modern state, with its tools of power and control (the census, the tax system, the emergence of identification systems), local communities were responsible for keeping accounts of families, and this information was not particularly extensive, sometimes unreliable, and not always preserved. Even though historians have scoured parish records, court records, the holdings of Hesse's rulers, and personal inventories to piece together an account of where Staden lived and how, much remains unknown. Local historians published their findings in a special edition of *Hessiche Heimat* in 1956. For an example of a biography of a "minor" individual who was emblematic of his times, see García-Arenal and Wiegers, *A Man of Three Worlds.* For the relationship between Hessian rulers and the Holy Roman Emperor, see Vogler, *Europas Aufbruch in die Neuzeit,* 45–62.

3. The "Hanseatic League" is this organization's accepted name in English, although the German word *Hanse* itself means "league." For Hesse's main regions and towns, see Gräf, "Small Towns in Early Modern Germany," 184–94; and Wright, *Capitalism, the State, and the Lutheran Reformation,* 48.

4. Wright describes the landscape in *Capitalism,* 76. For the rivers of the region, see Blackbourn, *Conquest of Nature,* 4. The contemporary description by Fynes Moryson, *An Itinerary,* is available online: www.archive.org/details/fynesmorysons01moryuoft. For a comparison between the Amazon and Hessian rivers, see Blackbourn, *Conquest of Nature,* 4.

5. For the Hessian towns associated with the Staden family, see Grimmel, "Die Familie Hans Stadens." For the Moryson quote, see Moryson, *An Itinerary,* 5:12.

6. Hochstadt, "Migration in Preindustrial Germany," 200.

7. Dryander's words about Staden: "(wie in gemeynem Sprichwort ist) der Apfel schmeckt alwege nach dem Stam" (as the common saying would have it, the apple tastes of the tree). And further in regard to Staden's father: "eyn offreichtigen frommen und dapfferen Man / der etwan auch in guten Kunsten studirt," *WH,* Dryander's introduction, paragraph 1. In fact, Staden describes himself as reading while in Brazil; see *WH* 1.36.3.

8. Grimmel, "Die Familie Hans Stadens," 34.

9. For Gernand Staden, see Grimmel, "Die Familie Hans Stadens," 34. For widows and their property, see Wiesner, *Women and Gender in Early Modern Europe,* 59, 74–75; see also Cavallo and Warner, eds., *Widowhood in Medieval and Early Modern Europe.* For mortality rates, see Brady, *German Histories in the Age of Reformations,* 22. For citizenship and rights, see Rowlands, "Conditions of Life for the Masses," 40.

10. Chrisman, *Lay Culture, Learned Culture,* xxv.

11. Jutte, "Household and Family Life."

12. Rowlands, "Conditions of Life," 56. As Christine Johnson has shown, German merchants were engaged in widespread trade from Eastern Europe to the Iberian Peninsula before the travels of Columbus or de Gama; in the sixteenth century German commercial firms were heavily invested in trade with ports in the East; see Johnson, *German Discovery of the World,* 88–122.

13. so ist er samt seinen Altern hie in diesem Lande gesessen / nit wie der Landtfahrer und Lügener gewoheyt / von eiynem landt ins ander / ziegeuners weise umblauffe, *WH,* Dryander's introduction, paragraph 5.

14. For the Hanseatic League and Korbach, see Hammel-Kiesow, *Die Hanse,* 10. For the trade between German cities and Lisbon, see Pohle, *Deutschland,* 16–19. For salt and trade, see Kellenbenz, "Der Norden und die Iberische Halbinsel," 66.

15. For markets and Hessian towns, see Gräf, "Small Towns in Early Modern Germany," 190. For spices and their use, see Freedman, *Out of the East,* 2–18.

16. Sobral, "Expansion and the Arts."

17. Bedini, *Pope's Elephant,* 28–58. On the history of the symbolism of the elephant and rhinoceros in Western art, see also Heckscher, "Bernini's Elephant and Obelisk." For the rhinoceros, see Bedini, *Pope's Elephant,* 111–36.

18. For the parrot in art, see Verdi, *Parrot in Art,* 40, 90. On Dürer, see Massing, "Quest for the Exotic," 115–19; Bedini, *Pope's Elephant,* 119–23; Smith and Findlen, "Commerce and the Representation of Nature in Art and Science," 1–3.

19. For cabinets of curiosity as precursors to museums, see Impey and MacGregor, *Origins of Museums;* and Findlen, *Possessing Nature.* An example of exotic animals in prints was Albrecht Dürer's lifelike woodcut print of a rhinoceros; see Smith and Findlen, "Commerce." For exotic animals as pets, see Boehrer, *Parrot Culture,* 50–59.

20. Smoller, "Playing Cards." Such cards were to be found in elite and common households alike.

21. For Landgrave Philipp, see Cahill, *Philipp of Hesse and the Reformation,* 69. Staden uses the phrase: Dem Durchleuchtigen vnd Hochgebornen Fürsten vnd Herrn / Herrn Philipsen Landtgrauen zû Hesse, *WH,* Staden's dedication.

22. Cahill, *Philipp of Hesse,* 15–17.

23. Koenigsberger, "Empire of Charles V."

24. For the role of religion in subduing Hesse, see Wright, *Capitalism,* 10. For debates on religion and Philipp, see Cahill, *Philipp of Hesse,* 151–80. For Philipp's letter to his envoys, see Brady, *Protestant Politics,* 56. For the Schmalkaldic League, see Brady, *Protestant Politics,* 57.

25. The historian Johann Justus Winkelmann makes the claim (unfortunately without any further proof) that Staden fought in this war against the Turks in 1532 on behalf of the palatinate prince, Friedrich II, serving as a supply master, quoted in Pistor, "Hans Staden zu Homberg," 6. On warfare, see Gunn, "War, Religion, and the State," in Cameron, *Early Modern Europe,* 102–33, quotation from 112.

26. Hale, *Artists and Warfare in the Renaissance,* 12–13. "The Siege of Muenster (Overview)," in Strauss, *Illustrated Bartsch,* 13:455–56.

27. "The Siege of Muenster (Overview)," in Strauss, *Illustrated Bartsch*, 13:458–59; Hale, *Artists and Warfare*, 13.

28. Hale, *Artists and Warfare*, 42–72, 65–66, 73. Hale describes it as a kind of topical, informative, and editorialized journalism; see *Artists and Warfare*, 62.

29. "[Lansquenet with Musket] C.2," in Strauss, *Illustrated Bartsch*, 13:383.

30. Philipp was released in 1552. See Martel, "Staden's Captive Soul," 57; Schmölz-Häberlein and Häberlein, "Hans Staden," 750. For the conditions necessary to proclaim victory, see Gunn, "War, Religion, and the State," 112.

31. For population figures, see Cristóvão Rodrigues de Oliveira, *Lisboa*, 101. For numbers of seafarers, see Oliveira, *Lisboa*, 97; see also Dutra, "Social and Economic World of Portugal's Seafarers," 95. For ships leaving Lisbon for India, see Duncan, "Navigation between Portugal and Asia," 22. For Portugal's image in the West, see Brandão (de Buarcos), *Grandeza e abastança de Lisboa*, 24.

32. Domingues, *Os navios do mar oceano*, 243–66; Filipe Vieira de Castro, *Pepper Wreck*, 13–16; Mathew, *Portuguese Trade with India*, 78–82, 113–14; Boxer, *Portuguese Seaborne Empire*, 51–61; Schwartz, *Sugar Plantations*, 3–27.

33. For slaves in Portugal, see Saunders, *Social History of Black Slaves*, 33, 54–55; and Oliveira, *Lisboa*, 101. For slaves from Brazil and Asia, see Scammell, "Indigenous Assistance in the Establishment of Portuguese Power," 10–11. Also, the account of the shipwreck of the *São João*, along the coast of east Africa in 1552 describes 500 survivors, 180 of whom were Portuguese, and of the rest many were slaves, which, given the disembarkation from Cochin, suggests that some may have been East Asians. See "Relacão da muy notavel perda do galeão grande S. João," in Brito, ed., *História trágico-marítima*, 13.

34. On the early slave trade to the Americas, see Blackburn, *Making of New World Slavery*, 97–160. One of the few voices raised in criticism of the slave trade was Fernando Oliveira, who published *Arte da guerra do mar* in 1555. Oliveira did not believe that the origins of the slave trade could be reconciled with the preconditions set out in the theory of Just War as expounded by Christian theologians. As a result, there could be no theological basis for the trade. He argued that the Portuguese had created the demand for slaves and, by extension, the maritime slave trade; see Oliveira, *Arte da guerra do mar*, 23–25. Ivana Elbl estimates that the average minimum volume of the Crown's share of the trade was 1,100 slaves per year between 1486 and 1521; see Elbl, "Volume of the Early Atlantic Slave Trade," 47. For Bartolomé de Las Casas's critique of Indian slavery, see Las Casas, *Devastation of the Indies;* and Hanke, *Spanish Struggle for Justice*.

35. Vogt, *Portuguese Rule on the Gold Coast*, 35–40.

36. For the Rua Nova dos Mercadores, see Brandão, *Grandeza*, 97. For goods available in Lisbon, see Góis, *Lisbon in the Renaissance*, 27; and Castro, *Pepper Wreck*, 15–16. For African imports, see Vogel, "Africa and the Renaissance," 84–89, 104. For Sri Lankan goods, see, e.g., the mid-sixteenth-century wood and ivory chest in the British Museum, Asia OA 1892.2–16.25, Room 33 Asia, www.britishmuseum.org.

37. The original manuscript has been lost and is only available as a copy in the Bavarian State Library in Munich; see Pohle, *Deutschland und die überseeische Expansion*, 43.

38. Pohle, *Deutschland und die überseeische Expansion*, 135, 149–50.

39. Pohle, *Deutschland und die überseeische Expansion*, 33.

40. Mathew, *Indo-Portuguese Trade,* 1–60.

41. Fernández-Armesto, "Portuguese Expansion in a Global Context," 496–98; Castro, *Pepper Wreck,* 17; Mathew, *Indo-Portuguese Trade,* 82–83; Bedini, *Pope's Elephant,* 32.

42. For the numbers of people leaving Portugal annually, see Boxer, *Portuguese Seaborne Empire,* 52. For pensions granted for service, see Pohle, *Deutschland und die überseeische Expansion,* 34. For special rights, see "Preuilegio dos bombardeiros alemaes," royal edict July 15, 1507, cited in Pohle, *Deutschland und die überseeische Expansion,* 135. For foreigners in service in the sixteenth century, see Pérez-Mallaína, *Spain's Men of the Sea,* 79. On the gunners and master gunners at sea, although for a slightly later period, see Phillips, *Six Galleons for the King of Spain,* 144–46.

43. For the sense of desperation that might lead one to go to sea, see Pérez-Mallaína, *Spain's Men of the Sea,* 23. For the status of seafarers, see Dutra, "Social and Economic World," 96.

44. Duarte Coelho was the donatário of the colony, which gave him extensive powers. He did not particularly appreciate the *degredados,* describing them as worse than the "peste," see Duarte Coelho to King João III, Olinda, 20 December 1546 in Gonsalves and Albuquerque, *Cartas de Duarte Coelho a El Rei,* 89. On the *degredados,* see Amado, "La séduction de l'autre"; Coates, *Convicts and Orphans;* and Pieroni, *Os excluídos do reino.*

45. On the upward mobility of men who served the Portuguese crown in Africa, Asia, or Brazil, see Dutra, "Duarte Coelho Pereira," 418–19. On the desire of hidalgos to emulate forebears, see the statement of the foot soldier Bernal Díaz del Castillo at the beginning of his own *Historia verdadera:* "My ancestors having always been servants of the Crown, and my father and one of my brothers being in the service of the Catholic Kings, Don Ferdinand and Doña Isabella, I wished in some sort to emulate them," *Conquest of New Spain,* 15.

46. Domingues, *A Carreira da Índia,* 64–68; Pérez-Mallaína, *Spain's Men of the Sea,* 79; Phillips, *Six Galleons,* 144–46. The names of the German men were Hans von Bruchhausen and Heinrich Brant; see Oberacker, *Der deutsche Beitrag zum Aufbau der brasilianischen Nation,* 22.

47. For mastering the currents, see Thornton, "Portuguese in Africa," 139–40. The astrolabe, originally a Greek invention, was refined in the Muslim world between the seventh and seventeenth centuries and was used on land to measure the location of stars. Astrolabes were made in medieval Spain, and treatises on the use of the astrolabe were translated into Latin in the twelfth and thirteenth centuries. See Gingerich, "Islamic Astronomy."

48. See *"Treaty between Spain and Portugal concluded at Tordesillas, June 7, 1494. Ratification by Spain, July 2, 1494. [Ratification by Portugal, September 5, 1494],"* in Davenport, *European Treaties,* 84–100. According to this line of demarcation, Brazil lay within Portugal's sphere. While the treaty established an agreement between Spain and Portugal, it did nothing to resolve conflicts with other kingdoms, such as France or England. Unwilling to accept the Papal Bulls that restricted trading rights in Africa to the Portuguese, or the Treaty of Tordesillas, French monarchs authorized French merchants to openly trade as if the sea were free, a *mare librum.* See Guénin, *Ango et ses pilotes.*

49. For the French attack in 1531, see Sousa, *Diario da navegação de Pero Lopes de Sousa,* 2:19–43. For figures on French ships, see Bonnichon, *Des cannibales aux castors,* 27–32.

50. Pérez-Mallaína, *Spain's Men of the Sea,* 63; Phillips describes the specialized work on board ship in the early seventeenth century in *Six Galleons,* 119–51.

51. "Too many guns," was the response of maritime archaeologist Filipe Vieira de Castro when he reviewed the image for us (personal communication). Léry, *History of a Voyage to the Land of Brazil*, 14.

52. Léry, *History*, 8–14.

53. On the Portuguese in Morocco, the role of Cabo de Gué, and the Sa'did conquest, see Cornell, "Socioeconomic Dimensions of Reconquista and Jihad in Morocco."

54. Wir fuhren hinbei / so kompt eyn Schiff auss dem Hauingen / wol geladen / Dem fuhren wir nach unnd uberkamen es / Aber das Volck entfure uns mit dem Botte, *WH* 1.2.3.

55. For details on this trading post, see the suit brought by Bertrand d'Ornesam, Baron of Saint Blanchard, against the Archbishop of Funchal [Portugal] Dom Martinho, and Antonio Correa, Bartholomeu Ferraz, Gonçalo Leite, Gaspar Palha, and Pero Lopes de Sousa, as transcribed in Sousa, *Diario da navegação*, 2:19–43. See also Marchant, *From Barter to Slavery*, 39 n. 55. Alonso de Santa Cruz, who sailed with Sebastian Cabot to the Río de la Plata in 1525–27, later wrote that the Portuguese had an "asiento" at Pernambuco that they called a "factoria"; see Santa Cruz, *Islariò general de todas las islas del mundo*, 1:543. For the failure of most settlements, see H. B. Johnson, "Portuguese Settlement, 1500–1580," 13–19. For Coelho's land grant, see Dutra, "Duarte Coelho Pereira," 415–41. For the sugar plantations, see Schwartz, *Sugar Plantations*, 7–15.

56. For *resgate*, see Metcalf's discussion of *resgate*, slave raiding, and the debate over Indian slavery in sixteenth-century Brazil in *Go-betweens*, 157–93. According to his grant of donation, Coelho was permitted to bring twenty-four slaves from the Brazilian slave trade, known as *resgate*, to Lisbon each year; on these slaves, he would pay no duty; see "Carta da doação da Capitania de Pernambuco a Duarte Coelho" [1534] in *Documentos para a história do açúcar*, 1:13. On the slave raiding, see Coelho to King João III, Olinda, 20 December 1546, in Gonsalves de Mello and Albuquerque, *Cartas de Duarte Coelho a El Rei*, 87–91.

57. Staden refers to the North African slaves who took part in the siege as "Moors," which suggests that they were Muslim; see *WH* 1.3.2.

58. Pérez-Mallaína, *Spain's Men of the Sea*, 1–10; Phillips, *Six Galleons*, 11.

59. For the shift from Lisbon to Seville, see Pohle, *Deutschland und die überseeische Expansion*, 255; see also Harreld, *High Germans in the Low Countries*. For the German colony in Seville, see Rolf Walther, "Fremde Kaufleute in Sevilla," 46.

60. Sagten viel wie Goldtreich es sein solt, *WH* 1.5.5. James Lockhart estimates the size of Atahualpa's ransom at 1.5 million pesos, of which the king received his royal fifth. Each man received a share, depending on his rank, and only a few were allowed to return immediately to Spain; see Lockhart, *Men of Cajamarca*, 13. und das Goltreiche lande Pirau genant / welchs vor etlichen jaren funden ist worden / und Brasilien / ist alles eyn fuss feste landt, *WH* 1.5.5.

61. Juan de Sanabria was appointed Adelantado of Rio de la Plata in 1547, with the provision that he was to take 250 soldiers and 100 families and found two coastal settlements, one at Santa Catarina Island and the other at the entrance of the Rio de la Plata. After his death, his rights passed to his son, Diego de Sanabria, in 1549. See Franco, "Introdução," in Hans Staden, *Duas viagens ao Brasil*, 5–24; Obermeier, "As relações"; and Azara, *Descripcion é historia del Paraguay*, 138–40. For how Salazar came to lead the expedition, see Obermeier, "As relações," 324–25.

62. Pérez-Mallaína, *Spain's Men of the Sea,* 8–9.

63. Staden gives the date of departure as the fourth day after Easter 1549 (*WH* 1.6), but the accepted date for the Sanabria expedition under Salazar is April 10, 1550; see Franco, "Introdução," 5; Obermeier, *Hans Staden,* 320 n. 27. In 1550, Easter fell on the sixth of April; see "Dates of Easter Sunday and Perpetual Calendar, 1550–2049," compiled by Brian Pears, www.genuki.org.uk/big/easter. For the inexperience of the pilot, see Juan de Salazar to the king of Spain, Laguna de Enbiaça [Santa Catarina, Brazil], 1 January 1552, in Obermeier, "Hans Staden und Ulrich Schmidel," 102–8. Franco writes that the head pilot was to have been the Portuguese Gonçalo da Costa, who was experienced in the south Atlantic, but that he was replaced by the Biscayan Sanches, see "Introdução," 6.

64. In Portugal, the use of the astrolabe on board ship was standard since at least the time of Bartolomeu Dias, see Pereira, *Esmeraldo de Situ Orbis,* 25–30; Cortés, *Arte of Navigation;* Silva, *A astronomia e 'Os Lusíadas,'* 145–88; Figueredo, "Geographical Discoveries and Conquests of the Portuguese"; Winter, "Origin of the Sea Chart"; and Matos, "A navegação atlântico dos portugueses," 87–92.

65. Pérez-Mallaína develops this argument about the transformation of the sailor from a co-participant in the business of the sea to a simple proletarian in *Spain's Men of the Sea,* 191–97.

66. Pérez-Mallaína, *Spain's Men of the Sea,* 83–84; Sandman, "Mirroring the World." As for soldiers having opinions, the classic example of this is Bernal Díaz del Castillo's account of the conquest of Mexico. Díaz del Castillo makes clear that the soldiers were often consulted and that Cortés needed to win them over to his side; see Díaz del Castillo, *Conquest of New Spain.*

67. For the numbers on the *San Miguel,* see Salazar to the king of Spain, in Obermeier, "Hans Staden und Ulrich Schmidel," 110–17. For status on board ship, see Pérez-Mallaína, *Spain's Men of the Sea,* 83. For the lack of medical personnel, see Salazar to the king of Spain, in Obermeier, "Hans Staden und Ulrich Schmidel," 108. On brigantines and caravels, see Domingues, *Os navios,* 259–66, 274–75.

68. Boxer, *Portuguese Seaborne Empire,* 88–89; Garfield, "History of São Tomé Island," 3–65.

69. For the honor of the women, see Salazar to the king, 1552, in Obermeier, "Hans Staden und Ulrich Schmidel," 102. In both letters to the king, Salazar writes that the pilot's charts did not show São Tomé; see Obermeier, "Hans Staden und Ulrich Schmidel," 102, 112. For how they stocked up with food and water, see Salazar to the king, 1552, in Obermeier, "Hans Staden und Ulrich Schmidel," 102–4; Franco, "Introdução," 6.

70. For such men, see Pérez-Mallaína, *Spain's Men of the Sea,* 208; see also Obermeier, "As relaçoes," 317–41.

71. Obermeier, "As relações," 325.

72. Ibid., 325–26.

73. Ibid., 324–27.

74. "Relação da muy notavel perda do galeão grande São João," in Brito, *História trágico-marítima,* 3–23; available in English as Boxer, ed. and trans., *Tragic History of the Sea.*

75. According to a Jesuit letter, Tomé de Sousa was in São Vicente in February 1553; see A Brother in Brazil [São Vicente] to Brothers in Portugal, 10 March 1553, in Leite, *Monu-*

menta Brasiliae, 1:431. For Sousa's claims, see Tomé de Sousa to the king, 1 June 1553, in Dias, Vasconcellos, and Gameiro, *História da colonização portuguesa do Brasil,* 3:365–66. For this expedition, see also Guzmán, *Historia Argentina;* ebook version, bk. 2, chap. 15.

76. For details about the *engenhos,* see Luís de Góis to King João III, Santos [São Vicente], 12 May 1548, in Dias, Vasconcellos, and Gameiro, *História da colonização portuguesa no Brasil,* 3:259. The first sugar plantations were almost entirely worked by Indian slaves, and African slaves were few and performed only the more specialized tasks in the mills. Slave raiding was the cause of much resistance on the part of indigenous groups; see Metcalf, *Go-betweens,* 174–80. For the numbers of slaves working in São Vicente, see Luís de Góis to King João III, in Dias, Vasconcellos, and Gameiro, *História da colonização portuguesa no Brasil,* 259.

77. Manoel da Nóbrega to Simão Rodrigues, São Vicente, 12 February 1553, in Leite, *Monumenta Brasiliae,* 1:420–23; Nóbrega to Simão Rodrigues, São Vicente, March 1553, in Leite, *Monumenta Brasiliae,* 1:457; Nóbrega to Luís Gonçalves da Câmara (in Lisbon), São Vicente, 15 June 1553, in Leite, *Monumenta Brasiliae,* 1:492; José de Anchieta to Inácio de Loyola, 1 September 1554, in Leite, *Monumenta Brasiliae,* 2:102–6; see also Metcalf, *Go-betweens,* 104–6.

78. Staden calls him Diego de Praga, and a Diego da Braga appears as a resident of São Vicente in 1550; see Obermeier, *Hans Staden,* 330 n. 43. For the Jesuits and mamelucos, see Metcalf, *Go-betweens,* 95–98. The etymology of *mameluco* is the Arabic *mamluk,* "to be possessed," and seems to have been adopted in Brazil to describe the mestizos of Brazil as freed slaves, since they were the children of Indian women who were held as de facto slaves. It is a direct reference to the Mamlukes of Egypt, who were thought to be descended from emancipated white slaves known for their military service. See *Oxford English Dictionary Online,* s.v. "Mameluke."

79. Nóbrega describes the desirability of establishing a church on the Piratininga plateau in his letter to the king of October 1553; and by 1554, José de Anchieta began to write regularly from Piratininga; see the correspondence of October 1553 through September 1554 in Leite, *Monumenta Brasiliae,* 2:16–123, passim. The founding of São Paulo is traditionally celebrated as January 25, 1554. It is impossible to know how the Tupinikin and the Tupinambá interacted before the arrival of Europeans, but the overlay of competing European powers on the groups did nothing to allay the hostilities that existed between them. See Monteiro, "Crises and Transformations of Invaded Societies."

80. See *WH* 1.15.

81. Tomé de Sousa to the king, 1 June 1553, in Dias, Vasconcellos, and Gameiro, *História da colonização portuguesa do Brasil,* 3:365. Sousa's account confirms what Staden says: that after Bertioga had been burned, it was rebuilt, and that Tomé de Sousa ordered a better fort to be built; see *WH* 1.16.

Chapter 2 · The Lying Captive

1. Nun helff Gott meiner Seelen, *WH* 1.18.4. und rissen mir die Kleyder vom leib / Der eyne die halslapen / der ander den hut / der dritte das hembd, *WH* 1.18.4.

2. Some of the few captives who did write about their experiences are discussed in Voigt, *Writing Captivity.* For slavery in Africa, see Miller, *Way of Death,* 379. For the absence of

original voices in the historical record, see Lovejoy, "Extending the Frontiers of Transatlantic Slavery," 65. Lovejoy's review of *Extending the Frontiers,* edited by Eltis and Richardson, argues that analyses drawn from the Voyages Transatlantic Slave Trade database (www .slavevoyages.com), one of the most important sources for understanding the slave trade, tend to adopt the perspective of the slave ship—the European shippers and their American destinations—and not that of the slaves who became victims of a massive forced migration.

3. The letters and reports of the Jesuits, who well understood the need to speak the indigenous languages for evangelism, described a common language, often referred to as the "Brazilian" language. José de Anchieta clearly stated that this language was shared by Tupi and Guarani peoples and described it as a common language used along the coast and up to 200 leagues into the interior; see Anchieta, "Informação do Brasil," 310. Ulrich Schmidel, a German who had spent twenty years in Paraguay before passing through São Vicente on his way to Antwerp, described the language of the Tupi as "with a few small differences the same as that of the Carios [Guarani]"; see Schmidel, *Relatos de la conquista del Río de la Plata y Paraguay,* 104. On Schmidel's manuscript, see Huffines, "Original Manuscript of Ulrich Schmidl," and the new critical edition (German/Spanish) by Obermeier, *Reise in die La Plata-Gegend.*

4. Léry, *History,* 115. For Staden's description of the capture, see *WH* 2.27. Other early European descriptions of Tupi warfare are similar to Staden's and emphasize the ferocity of the Tupi warrior in hand-to-hand combat, see Léry, *History,* 112–21; and Thevet, *Les singularités de la France Antarctique,* 156–60.

5. und wollten nun irer freunde tod wol an mir rechen," *WH* 1.18.4; and auff das mich auch ire weiber lebendig sehen / und ihre fest mir mir hetten," *WH* 1.18.6.

6. For Tupi warriors and chiefs, see Léry, *History,* 113. The first Jesuits in Brazil also remarked on the oratorical skill of indigenous chiefs; see Metcalf, *Go-betweens,* 250. "Kawewi Pepicke," or, in modern spelling, *cauim pepica.* Cauim was the name given to the alcoholic drink made from fermented manioc; hence, the term *manioc beer* has evolved. Staden's words: und mich dan mit eynander essen, *WH* 1.18.6.

7. See Arens, *Man-Eating Myth,* for the clearest statement of the creation of a myth of cannibalism; see also Obeyesekere, *Cannibal Talk.* However, the consensus of modern historians and anthropologists is that the accounts of cannibalism by Staden and other sixteenth-century observers such as Jean de Léry, André Thevet, Manoel da Nóbrega, and others are valuable as a means to understand both European thought and the customs of the Tupi, recognizing that all accounts are colored with bias and must be used with care. See Lestringant, *Cannibals;* Castro, *From the Enemy's Point of View,* 274–305; and Whitehead and Harbsmeier, *Hans Staden's True History,* xv–civ. Conklin, *Consuming Grief,* xxiv.

8. Léry, *History,* 112.

9. For the context of cannibalism ceremonies, see Pedersen, "European Indians and Indian Europeans," 386–87. See also Whitehead and Harbsmeier, *Hans Staden's True History,* xlvi–xlvii. The other German witness was Ulrich Schmidel; see his *Relatos de la conquista,* 104.

10. For a summary of Jesuit descriptions, see Whitehead and Harbsmeier, *Hans Staden's True History,* xxv–xxviii. Correa claimed at the end of his description not to have described

even half of the ceremony. See Pero Correa to João Nunes Barreto (in Africa), São Vicente, 20 June 1551, in Leite, *Monumenta Brasiliae*, 1:227–29.

11. "Full of fear": so grosser angst und jamer war, *WH* 2.20.3. The chorale theme *Aus tiefer Not schrei ich zu dir* ("Out of the Depths") is attributed to Martin Luther and first appeared in print in Luther's *Geystliche Gesangk-Buchleyn*, ed. Johann Walter, published in Wittenberg (1524). The text comes from Psalm 130. "See how he cries": jetzt jammert es ihn, *WH* 1.20.3. verspotteten mich und hiessen mich / auff ire sprache / Schere inbau ende / Du bist mein gebunden Tier, *WH* 1.20.4. When Staden says that they called him "my bound animal [pet]," he uses the Tupi words *Schere inbau ende* [Chê reimbaba indé], which anthropologist Carlos Fausto has shown has a wide distribution throughout Lowland South America. The notion of a bound animal, or wild pet, can define a shaman's relationship with spirits, the relationship between the captor and the captive, or in nature the bond between spirit owners and their animal. Staden was employing specific language referring to a specific kind of relationship that he could only have known about from his own experience which, Fausto argues, further underscores the ethnographic veracity of his tale; see Fausto, "Of Enemies and Pets," and personal communication.

12. Ich ewer essenspeise komme, *WH* 1.21.2.

13. Den Schlag reche ich an dir von meines Freunds wegen / Den die / darunter du gewesen bist / getödtet haben, *WH* 1.21.5.

14. wann man mich essen wolte / und jme also eynen namen mir mir machen, *WH* 1.22.2. Chapter 22 is titled "What Their Greatest Honor Is," and in it Staden writes that honor derives from capturing and killing enemies and that after each enemy is captured and killed, a new name is taken. Thus, the most prominent in Tupinambá society are those with the most names. Eduardo Viveres de Castro argues that killing enemies was vital to the reproduction of Tupinambá society, a culture in which warfare was idealized and boys became men, and able to procreate, only after killing their first enemies: "Without enemies, there would be no proud recitation of names, no bodies laboriously marked with commemorative incisions, no mouths ornamented with precious stones for authoritative public speech, no honorable destinies in the afterlife. Without dead enemies, there would be, literally, no one living: there would be no legitimate children," Castro, *From the Enemy's Point of View*, 279. "Not yet": Noch nit, *WH* 1.22.3.

15. das die Portugaleser / denen byeden so geuder waren / und mich gefangen hatten / jenem vatter enem arm abgeschossen hatten / also das er gestorben were / und desselbigen ires vatterstod / wolten sie nun an mir rechen, *WH* 1.25.1.

16. On running away as a resistance to slavery, see Reis and Gomes, *Liberdade por um fio*.

17. Neil Whitehead notes that "Staden himself was able to sustain a cultural performance of some felicity before his Tupi captors through his manipulation of indigenous concepts and categories in a way which saved his life," in "Hans Staden and the Cultural Politics of Cannibalism," 744. Similarly, H. E. Martel describes Staden as a "practiced chameleon" who "demonstrated his willingness to lie and perform an identity not his own," a classic description of many transactional go-betweens; see Martel, "Staden's Captive Soul," 58.

18. Staden describes the maracas in *WH* 2.23, and Léry also describes them in detail in *History*, 61. Jesuits recognized the importance of the maracas and even adopted them in their early preaching among indigenous groups in Bahia; see Metcalf, *Go-betweens*, 100;

205. Da sagte ich / die dinger haben keyne maacht / und konnen auch nicht reden / und liegen / das ich eyn Portugaleser bin / soder ich bin der Frozosen freund und verwanten eyer / Und das land da ich daheyme bin / heysset Allemanien, *WH* 1.24.1. Daruff sagten sie / Das muste ich liegen / dann wan ich der Franzosen freund were / was ich dann unter den Portugalesern her, *WH* 1.24.1.

19. Zagorin, *Ways of Lying,* 3. Zagorin, "Historical Significance," 887.

20. Zagorin, *Ways of Lying,* 2–3. Zagorin, "Historical Significance," 879–84; and *Ways of Lying,* 38–62.

21. Zagorin, "Historical Significance," 885–86. Machiavelli, *The Prince,* 51.

22. da kamen die Wilden zu mir gelauffen / und sagten: Hie ist nu eyn Franzoß kommen / num wollen wir sehen ob du auch eyn Franzoß seist oder nit, *WH* 1.26.1.

23. Er ist ye eyn Christ / er wird wol zum besten reden, *WH* 1.16.1.

24. eyn junger geselle, *WH* 1.26.2. Carautá-uára is Karwattuware in Staden's spelling. und ich kundte inen nicht wohl verstehn. Wie ich im num nicht antworten kundt, *WH* 1.26.2.

25. "Kill him and eat him . . .": Totet und esset inen / den bößwicht / Er ist eyn rechter Portugaleser / euwer unnd mein feindt, *WH* 1.26.2. "They want to eat you": Sie wollen dich essen, *WH* 2.26.2.

26. Nóbrega to Dr. Martín de Azpilcueta Navarro (in Coimbra), Salvador, 10 August 1549, in Leite, *Monumenta Brasiliae,* 1:136–37.

27. "Cursed are those . . .": Vermaledeiet sei der mensch so sich auff menschen verlasset, *WH* 1.26.2.

28. Marakayas in Staden's spelling; also referred to in sixteenth-century sources as Maracajás or Maragaiás.

29. "I thought . . .": Ich gedacht / so würden sie auch mir mir umbgehn, *WH* 1.28.2. "Here I bring . . .": Hie bringe ich den Schlauen den Portugaleser her / un meynte es were ein fein ding anzusehen / wann eyner seinen find in seiner gewalt hette, *WH* 1.28.2.

30. "Have you . . .": Bistu kommen unser feindt? *WH* 1.28.2. "I have come . . .": Ich sagte: "Ich bin kommen / aber ich bin nicht ewer feindt," *WH* 1.28.2. "Are you . . . ": Bistdu der Konyan Bebe: Lebestu noch: ja sagte er ich lebe noch. Wolan sagt ich / Ich hab vil vo dir gehort / wie du so eyn weydlicher man seist, *WH* 1.28.2.

31. "Yes, it's true . . .": Ja es ist war / Ich bin lang auß dem lande geweßt / und hab die Sprach vergessen, *WH* 1.28.2. "already helped . . .": Er hette schon fünff Portgaleser helffen fangen und essen / die alle gesagt hetten sie weren Franzosen / und hettens doch gelogen, *WH* 1.28.3.

32. Er fragte mich vil / und sagte mir vil, *WH* 1.28.4.

33. Ihr haltet mich für eynen Portugaleser / eweren feindt / gebet mir nun eynen bogen mit pfeilen / und lasset mich loß gehen / so wil ich euch helffen die hütten verthedingen, *WH* 1.29.2.

34. Ich sehe im an er ist zornig. Er sihet nach deiner hütten, *WH* 1.30.1.

35. O mein Herr und Gott hulf mir dieses elend zum siedlingen end, *WH* 1.28, woodcut. See figure 31 (right).

36. wollen dich etwan kauffen, *WH* 1.32.2.

37. Mein bruder leßt sich beduncken / das dein Gott musse zornig sein, *WH* 1.33.1.

38. Ich sagt im ja / mein Gott ist zornig / das er mich wolte essen, *WH* 1.33.1. das er wider herkome in seine hütten / so wolle ich mit meine Gott reden / er solle gesundt werden, *WH* 1.33.1.

39. Er solte sterben, *WH* 1.34.6. Auch so haben wir schon etliche Portugaleser gehabt und gessen / aber ir Gott wurd so zornig nicht / als deiner, *WH* 1.34.6.

40. On the demographic catastrophe that befell the Americas after 1492, see Kiple and Beck, *Biological Consequences of European Expansion,* vol. 26; Alchon, *A Pest in the Land;* Cook and Lovell, *Secret Judgments of God;* and Denevan, *Native Population of the Americas.* There is little written on Brazil; see Metcalf, *Go-betweens,* 119–55.

41. "would not let me go . . .": sie wollten mich niemant lassen / mein eygen vatter oder brüder keme dann dahin / unnd brechte inen eyn schoffvoll guts, *WH* 1.35.5. "Why did he not . . .": warumb hat er dir nicht eyn messer geben / das du mir geben hettest, *WH* 1.35.7. "That the Frenchmen . . .": Die Franzosen dochten zuhandt so wenig als die Portugaleser, *WH* 1.35.7.

42. viel gezeuges, *WH* 1.35.2.

43. "Bring a ship . . .": Schiff mit vilen Gütern, *WH* 1.35.4. "He surely . . .": Er muß gewiss eyn Frantzsoß sein / lasset uns inen nun vortan besser halten, *WH* 1.35.9.

44. hetten dir ye eyn hembd geben / dieweil du nacket gehest / Aber sie achten nichts auff dich (wie es auch war), *WH* 1.40.2.

45. Meynet ir das ich euch so entlauffen wolte / Ich bin da im bot gewesen / und meinen landtsleuten gesagt / das sie sich darauff schickten / wann ir auß dem krieg kemet / und mich dahinbringet / das sie dann viel wahr bei eynander hetten/und euch geben, *WH* 1.40.5.

46. Ich kannte sie alle mit eynander, *WH* 1.41.10.

47. "he spoke and acted . . . ": Ja sagte er / mit jnen hette man sie besser. Vnd er fuehrete solche rede als ob er solte zur kirmess gehen, *WH* 1.41.2. Stewart, *Before Bruegel,* 9, 61. See Villas-Bôas, "Anatomy of Cannibalism," on the association between the cannibalism ceremony and European festivals.

48. er wil sterben / Wir wollen inen / ehe dann er stirbet todt schlagen, *WH* 1.39.6.

49. neyn/thuts nit / er wirt villeicht widerumb gesundt werden, *WH* 1.39.7. Staden describes how he looked from his illness as "scheußlich," *WH* 1.39.7.

50. Also wirt mein Gott mit allen Schelcken thun / so mir leydt gethan haben und thun werden, *WH* 1.39.8.

51. ich sagte das musten sie stellen in den willen / des himlischen vatters/und seines lieben Sons Jesu Christi / des gecreutzigten vor unser Sünd / in welches namen wir getauft sein . . . und was der almechtige Gott mit uns angahet / darmit müssen wir zufrieden sein, *WH* 1.42.5.

52. Sie sollten gessen werden, *WH* 1.43.11. Es schmeckt gut, *WH* 1.43.2.

53. For metaphor and joking, see Castro, *From the Enemy's Point of View,* 270–72. Die Wilden waren mir sehr gunstig. Ja / Wir zogen auß / gleich wie tapffere leut pflegen / euch unsere feinde zufangen und zuessen. Nun habt ir die oberhant kriegt / habt uns gefangen / aber wir fragen nichts darnach / Die wehrhafftigen dapffern leut sterben in irer feindelandt. So ist auch unser lant noch groß / die unsern werden uns an euch wol rechen. Ja sagten die andern / ihr habt der unsern schon vil vetilget / das wollen wir an euch rechen, *WH* 1.43.3.

54. Castro, *From the Enemy's Point of View,* 274. Castro writes that "Tupinamba society should be understood as including its enemies" and that in Tupi society "one is always, and before all else, the enemy of someone, and this is what defines the self," 283–84.

55. Iteronne in Staden's original account, which is generally accepted as Niteroi. Niteroi is across the Guanabara Bay from the city of Rio de Janeiro. Taquaraçu-tiba is Tackwara

Sutibi in Staden's original account. Abati-poçanga is Abbati Bossange in Staden's original account.

56. Wilhelm de Moner in Staden's original account, which we have transcribed as Guillaume de Monet. Coó-uara-açu is Sowarasu in Staden's original account. Perrault is Perot in Staden's original.

57. weil sie sic him Guten von den Wilden trennen wollten, *WH* 1.50.3. So halff mir der allmechitge Herr / der Gott Abraham / Isaac und Jacob / auß der gewalt der Tyranne, *WH* 1.50.5.

58. For the value of a ducat in Brazil, see Schwartz, *Sugar Plantations,* 498. For the value of a female slave, see "Will of Mem de Sá, 1569, in Instituto do Açúcar e do Álcool," in *Documentos para a história do açúcar,* 3:19. For the value of Indian slaves, see Schwartz, *Sugar Plantations,* 70. For expected profit, see "Relação de Leonardo de Cá Masser, 23 de Outubro de 1505," in Amado and Figueiredo, *Brasil 1500,* 401. Masser was a Venetian who went to Lisbon to report back to the Senate on the Portuguese commercial activities in India and the New World.

59. das ich möchte wierub in Christen landtschaft kommen / und seine an mir erzeygre wohthat andern leuten auch verkünden, *WH* 1.52.2.

60. Mouette, "Les balbutiements de la colonisation française au Brésil."

61. Brunelle, *New World Merchants of Rouen,* 17–18.

62. Ibid., 9–10.

63. Ibid., 17.

64. Wintroub, "Civilizing the Savage and Making a King," 468.

65. For the French colony at the Guanabara Bay, see Ronciére, *Histoire de la Marine Française,* 4:13. Staden says Meonsorial Miranth, which was translated as Royal Governor by Malcolm Letts in his English translation of Staden's account; see Letts, *Hans Staden: The True History,* 122. The recent critical edition by Obermeier transcribes Staden's words as "mon sieur L'Admiral," which would refer to Admiral Gaspard de Châtillon-Coligny or possibly Villegagnon. See Obermeier, *Hans Staden,* 371 n. 134.

66. This inconsistency was brought out by Neil Whitehead at the conference "Hans Stadens Wahrhaftige Historia von 1557—Dekonstruktion und Rekonstruktion des ersten Brasilienbuches," Regionalmuseum, Wolfhager Land, March 9–11, 2007.

67. Montaigne, "Of Cannibals," in *Complete Essays of Montaigne,* 1:152.

68. Ibid. Montaigne's putdown of the king's cosmographer is likely a reference to André Thevet, a Franciscan, who embarked with Villegagnon as a chaplain and who therefore visited Brazil shortly after Staden returned. Thevet wrote about his observations of Brazil and the Tupinambá in *Les singularités de la France Antarctique,* which was published in France later in the same year that Staden's book appeared in Germany. Montaigne disliked Thevet's approach because he ranged too widely and wrote equally authoritatively about what he knew and did not know. Montaigne greatly preferred Jean de Léry, whose *Histoire d'un voyage fait en la terre du Brésil* (Geneva: 1587) was also based on his residence in Brazil (in 1556–58), and was deeply critical of Thevet, see Janet Whatley's introduction to Léry's *History,* xix–xxi, xlv–lxii, 221. Montaigne, however, does not acknowledge his own debt to Léry.

69. Whitehead and Harbsmeier suggest that Staden told his story orally and that another wrote it down; see *Hans Staden's True History,* lxxv. Frank Lestringant argues that

Thevet and Léry were also humble men, although not as ordinary as Staden, and that neither was educated as a humanist would have been; see "Les indiens tupinamba vus par Staden, Thevet et Léry," in Obermeier and Schiffner, *Die Warhaftige Historia*, 53–56. However, their books are considerably more sophisticated than Staden's, both in terms of the writing style and the images that accompany the text. In Thevet's case, Lestringant attributes this to the fact that he had a co-author, while Léry wrote his book some twenty years after visiting Brazil, during which time he had studied theology, read widely, and served as a minister during France's religious wars. Montaigne's essays on lying were "Of Liars," "Of Giving the Lie," and "Of Presumption." Quotations here are from *Essays* 1:23; 2:505; and 2:491.

70. On the booksellers, see McCusker, "Demise of Distance," fig. 1; on the burgeoning art market in Antwerp, the largest public art market in Europe, see Ewing, "Marketing Art in Antwerp"; on woodcuts, see Stewart, *Before Bruegel*, 261.

Chapter 3 · The Traveler Returns

1. b E. F. G. zu jrer gefelligen gelegenheyt / . . . / durch mich durchzogene Land und Meer / sich woellen vorlesen lassen / vmb wunderbarer geschicht willen, *WH*, Staden dedicatory letter, paragraph 4. darinne mit hilff Gottes / . . . / der Almechtige Gott in noeten / bei mir erzeygt hat, *WH*, Staden dedicatory letter, paragraph 4.

2. Metcalf, *Go-betweens*, 10.

3. Pfister and Brázdil, "Climatic Variability in Sixteenth-Century Europe."

4. Wright, *Capitalism, the State, and the Lutheran Reformation*, 170.

5. For the making of the Hessian Protestant state, see Jagusch, *Mit dem Glauben Staat machen*. For the consolidation of Prostestantism in Germany, see Brady, "Emergence and Consolidation of Protestantism," 28. For the concept of social discipline, see Hsia, *Social Discipline in the Reformation*, 11.

6. For Philipp's captivity and return, see Egelhaaf, "Landgraf Philipp von Hessen," 30. For the founding of the university in Marburg, see Unckel, "Die Entwicklung des Schulwesens." For Dryander's role in the seizure of Church funds, see Schachtner, "Johannes Dryander," 796; see also Hirsch, "Dryander, Johannes," 440.

7. For states and censorship, see Harley, "Silences and Secrecy," 59. For publishing in Hesse, see Villas-Bôas, "Travel writing and religious dissent," 37. For the first banned texts in Hesse, see Obermeier, "Hans Stadens Brasilienbuch," 34.

8. Some scholars prefer the phrase "princely reformation" to identify the role that German princes placed in promoting the cause of the Reformation in their lands and in instigating a series of reforms that increased the power of the prince (prior to the later phase, which includes the Counter-Reformation); see Schulze, *Fürsten und Reformation*. For social discipline in Hesse, see Hancock, "Philipp of Hesse's View of the Relationship of Prince and Church," 161.

9. So the admiral in France; investors in London and Antwerp.

10. The issue of reforming Christian charity and addressing the problem of begging was central to the Reformation and linked to changing perceptions about the moral and social causes of poverty. See Wright, *Capitalism, the State, and the Lutheran Revolution*, 177–79; and "Reformation Contributions to Public Welfare Policy," 1170. Midelfort notes that the

hospitals were jammed full by the 1590s but that more poor and indigent clamored to be admitted; see Midelfort, *History of Madness,* 340. For the purpose of hospitals, see Wright, "Reformation Contributions," 1166–67.

11. Staden wrote letters to two nobles—Count Wolrad II of Waldeck (1509–78) and Count Philip Ludwig I of Hanau (1553–80)—sending them copies of his book and, in the first instance, asking for an intervention on the behalf of a "poor widow in Korbach"; see Menk, "Die beiden Widmungsschreiben Hans Stadens," 69–70; and Obermeier, *Hans Staden,* ii. Shayne Legassie argues that travel literature is a part of "real world power struggles," as knowledge about far-away places can be used to assert claims to political and social precedence; see Legassie, "Differently centered worlds," 6. For the context of Staden's story, see Menninger, *Macht der Augenzeugen,* 186.

12. See introduction above.

13. und lange zeyt zuvor her von hochgemeltem f. unserm gneidigen herzn / in meiner und anderer vil / gegenwerktigkeyt / den Hans Staden / examinirt / und von allen Stücken seiner Schiffart un Gefencknis gründlich ausgefragt und erforst, *WH,* Dryander introduction, paragraph 28.

14. Annerose Menninger argues that Staden's story was tailored to fit Philipp's experiences as a captive; see "Hans Stadens 'Wahrhaftige Historia,' " 523–24. For Staden's testimony of faith, see Villas-Bôas, "Travel writing," 49.

15. das ich doch zuvor / seine Arbeyt und Schrifft dieser Historien ubersehen / Corrigiren / und wo es von noeten ist/verbessern, *WH,* Dryander introduction, paragraph 2. In reviewing the extensive literature regarding Dryander's role in shaping Staden's *True History,* Michael Harbsmeier argues that one can only make an educated guess about his influence. He notes that scholars initially ignored Dryander's role altogether, then began to question his motives, and finally even argued that there could be no single author of the book at all. Harbsmeier himself thinks that Dryander shaped the form of the text and served thus as Staden's learned shadow, like so many scribes who wrote down traveler's tales (it should be noted that before the invention of print having a scribe was a sign of status rather than a symbol of illiteracy or poverty); see Harbsmeier, "Johannes Dryander: Hans Stadens gelehrter Schatten?" 120–42.

16. Wer liegen will / der liege fern her / vnd vber feldt, *WH,* Dryander introduction, paragraph 9.

17. Darzu so ist er samt seinen Altern hie in diesem Lande gesessen / nit wie der Lndtfahrer und Lügner gewonheyt / von eymen landt ins ander / ziegenuners weis / umblauffe, *WH,* Dryander introduction, paragraph 5.

18. The engraving appeared in *Bibliotheca chalcographica, hoc est Virtute et eruditione clarorum Virorum Imagines,* a collection of 438 engravings of humanists and reformers, including Desiderius Erasmus (ca. 1469–1536), Philip Melanchthon (1497–1560), and Ulrich Zwingli (1484–1531); see Boissard and de Bry, *Bibliotheca chalcographica.* Schachtner, "Johannes Dryander," 789.

19. Bietenholz and Deutscher, *Contemporaries of Erasmus,* 406.

20. For the smaller as an image of the whole, see Crowther-Heyck, "Be Fruitful and Multiply," 917. For the first autopsies in Germany, see Völker and Bauer, "Medizin and Chemie," 489. For public dissections in Marburg, see Herrlinger, "Dryander, Johannes."

21. For an annotated digital version of Vesalius's work, see http://vesalius.northwestern .edu/index.html. Charles Singer, "Brain Dissection before Vesalius," quotes Vesalius as calling Dryander "slave of the sordid printer of Marburg and Frankfurt" (262). See Preface, http:// vesalius.northwestern.edu/index.html.

22. Clark, "Foiling the Pirates," 301.

23. Völker and Bauer, "Medizin and Chemie," 490.

24. For the relationship between Egenolff and Kolbe, see Dommer, *Die aeltesten Drucke,* 17–19. For an overview of the Kolbe press's publications, see Bredehorn, "Die Marburger Frühdrucke," 22–23. For a view on the importance of sales to the printing of early modern books, see Hirsch, *Printing, Selling and Reading,* 29. Landgrave Philipp instructed Kolbe in 1548 that he was to use the kind of presses, paper, and ink that were proper for a printer of his standing and to do so better than he had done previously. See Reske, *Die Buchdrucker,* 604.

25. Schachtner, "Dryander," 789. For maps of Hesse, see Meurer, "Cartography in the German Lands," 1227 n. 346. For *navigatio,* see Neuber, *Fremde Welt im europäischen Horizont,* 35.

26. For later prints and reproductions, see note 4 in the introduction. Karl Fouquet lists eight further reprints and editions after the first two in 1557 (Marburg and Frankfurt): a 1558 Dutch translation in Antwerp, a 1561 Low German translation in Hamburg, a 1563 Antwerp edition, a 1567 Frankfurt edition (as part of a collection edited by Sebastian Franck), and an additional Frankfurt edition of that same year. In 1592, Theodor de Bry included Staden's work in his edited collection of works about voyages to the New World (which were translated into Latin). See Fouquet, "Die Ausgaben der 'Wahrhaftigen Historia,'" 211–31. *Fressen* is the German word describing how animals eat; *essen* is the German word "to eat." Wolfgang Neuber notes that an early catalogue of the Frankfurt book fair lists the book as the men-eater book; see *Fremde Welt,* 254.

27. Later editions of Staden's book were sold at the Frankfurt book fair, see Obermeier, "A viagem," 292.

28. Hackenberg, "Books in Artisan Homes," 78.

29. Mancall, ed., *Travel Narratives,* 8. Prior to Columbus's journeys, many of the Europeans who made trips and published reports about them were either pilgrims or captives (or both), and their accounts were stories about their visits to holy sites and descriptions of their travels to places like Jerusalem. Some even traveled in disguise to Mecca and Medina—in disguise because non-Muslims were forbidden to visit the holy places of Islam. Lodovico de Varthema of Bologna left Venice in 1502 and traveled throughout the Middle East and onward to India. Returning to Rome in 1508 aboard a Portuguese ship, he published his *Itinerario* in 1510. Varthema's book was especially popular in German-speaking lands and was printed and reprinted numerous times. See Varthema, *Reisen im Orient,* 23–30.

30. Fernandes expressed his awe at the Portuguese expeditions in Africa and his appreciation of Portuguese trade efforts; see Pohle, *Deutschland und die überseeische Expansion,* 219. For Dürer's drawing of the rhinoceros, see Massing, "Quest for the Exotic," 115–19.

31. For the origins of the business newspaper, see McCusker, "Demise of Distance," 295–301.

32. For *Neue Zeitungen,* see Pohle, *Deutschland und die überseeische Expansion,* 279. For Columbus's and Vespucci's letters in Germany, see Neuber, *Fremde Welt,* 235. For the Fuggers

and Welsers and their desire for information, see Neuber, *Fremde Welt*, 238; Pohle, *Deutschland und die überseeische Expansion*, 230; and Johnson, *German Discovery*, 95–100.

33. The quote regarding the *Cosmographia* is from Johnson, *German Discovery*, 32. On the title page the traveler wears a turban, but he is otherwise dressed as a Tupinambá Indian, showing that in the European imagination, the Tupinambá were sometimes interchangeable with Muslims; see Voigt, *Writing Captivity*, 43–50; Lopes, *Wonderful Things Never Yet Seen*, 42–43.

34. For Schmidel's account as it compares to that by Staden, see Obermeier, "Hans Staden und Ulrich Schmidel." Obermeier also provides an overview of the research on Schmidel in "Die Geschichte der Ulrich-Schmidel Forschung."

35. Historian Roger Chartier notes that well into the eighteenth century a dedication was the best way to win the goodwill of the sovereign; see "Prince Patronage and the Economy of Dedication," 33. Die sollen dem HERN dancken / vmb seine guete / vnd vmb seine wunder / die er an den menschen kindern thut, *WH*, Staden's dedication.

36. TenHuisen, "Providence and Passio," 217.

37. Gernot Gerlach argues that Staden frames his story around the word of God, a thoroughly Protestant undertaking; see Gerlach, "Nun helff Gott meiner seelen." "Stands there praying": und ich fieng an mit weynenden augen zusingen außgrundt meines hertzen den Psalmen: Auß tiefer not schrei ich zů dir &c. / Da sagten die Wilden: Sihe wie schreiet er / ytzt jamert jn, *WH* 1.20.3. For Psalm 130 and Luther, see Leaver, *Luther's Liturgical Music*, 149.

38. Da wurd ich ingedenck des spruchs Jeremie cap. xxij. der da saget: Vermaledeiet sei der mensch so sich auff menschen verlasset, *WH* 1.26.2. Nun bitten wir den heyligen geyst, *WH* 1.26.2.

39. Greenblatt, *Marvelous Possessions*, 135. It is important to distinguish between the literary conventions used by Staden to narrate his captivity and return, and the actual experiences he may have had while in Brazil. While we can never fully discern what actually happened and what Staden relates (because the story conforms to certain stereotypical beliefs, conventions, and expectations), we can be sure that Staden is convinced that the best framework in which to tell his story is that of the tortured martyr.

40. "A black cloud": So erhebet sich eyn grosse schwarze wolcke / unkomet hinter uns her, *WH* 1.20.5. "Speak to your God": Rede mit deinem Gott / das uns der grosse regen und wint keynen schaden thu, *WH* 1.20.5. "Oh almighty God": O du Almechtige Gott / du hymlicher und erdriche gewalthaber / der du von anbegin / denen / die deinen namen anruffen / gehoffen und sie ehören hast / unter den Gottlosen / erzeyge mir deine barmhertizgkeyt / auff das ich erkennen möge / das du noch bei mir seiest / und die Wilden heyden / so dich nit kennen / sehen mögen / das du mein Gott mein gebet erhöret hast, *WH* 1.20.7.

41. Wie der Almechtige Gott eyn zeychen thet, *WH* 1.46. und ich hatte den wilden befolen / sie solten es nicht auffrihen / es möchte inen ungluck davon kommen, *WH* 1.46.1.

42. "They came in my hut": Sie kamen in meine huetten / begerten / Jch solte mit meinem Gott machen / das der regen auff hoerete / Dann wo es nicht auffhoerete / wuerde es jre pflantzung verhindern / Dann jre pflantz zeit war da, *WH* 1.46.1. "It's your own fault": Jch sagte es were jr schuldt / sie hetten meinen Gott erzuernet / das sie das holtz hetten außgeraufft. Dann bei dem holtz pflegte ich mit meinem Gott spraach zuhalten, *WH* 1.46.2.

43. *WH* 1.47.

44. "I had to think about": mit dem wurd ich ingedenck / des leidens unsers Erlösers Jesu Chrsti wie der von den schnoden Juden unschuldig leyd, *WH* 1.22.3. "Oh my Lord": O mein Herr und mein Gott / hilff mir dieses ellends zu eynem seligen end, *WH* 1.30, woodcut caption. Kennet Pedersen has argued that Staden "escaped the fate of being eaten when he began to play the role of a great shaman"; see "European Indians and Indian Europeans," 408.

45. "Always lied about me": welcher mich stets belog, *WH* 1.39.8. "Because of the lies": yetzt aber der luegen halben so er auff mich gelogen hat / ist mein Gott zornig worden, *WH* 1.39.8. "I ask the reader": Bitte dero halben den Leser das er wölle achtung haben auff mein schreiben / Dann ich thu diese muehe nit der gestalt / das ich lust hette etwas newes zu-schreiben / sondern alleyne die erzeygte wolthat Gottes an den tag zubringen, *WH* 1.39.8.

46. "My prayer": Mein gebet zû Gott dem hern dieweil ich in der Wilden leut gewalt war mich zû essen, *WH* 1.53.5. "Only my God can release me": Sonder alleyne / das deine gewaltige hand geholffen habe / dañ jtzt kan mir keynes menschen gewalt helffen / vnd wenn du mir geholffen hast / auß jrer gewalt, *WH* 1.53.5.

47. "Do not fear": seit getrost / gute newe zeitungs / lasset mich neher kommen so wil ich euch bericht geben, *WH* 1.10.4. Harbsmeier, *Wilde Volkerkunde,* 100.

48. *WH* 1.51.

49. Kiening, *Das wilde Subjekt,* 60.

50. In enjoying the role of go-between, Staden resembles Georg Simmel's *tertius guadens* ("the third who rejoices"); see Metcalf, *Go-betweens,* 3, 260.

51. wie in dieser Historia / da die leuthe alle in der Jnsell nacket gehen / keyn heusslich vihe zur narung / keynerley dinge so bei vns im Brauch / den Leib zuerhalten / haben / als kleyder / Bette / Pferde / Schwein oder Kuehe / noch Wein oder Bier &c. sich vff jhre weise enthalten / vnd behelffen müssen, *WH,* Dryander's introduction, paragraph 22. Neuber, *Fremde Welt,* 96–97. Luciana Villas-Bôas argues that the *Beschreibung* "mirrors the composition of Pliny the Elder's *Natural History,* one of the most influential models for formalizing the selection and description of collections in the Renaissance"; Villas-Bôas, "Travel writing," 160.

52. Neuber, *Fremde Welt,* 66.

53. Pagden, *European Encounters with the New World,* 20–36.

54. "Begging that it may": habe ich diese meine præfation oder vorred E. G. vndertheniglich woellen zuschreiben / Welch E. G. gnediglich also vô mir woelle annemen / bis so lang ich etwas trifftigers / in E. G. namen / in truck verfertigen werde, *WH* 1, Dryander's introduction, paragraph 28. Michael Harbsmeier coins the phrase "learned shadow"; see Harbsmeier, "Johannes Dryander," 120 and above, note 15.

55. H. E. Martel makes a similar argument about Staden's integration; see Martel, "Staden's Captive Soul," 51–69. "Yelled and shot": Ich reiff vnd schoß vnd machts auff ihre weiß wie ich best kond [emphases ours], *WH* 1.29.2.

56. Jch wolte durch das Stacket kommen / welchs vmb die huetten hergieng / vnd zû die andern lauffen / dann sie kanten mich wol, *WH* 1.29.2.

57. "Brief account": Warhafftiger kurtzer bericht / handel vnd sitten der Tuppin Inbas / derer gefangner ich gewesen bin, *WH* 2, title. "Who waits upon him": geben jme eyn weib das jnen verwaret / vnnd auch mit jme zuthun hat, *WH* 2.29.1. "Of bees": Von Binen oder

Jmen des lands, *WH* 2.35. "Honey when I was naked": auch hab ich selbs den honig nacket gelanget / aber ich muste das erstemal / von grossem wehe zû eynem wasser lauffen / vnd sie darinne abwaschen / solte ich jrer loß werden von dem leibe, *WH* 2.35.3.

Chapter 4 · Staden's Images

1. Fraktur first appeared in Frankfurt in 1522, and one of Albrecht Dürer's books on the proportions of the human figure was set in Fraktur in Nuremberg in 1528. The font soon became known as "the German letter," and over the course of the sixteenth century the narrow and pointed letters of Fraktur (which could pack more words onto a page) would gradually replace Schwabacher; see Dowding, *Introduction to the History of Printing Types*, 214–15. On the use of italic by humanists, see Dowding, *Introduction*, 5. Whether intentional or not, Dryander, the humanist, is distinguished from Staden and Landgrave Philipp by the italic type. For the use of red ink in the production of manuscripts and books (first used in 1457), see Hirsch, *Printing, Selling, and Reading*, 49. For books in sixteenth-century Germany, see Clair, *History of European Printing*, 138. "Sete katii" is translated as "it is good" in Obermeier, *Hans Staden*, 179; on the title page and woodcut, see also Obermeier, "Die Illustrationen in Stadens *Warhaftige Historia*," 38.

2. Shevlin, "To Reconcile Book and Title," 48; Smith, *Title-Page*, 18, 23, 75–78.

3. Obermeier (citing Neuber) gives an approximate price of 14.4 or 16.4 denaren for the book, making it accessible to all readers; see *"A viagem,"* 292. Images were seen as a means to teach religious doctrine to the illiterate, as noted by Pope Gregory the Great in the fifth century and frequently repeated, see Burke, *Eyewitnessing*, 48. Moralized Bibles were a huge compendia of biblical illustration that were highly detailed and carefully prepared; see Lowden, *Making of the Bibles Moralisées*. For the first illustrated Bible printed in Germany, see Füssel, "Early Modern German Printing," 233–34. For the reading public targeted by printers, see Hirsch, *Printing, Selling, and Reading*, 121. For block books, see Steinberg, *Five Hundred Years of Printing*, 70. Illustrated books were a distinctive feature of the German book trade, and German books incorporated illustrations as early as the 1460s when Albrecht Pfister of Bamberg left spaces in the text for woodcuts to be inserted; see Clair, *History of European Printing*, 25, 138.

4. Copperplate engraving, for example, required twice as much work, and the text and the illustrations had to be printed separately. As a result, woodcut illustrations that could be included alongside of text were favored by printers in the sixteenth century; see Bucher, *Icon and Conquest*, 4. For the process of cutting, see Stewart, *Before Bruegel*, 242. For woodcutters and their tools, see Hind, *Introduction to a History of Woodcut*, 1:7–8.

5. Dommer, *Die aeltesten Drucke*, 158.

6. Schedel, *Liber chronicarum;* for a recent annotated version of the chronicle, see Schedel and Füssel, *Chronicle of the World*. For Wolgemut, see Panofsky, *Albrecht Dürer*, 1:19–20.

7. Münster, *Cosmographia;* McLean, *Cosmographia of Sebastian Münster;* Gerald Strauss, *Sixteenth-Century Germany*, 116–17; Grafton, *New World, Ancient Texts*, 97–111. Another important cosmography published in Germany before Münster's was Sebastian Franck's *Weltbuch* (1534).

8. For the recycling of images, see, e.g., Tedeschi, "Publish and Perish," 45–46. Indeed, some of the 52 woodcuts in the *True History* are used more than once. For readers' interpretation and reading of images, see Eisenstein, *Printing Press,* 53, and Strauss, *Sixteenth-Century Germany,* 139.

9. C. R. Johnson, *German Discovery,* 32–37.

10. For a discussion of the use of the Varthema images in the Frankfurt edition, see Voigt, *Writing Captivity,* 43–50. See also Villas-Bôas, "Travel writing," 101–7.

11. Voigt, *Writing Captivity,* 43–50; Lopes, *Wonderful Things Never Yet Seen,* 42–43; Neuber, "Travel Reports in Early Modern Germany," 741.

12. Neuber, "Travel Reports," 741.

13. For Egenolff, see Clair, *History of European Printing,* 131. Strauss, *Sixteenth-Century Germany,* 140. See, more generally, Hirsch, *Printing, Selling, and Reading,* 49.

14. See, e.g., Conradus de Megenberg, *Naturbuch* (Frankfurt am Main: Christian Egenolff, 1540), and Dryander's *Artzenei Spiegel* (Frankfurt am Main: Christian Egenolff, 1547).

15. McLean, *Cosmographia,* 173, 152–53.

16. "intimate familiarity," from Whitehead and Harbsmeier, *Hans Staden's True History,* lxxv; "more authentically personal expression," from Whitehead, "Hans Staden and the Cultural Politics of Cannibalism," 748; "exceptional for the wealth," from Whitehead, "Hans Staden and the Cultural Politics of Cannibalism," 745. Obermeier, "Die Illustrationen." In *Cannibals,* Lestringant suggests that an illustration in Thevet's *Les singularités* "might be an imitation *of a picture by Hans Staden*" (58, emphasis ours); while a caption to an illustration reads: "The cannibal prisoner defies his captors, as portrayed *by (a) Hans Staden,* who was himself held prisoner by the Tupinikin Indians and feared for his life" (105, emphasis ours).

17. Obermeier, *Hans Staden,* xxv–xxvii. Burke, *Eyewitnessing,* 15–16. On artists at sea, see Quinn, "Artists and Illustrators in the early Mapping of America," and Wallis, "Role of the Painter in Renaissance Marine Cartography," 2:515–23. On soldiers as artists, see Burke, *Eyewitnessing,* 148.

18. Delano-Smith, "Signs on Printed Topographical Maps." Hildegard Binder Johnson argues that the 1507 World Map by Waldseemüller was printed by Johannes Grüninger in Strassburg; see Johnson, *Carta Marina,* 22–24.

19. The fort where Staden served is on the northern end of Santo Amaro Island, and thus the first image seems to be inverted. However, since Staden's fold-out map (see discussion below) is oriented with south at the top, the second image could be the one that was inverted.

20. Whitehead argues that Staden's illustrations would not have seemed shocking to a German public, given what they were used to seeing; see Whitehead, "Ethnographic Lens in the New World"; see also Spinks, "Wondrous Monsters."

21. For Columbus's letter to Santángel, see *The Spanish Letter;* for the quotation from the *Mundus Novus,* see Formisano, *Letters from a New World,* 50.

22. For German print culture, see Johnson, *German Discovery,* 19–24. In his own words Anghiera wrote that "the printing-press has distributed [his writings] to the public," Anghiera, *De Orbe Novo,* 1.2.5. Anghiera's "Decades" had early editions in Basel, Cologne, and Nuremberg.

23. See Lestringant, *Cannibals,* 17–19.

24. Whitehead makes a similar observation—that the depictions of cannibalism are not very similar to the ways cannibalism was depicted in sixteenth-century Germany, see "Ethnographic Lens," 86 n. 9, and *Hans Staden's True History,* lxxv n. 100. For the images of cannibalism that accompanied the publication of Vespucci's letters in Germany, see Wolff, *America,* 20; and König, "Newly Discovered Islands," in Wolff, *America,* 106–7. The c. 1506 map with the image of cannibalism is known as the "Four Finger," or as the Kunstmann II world chart; see Kupčík, *Munich Portolan Charts,* 28–34; the cardinal's heraldic crest appears over South Africa and was identified by Emma Treadway in "Vespucci's Earthly Paradise and the Four-Finger Map." Susi Colin discusses how images of cannibalism became popularized on maps in "Woodcutters and Cannibals," in Wolff, *America,* 175–81.

25. Colin, "Woodcutters and Cannibals," in Wolff, *America,* 175–81; Johnson, *Carta Marina,* 58–65, 92. Grynaeus and Huttich, *Novus orbis regionum.*

26. See Lestringant, *Cannibals,* 18–19, 23–31. While Obermeier argues that this image of cannibalism on the title page was related to other images of cannibalism in sixteenth-century Germany, we find that it is different; see Obermeier, "Die Illustrationen," 38. On the Dieppe, or Norman school of cartography, see Helen Wallis's introduction to *The Maps and Text of the Boke of Idrography,* 35–72; Tony Campbell, "Egerton MS 1513"; and Toulouse, "Marine Cartography and Navigation in Renaissance France."

27. Vnd wann dis nicht sein vornemens were (welchs dan erbarlich vnd recht ist / so wolte er viel lieber dieser muehe vnd arbeyt / verseumnis / auch angewentes kostens / der nicht gering vff diesen Truck vnd Formen zu schneiden ergangen ist / enthaben sein, *WH,* Dryander's introduction, paragraph 27: "His intention is both honorable and just, and if this were not the case, he could have spared himself the associated cost—which is not inconsiderable—needed to print and cut the forms."

28. Ist so geformirt wie volget, *WH* 2.23.1. On the importance of the added caption and how it serves as an intermediary, see Bucher, *Icon and Conquest,* 26.

29. Brant, *Doctor Brants Narrenschiff* (1509).

30. Obermeier suggests that D.H. may stand for the phrase "Domino Honorem," or "praise be to God," *Hans Staden,* 182 n. 16; while Dommer postulates that D.H. and A.I.I. may indicate the name of the illustrator and woodcutter; see *Die Aeltesten Drucke,* 158. It was certainly common for artists and woodcutters to sign their work; however, we were unable to identify an artist or a woodcutter in Nagler, *Die Monogrammisten.*

31. Nautical archaeologist Felipe Vieira de Castro brought the detail of the flags' directions to our attention; personal communication.

32. Francisco Contente Domingues, an authority on Portuguese ships, explains that none of the ships resemble actual sixteenth-century vessels; personal communication.

33. Unger, *Ships on Maps,* 176.

34. Was hilft der wechter in der statt / Dem geweltigen Schiff im meer sein fart / So sie Gott beyde nicht bewart, *WH* 1.

35. Woodward, "Techniques of Map Engraving," 1:609; see also Bagrow, *History of Cartography,* 125–40.

36. Delano-Smith, "Signs on Printed Topographical Maps," 528–90.

37. Unfortunately, many of the fold-out maps were removed, and it is not clear exactly where the map was originally bound. The copy at the Lilly Library, for example, is missing the map; the copy at the John Carter Brown library has a facsimile of the original map; while the copy at the Biblioteca Nacional in Rio de Janeiro, which is of the second printing (1557), has the map at the end of the book. Breydenbach, *Peregrinatio in terram sanctam.* Metcalf, "Mapping the Traveled Space."

38. Delano-Smith, "Signs on Printed Topographical Maps," 528–90. The *Romweg* map by Erhard Etzlaub and the *Landstrassen,* a traveling map of Germany, were both oriented with South at the top; see Metcalf, "Mapping the Traveled Space," 4–5.

39. Die Landschafft mit den genanten bauingen / so ich zum teyl in America gesehen hab / in wie vil gradus sie leigen / Auch wie die Irwoner heyssen / vnd ire lande sich zusamen strecken / Das hab ich nach meim besten ingedenck hirinnen abgeteylet / eynem yedern verstendigen leichtlich zu zuuerstchen.

40. The assignment of territories to indigenous groups in Brazil is a unique feature of Staden's map. Not beholden to the territorial ambitions of Portugal, Spain, or France, he was free to depict the ownership of lands in Brazil as he wished, and he assigned them to autonomous and independent indigenous groups; see Metcalf, "Mapping the Traveled Space."

41. Neuber, "Travel Reports," 756.

42. As Lestringant notes, Thevet is more the compiler than the author of *Les singularités,* given that he was in Brazil only a short time and contracted a severe fever while there, which continued even after he returned to France. He used the detailed notes compiled by Villegagnon or his secretary that were drawn from information gleaned from the *truchments* living around the Guanabara Bay (possibly even before Villegagnon's arrival). Joining Thevet in the writing of the text was Mathurin Héret, a Greek scholar, who added the classical references to the ethnographic description. See Lestringant's introduction to Thevet, *Les singularités,* 21–22.

43. Thevet describes warfare in chapter 39 of *Les singularités,* 156–60. On his method, see Lestringant's introduction to *Les singularités,* 7–9, and his more extensive "Euhemerist Tradition," 173–88.

44. On the single scene, multi-scene, and simultaneous portrayal of events in a single illustration, see Bucher, *Icon and Conquest,* 28–29.

45. O mein Herr und Gott hulf mir dieses elend zum siedlingen end.

46. McLean, *Cosmographia,* 249–61; Strauss, *Sixteenth-Century Germany,* 132.

47. In a 1503 nude sketch, Dürer points to a yellow spot on his torso "where it hurts me." While art historians traditionally see the drawing as having been prepared for a physician, some also argue that Dürer is making a clear reference to the wounds of Christ. In his self-portrait of ca. 1505, Dürer depicts himself as completely naked. In the 1522 self-portrait known as "Man of Sorrows," Dürer presents himself sitting naked with the scourge and whip, echoing the passion of Christ. See Robert Smith, "Dürer as Christ?" and Koerner, *Moment of Self-Portraiture,* especially 63–79 and 160–86. For another interpretation of the meaning of Staden's nakedness that emphasizes Staden's helplessness and naiveté, see Whitehead and Harbsmeier, *Hans Staden's True History,* lxviii–lxx. Another interpretation is offered by Benjamin Mark Allen, who argues that nakedness is a theme of captivity narratives

(including Staden's) and that it serves to underscore the shame of the captive; see Allen, "Naked and Alone in a Strange New World," 150–52.

48. On the bound pet, see Fausto, "Of Enemies and Pets," 933–56. This custom of giving captives women is documented in Jesuit letters, see Pero Correa to João Nunes Barreto, 20 June 1551, in Leite, *Monumenta Brasiliae,* 1:227–29 and José de Anchieta to Diego de Laínez, 1 June 1560, in Leite, *Monumenta Brasiliae,* 3:262. Jean de Léry and André Thevet both remark that the male captives are given wives who treat them well and minister to all of their needs, see Léry, *History,* 122, and Thevet, *Les singularités,* 160.

49. Zika, "Cannibalism and Witchcraft in Early Modern Europe"; see also Sullivan, "Witches of Dürer and Hans Baldung Grien," 334–43.

50. Bucher, *Icon and Conquest,* 15–17, 46–64; see also Whitehead, "Ethnographic Lens," 96–100. Theodor de Bry was born in Liège in 1528. A Protestant, he took up residence in Strasbourg in 1560 and later in Frankfurt in the 1580s. His first volume of the Great Voyages series, *Americae tertia pars,* appeared in Frankfurt in 1590. Volume 3 (1592) contains the Hans Staden and Jean de Léry accounts of Brazil.

51. Sadlier, *Brazil Imagined,* 52–61.

52. See Whitehead and Harbsmeier, *Hans Staden's True History,* xli–lxx; Whitehead, "Cultural Politics of Cannibalism"; Gareis, "Cannibals, *Bons Sauvages,* and Tasty White Men"; Villas-Bôas, "Anatomy of Cannibalism"; Klarer, "Cannibalism and Carnivalesque"; Martel, "Hans Staden's Captive Soul"; and Schreffler, "Vespucci Rediscovers America"; quotations from Obeyesekere, citing Roy Harvey Pearce, in *Cannibal Talk,* 11.

Epilogue

1. Grimmel, "Die Familie Hans Stadens," 35. See further Obermeier, *Hans Staden,* 179 n. 4.

2. Winckelmann, *Der Americanischen Neuen Welt Beschreibung.* Personal communication from Wolfgang Schiffner about Winckelmann's biography.

3. Egelhaaf, "Landgraf Philipp der Großmütige," 30.

4. Lyncker, "Geschichte der Stadt Wolfhagen," 93. Grimmel, "Die Familie Hans Stadens," 35.

5. Reske, *Die Buchdrucker,* 604.

6. Hanigan, Ragen, and Foster, "Dryander of Marburg," 495.

7. Quotation from the letter of the pilot Nicholas Barré, from Antarctic France [Rio de Janeiro], [1555], in Lescarbot, *Histoire de la Novvelle-France,* 1:299–300. Thevet was in Brazil for ten weeks between November 10, 1555, and January 31, 1556, and he appeared to have been sick for most of that time, see Thevet, *Les singularités,* 19–20, 150, 167.

8. Thevet, *Les singularités,* 150. Some scholars identify this chief as Pindobuçu, the same one whom Anchieta met in Ubatuba, see Leite, *Monumenta Brasiliae,* 4:132 n. 24. Letter of Barré, in Lescarbot, *Histoire de la Novvelle-France,* 1:304. On the population decline of the coastal region, see Dean, "Indigenous Populations."

9. On the size of the expedition, see Léry, *History,* 7; Léry writes at length on Thevet and Villegagnon, see *History,* xlv–lxii, 33–50.

10. Belchior, "Estácio de Sá," 83–85.

11. Forsyth, "Beginnings of Brazilian Anthropology," 157–59; Anchieta to Laínez (in Rome) São Vicente, 8 January 1565, in Leite, *Monumenta Brasiliae,* 4:169–71. Iperoig is the name of the main beach of Ubatuba.

12. Indian warriors from Espírito Santo (a Portuguese colony on the coast north of the Guanabara Bay) and mamelucos from Piratininga in São Vicente made up Sá's army; see Anchieta to Diogo Mirão (in Lisbon) Bahia, 9 July 1565, in Leite, *Monumenta Brasiliae,* 4:241–55. See also Belchior, "Estácio de Sá," 88–91; and Forsyth, "Beginnings of Brazilian Anthropology," 157–59.

13. Léry mentions Staden's account in his 1600 and 1611 editions; see Lestringant, "Les indiens tupinamba vus par Staden, Thevet et Léry," in Obermeier and Schiffner, *Die War-haftige Historia,* 67–68. Samuel Purchas, *Hakluytus posthumus, or Purchas his Pilgrimes: Con-tayning a History of the World in Sea Voyages and Lande Travells by Englishmen and Others,* 20 vols. (Glasgow, J. MacLehose and sons, 1905–7), 17:56.

14. Andrade, "Manifesto Antropófago." See Bellei, "Brazilian Anthropaphagy Revisited."

15. Certeau, "Travel Narratives of the French to Brazil," 223.

Alchon, Suzanne Austin. *A Pest in the Land: New World Epidemics in a Global Perspective.* Albuquerque: University of New Mexico Press, 2003.

Allen, Benjamin Mark. "Naked and alone in a strange New World: Early modern captivity and its mythos in Ibero-American consciousness." Ph.D. diss., University of Texas at Arlington, 2008.

Amado, Janaína. "La séduction de l'autre: premiers intermédiaires de l'empire portugais." In *Naissance du Brésil moderne, 1500–1808,* edited by Kátia de Queirós Mattoso, 237–48. Paris: Presses de l'Université de Paris-Sorbonne, 1998.

Amado, Janaína, and Luiz Carlos Figueiredo, eds. *Brasil 1500: Quarenta Documentos.* São Paulo: Imprensa Oficial, 2001.

Anchieta, José de. "Informação do Brasil e de suas Capitanias 1584." In *Cartas: informações, fragmentos históricos e sermões,* Cartas Jesuíticas III, 309–56. Belo Horizonte: Itatiaia, São Paulo: Editora da Universidade de São Paulo, 1988.

Andrade, Oswald de. "Manifesto Antropófago." *Revista de Antropofagia* 1 (1928): 11–19.

Anghiera, Pedro Martyr de. *De Orbe Novo.* Translated by Francis Augustus MacNutt. 2 vols. New York: Putnam's Sons, 1912.

Arens, William. *The Man-Eating Myth: Anthropology and Anthropophagy.* New York: Oxford University Press, 1979.

———. "Rethinking Anthropophagy." In *Cannibalism in the Colonial World,* edited by Francis Barker, Peter Hulme, and Margaret Iversen, 39–62. Cambridge: Cambridge University Press, 1998.

Aune, M. G. "Early Modern Travel Writing after Orientalism." *Journal for Early Modern Cultural Studies* 5 (2005): 120–38.

Azara, Don Félix de. *Descripcion é historia del Paraguay e del Rio de la Plata.* 2 vols. Madrid: Impr. De Sanchiz, 1847.

Bagrow, Leo. *History of Cartography.* 2nd ed. Chicago: Precedent Publishing, 1985.

Barker, Francis, Peter Hulme, Margaret Iversen, eds. *Cannibalism and the Colonial World.* Cambridge: Cambridge University Press, 1998.

Bedini, Silvio A. *The Pope's Elephant.* Nashville, TN: J. S. Sanders and Co., 1998.

Belchior, Elysio. "Estácio de Sá e a fundação do Rio de Janeiro." *História* 27 (2008): 77–99.

Bellei, Sérgio Luiz Prado. "Brazilian Anthropophagy Revisited." In *Cannibalism and the Colonial World,* edited by Francis Barker, Peter Hulme, and Margaret Iversen, 87–109. Cambridge: Cambridge University Press, 1998.

Bethencourt, Francisco, and Diogo Ramada Curto, eds. *Portuguese Oceanic Expansion, 1400–1800.* Cambridge: Cambridge University Press, 2007.

Bietenholz, Peter Gerard, and Thomas Brian Deutscher. *Contemporaries of Erasmus: A Biographical Register of the Renaissance and Reformation.* 2nd ed. Toronto: University of Toronto Press, 2003.

Blackbourn, David. *The Conquest of Nature: Water, Landscape, and the Making of Modern Germany.* New York: W. W. Norton, 2006.

Blackburn, Robin. *The Making of New World Slavery: From the Baroque to the Modern, 1492–1800.* New York: Verso, 1997.

Boehrer, Bruce Thomas. *Parrot Culture: Our 2500-Year-Long Fascination with the World's Most Talkative Bird.* Philadelphia: University of Pennsylvania Press, 2004.

Boettcher, Susan. "Review Essay: Luther Year 2003? Thoughts on an Off-Season Comeback." *Sixteenth Century Journal* 35 (2004): 795–809.

Boissard, Jean-Jacques, and Theodor de Bry. *Bibliotheca chalcographica, hoc est Virtute et eruditione clarorum Virorum Imagines.* Heidelberg: Clemens Ammon, 1669.

Bonnichon, Philippe. *Des cannibales aux castors: Les découvertes françaises de l'Amérique, 1503–1788.* Paris: France-Empire, 1994.

Boxer, C. R. *The Portuguese Seaborne Empire, 1415–1825.* New York: Knopf, 1969.

———, trans. and ed. *The Tragic History of the Sea.* 2nd ed. Minneapolis: University of Minnesota Press, 2001.

Brady, Thomas A. Jr., "Emergence and Consolidation of Protestantism in the Holy Roman Empire to 1600." In *Reform and Expansion 1500–1660,* edited by R. Po-chia Hsia, 20–36. Cambridge: Cambridge University Press, 2007.

———. *German Histories in the Age of Reformations, 1400–1650.* Cambridge: Cambridge University Press, 2009.

———. *Protestant Politics: Jacob Sturm (1489–1553) and the German Reformation.* Atlantic Highlands, NJ: Humanities Press, 1995.

Brandão (de Buarcos), João. *Grandeza e abastança de Lisboa em 1552.* Edited by José da Felicidade Alves. Lisbon: Livros Horizonte, 1990.

Brant, Sebastian. *Doctor Brants Narrenschiff.* Basel: N. Lamparter, 1509.

Braun, Georg. *Civitates orbis terrarum.* Antwerp: Theodor Graminaeus, 1575.

Bredehorn, Uwe. "Die Marburger Frühdrucke." In *Marburger Frühdrucke 1527–1566. Eine Ausstellung der Universitätsbibliothek Marburg,* edited by Uwe Bredehorn, 1–36. Marburg: Philipps-Universität Marburg, 1987.

Breydenbach, Bernhard von. *Peregrinatio in terram sanctam.* Speier: Peter Dratch, 1502.

Brito, Bernando Gomes de, ed. *História trágico-marítima* [1735–1736]. 2nd ed. Rio de Janeiro: Lacerda Editores, 1998.

Brunelle, Gayle K. *The New World Merchants of Rouen, 1559–1630.* Kirksville, MO: Truman State University Press, 1991.

Bucher, Bernadette. *Icon and Conquest: A Structural Analysis of the Illustrations of de Bry's Great Voyages.* Translated by Basia Miller Gulati. Chicago: University of Chicago Press, 1981.

Burke, Peter. *Eyewitnessing: The Uses of Images as Historical Evidence.* Ithaca, NY: Cornell University Press, 2001.

Cahill, Richard Andrew. *Philipp of Hesse and the Reformation.* Mainz: Verlag Philipp von Zabern, 2001.

Cameron, Euan, ed. *Early Modern Europe: An Oxford History.* New York: Oxford University Press, 1999.

Campbell, Mary B. *The Witness and the Other World: Exotic European Travel Writing, 400–1600.* Ithaca, NY: Cornell University Press, 1988.

———. *Wonder and Science: Imagining Worlds in Early Modern Europe.* Ithaca, NY: Cornell University Press, 1999.

Campbell, Tony. "Egerton MS 1513: A Remarkable Display of Cartographical Invention." *Imago Mundi* 48 (1996): 93–102.

Castro, Eduardo Viveiros de. *From the Enemy's Point of View: Humanity and Divinity in an Amazonian Society.* Translated by Catherine V. Howard. Chicago: University of Chicago Press, 1992.

Castro, Filipe Vieira de. *The Pepper Wreck: A Portuguese Indiaman at the Mouth of the Tagus River.* College Station: Texas A&M University Press, 2005.

Cavallo, Sandra, and Lyndan Warner, eds. *Widowhood in Medieval and Early Modern Europe.* New York: Longman, 1999.

Certeau, Michel de. "Travel Narratives of the French to Brazil: Sixteenth to Eighteenth Centuries." Translated by Katharine Streip. *Representations* 33 (1991): 221–26.

Chartier, Roger. "Princely Patronage and the Economy of Dedication." In *Forms and Meanings: Texts, Performances and Audiences from Codex to Computer,* 25–42. Philadelphia: University of Pennsylvania Press, 1995.

Chrisman, Miriam Usher. *Lay Culture, Learned Culture: Books and Social Change in Strasbourg, 1480–1599.* New Haven, CT: Yale University Press, 1982.

Clair, Colin. *A History of European Printing.* London: Academic Press, 1976.

Clark, Harry. "Foiling the Pirates: The Preparation and Publication of Andreas Vesalius's *De Humani Corporis Fabrica.*" *Library Quarterly* 51 (1981): 301–11.

Coates, Timothy J. *Convicts and Orphans: Forced and State-Sponsored Colonizers in the Portuguese Empire, 1550–1755.* Stanford, CA: Stanford University Press, 2001.

Colin, Susi. "Woodcutters and Cannibals: Brazilian Indians as Seen on Early Maps." In *America: Early Maps of the New World,* edited by Hans Wolff, 175–81. Munich: Prestel, 1992.

Conklin, Beth A. *Consuming Grief: Compassionate Cannibalism in an Amazonian Society.* Austin: University of Texas Press, 2001.

Cook, Noble David, and W. George Lovell, eds. *Secret Judgments of God: Old World Disease in Colonial Spanish America.* Norman: University of Oklahoma Press, 1992.

Cornell, Vincent J. "Socioeconomic Dimensions of Reconquista and Jihad in Morocco: Portuguese Dukkala and the Saʿdid Sus, 1450–1557." *International Journal of Middle East Studies* 22 (1990): 379–418.

Cortés, Martín. *The Arte of Navigation* [1561]. Facsimile edition. Delmar, NY: The John Carter Brown Library and Scholar's Facsimiles and Reprints, 1992.

Crowther-Heyck, Kathleen. "'Be Fruitful and Multiply': Genesis and Generation in Reformation Germany." *Renaissance Quarterly* 55 (2002): 904–35.

Daston, Lorraine, and Katherine Park. *Wonders and the Order of Nature, 1150–1750.* New York: Zone Books, 1998.

"Dates of Easter Sunday and Perpetual Calendar, 1550–2049." Compiled by Brian Pears. www.genuki.org.uk/big/easter.

Davenport, Frances Gardiner. *European Treaties Bearing on the History of the United States and Its Dependencies to 1648.* Washington, DC: Carnegie Institution, 1917.

De Bry, Theodor. *Americae tertia pars.* Frankfurt: Theodor De Bry, 1592.

Dean, Warren. "Indigenous Populations of the São Paulo–Rio de Janeiro Coast: Trade, Aldeamento, Slavery and Extinction." *Revista de História* 117 (1984): 3–26.

Delano-Smith, Catherine. "Signs on Printed Topographical Maps, ca. 1470–ca. 1640." In *Cartography in the European Renaissance.* Vol. 3, bk. 1, of *The History of Cartography,* edited by David Woodward, 528–90. Chicago: University of Chicago Press, 2007.

Denevan, William M. *The Native Population of the Americas in 1492.* 2nd ed. Madison: University of Wisconsin Press, 1992.

Dias, Carlos Malheiro, Ernesto de Vasconcelos, Roque Gameiro, eds. *História da colonização portuguesa do Brasil.* 3 vols. Porto: Litographia Nacional, 1921–1924.

Díaz del Castillo, Bernal. *The Conquest of New Spain.* Translated by J. M. Cohen. Hammondsworth, Middlesex: Penguin Books, 1963.

Documentos para a história do açúcar. 3 vols. Rio de Janeiro: Instituto do Açúcar e do Álcool, 1954.

Domingues, Francisco Contente. *A Carreira da Índia.* Lisbon: CTT Correios, 1998.

———. *Os navios do mar oceano: Teoria e empiria na arquitectura naval portuguesa dos séculos XVI e XVII.* Lisbon: Centro de História da Universidade de Lisboa, 2004.

Dommer, Arey von. *Die aeltesten Drucke aus Marburg in Hessen 1527–1566.* Marburg: N. G. Ellwert, 1892.

Dowding, Geoffrey. *An Introduction to the History of Printing Types.* London: The British Library and Oak Knoll Press, 1998.

Dryander, Johannes. *Anatomiae, hoc est, Corporis humani dissectionis pars prior . . .* Marburg: Apud Lucharium Ceruicornus, 1537.

———. *Annulorum Trium Diversi Generis Instrumentorum Astronomicorum.* Marburg: Ceruicornus, 1537.

———. *Artzenei Spiegel Gemeiner Innhalt derselbigen, Wes beide einem Leib und Wundartzet in der Theoric Practic unnd Chirurgei zusteht.* Frankfurt am Main: Egenolff, 1557.

Duncan, T. Bentley. "Navigation between Portugal and Asia in the Sixteenth and Seventeenth Centuries." In *Asia and the West: Encounters and Exchanges from the Age of Explorations: Essays in Honor of Donald F. Lach,* edited by Cyriac K. Pullapilly and Edwin J. Van Kley, 3–25. South Bend, IN: University of Notre Dame Press, 1986.

Dutra, Francis A. "Duarte Coelho Pereira, First Lord-Proprietor of Pernambuco: The Beginning of a Dynasty." *The Americas* 29 (1973): 415–41.

———. "The Social and Economic World of Portugal's Elite Seafarers, 1481–1600." *Mediterranean Studies* 14 (2005): 95–105.

Egelhaaf, Gottlob. "Landgraf Philipp der Großmütige." *Verein für Reformationsgeschichte* 83 (1904): 1–37.

Eisenstein, Elizabeth L. *The Printing Press as an Agent of Change.* Cambridge: Cambridge University Press, 1979.

Elbl, Ivana. "The Volume of the Early Atlantic Slave Trade, 1450–1521." *Journal of African History* 38 (1997): 31–75.

Eltis, David, and David Richardson, eds. *Extending the Frontiers: Essays on the New Transatlantic Slave Trade Database.* New Haven, CT: Yale University Press, 2008.

Ewing, Dan. "Marketing Art in Antwerp, 1460–1560: Our Lady's *Pand.*" *Art Bulletin* 72 (1990): 558–84.

Fausto, Carlos. "Of Enemies and Pets: Warfare and Shamanism in Amazonia." Translated by David Rodgers. *American Ethnologist* 26 (1999): 933–56.

Fernandes, Florestan. *A função social da guerra na sociedade Tupinambá.* São Paulo: Pioneira/ Editora da Universidade de São Paulo, 1970.

———. *Organização social dos Tupinambá.* São Paulo: Difusão Européia do Livro, 1963.

Fernández-Armesto, Felipe. *Amerigo: The Man Who Gave His Name to America.* New York: Random House, 2007.

———. "Portuguese Expansion in a Global Context." In *Portuguese Oceanic Expansion, 1400–1800,* edited by Francisco Bethencourt and Diogo Ramada Curto, 480–511. Cambridge: Cambridge University Press, 2007.

Figueredo, Fidelino de. "The Geographical Discoveries and Conquests of the Portuguese." *Hispanic American Historical Review* 6 (1926): 47–70.

Findlen, Paula. *Possessing Nature: Museums, Collecting, and Scientific Culture in Early Modern Italy.* Berkeley: University of California Press, 1994.

Formisano, Luciano, ed. *Letters from a New World: Amerigo Vespucci's Discovery of America.* Translated by David Jacobson. New York: Marsilio, 1992.

Forsyth, Donald W. "The Beginnings of Brazilian Anthropology: Jesuits and Tupinambá Cannibalism." *Journal of Anthropological Research* 39 (1983): 147–78.

———. "Three Cheers for Hans Staden: The Case for Brazilian Cannibalism." *Ethnohistory* 32 (1985): 17–36.

Fouquet, Karl. "Die Ausgaben der 'Wahrhaftigen Historia' 1557–1964." In *Hans Stadens Wahrhaftige Historia,* edited by Reinhard Maack and Karl Fouquet, 211–31. Marburg: Trautvetter and Fischer, 1964.

———. *Hans Staden: Zwei Reisen nach Brasilien.* 2nd ed. Marburg: Trautvetter, 1963.

Franck, Sebastian. *Weltbuch: Spiegel und Bildtniss des ganzen Erdtbodens.* Tübingen: U. Morhart, 1534.

Franco, Francisco de Assis Carvalho. "Introdução." In Hans Staden, *Duas viagens ao Brasil.* Translated by Guiomar de Carvalho Franco, 5–24. São Paulo: Editora da Universidade de São Paulo, 1942.

Freedman, Paul. *Out of the East: Spices and the Medieval Imagination.* New Haven, CT: Yale University Press, 2008.

Füssel, Stephan. "Early Modern German Printing." In *Early Modern German Literature 1350–1700,* ed. Max Reinhart, 217–46. Rochester, NY: Camden House, 2007.

García-Arenal, Mercedes, and Gerard Wiegers. *A Man of Three Worlds: Samuel Pallache, A Moroccan Jew in Catholic and Protestant Europe.* Translated by Martin Beagles. Baltimore: Johns Hopkins University Press, 1999.

Gareis, Iris. "Cannibals, *Bons Sauvages,* and Tasty White Men: Models of Alterity in the Encounter of South American Tupi and Europeans." *Medieval History Journal* 5 (2002): 247–66.

Garfield, Robert. "A History of São Tomé Island, 1470–1655." Ph.D. diss., Northwestern University, 1971.

Gerlach, Gernot. "'Nun helff Gott meiner seelen': Glaubenserfahrungen in der Reformationszeit." *Jahrbuch Martius Staden* 53 (2006): 23–34.

Gingerich, Owen. "Islamic Astronomy." *Scientific American* 254 (1986): 74–84.

Góis, Damião de. *Lisbon in the Renaissance.* Translated by Jeffrey S. Ruth. New York: Italica Press, 1996.

Gonsalves de Mello, José Antonio, and Cleonir Xavier de Albuquerque. *Cartas de Duarte Coelho a El Rei.* Recife: Imprensa Universitária, 1967.

Gräf, Holger. "Small Towns in Early Modern Germany: The Case of Hesse, 1500–1800." In *Small Towns in Early Modern Europe,* edited by Peter Clark, 184–205. New York: Cambridge University Press, 1995.

Grafton, Anthony. *New Worlds, Ancient Texts: The Power of Tradition and the Shock of Discovery.* Cambridge, MA: Belknap Press of Harvard University Press, 1992.

Greenblatt, Stephen. *Marvelous Possessions: The Wonder of the New World.* Chicago: University of Chicago Press, 1991.

Grimmel, D. "Die Familie Hans Stadens." *Hessische Heimat* 6 (1956/57): 34–36.

Grynaeus, Simon, and Johann Huttich. *Novvs orbis regionum.* Basel: Hervagivs, 1532.

Guénin, Eugène. *Ango et ses pilotes, d'après des documents inédits tirés des archives de France, de Portugal et d'Espagne.* Paris: Imprimerie Nationale, 1901.

Gunn, Steven. "War, Religion, and the State." In *Early Modern Europe: An Oxford History,* edited by Euan Cameron, 102–34. New York: Oxford University Press, 1999.

Guzmán, Ruy Díaz de. *Historia Argentina del descubrimiento, población y conquista de las provincias del Río de la Plata* [1612]. Buenos Aires: Imprenta del Estado, 1835; eBook version: Alicante: Biblioteca Virtual Miguel de Cervantes, 2001.

Hackenberg, Michael. "Books in Artisan Homes of Sixteenth-Century Germany." *Journal of Library History* 21 (1986): 72–91.

Hale, J. R. *Artists and Warfare in the Renaissance.* New Haven, CT: Yale University Press, 1990.

Hammel-Kiesow, Rolf. *Die Hanse.* Munich: C. H. Beck, 2002.

Hancock, Alton O. "Philipp of Hesse's View of the Relationship of Prince and Church," *Church History* 35 (1966): 157–69.

Hanigan, William C., William Ragen, and Reginald Foster. "Dryander of Marburg and the First Textbook of Neuroanatomy." *Neurosurgery* 26 (1990): 489–98.

Hanke, Lewis. *The Spanish Struggle for Justice in the Conquest of America.* Philadelphia: University of Pennsylvania Press, 1949.

Harbsmeier, Michael. "Johannes Dryander: Hans Stadens gelehrter Schatten?" in *Die Warhaftige Historia von 1557: Das erste Brasilienbuch, Akten des Wolfhagener Kongresses zu 450 Jahren Hans-Staden-Rezeption,* edited by Franz Obermeier and Wolfgang Schiffner, 120–42. Kiel: Westensee-Verlag, 2008.

———. *Wilde Völkerkunde: Andere Welten in deutschen Reiseberichten der Frühen Neuzeit.* Frankfurt am Main and New York: Campus, 1994.

Harley, J. B. "Silences and Secrecy: The Hidden Agenda of Cartography in Early Modern Europe." *Imago Mundi* 40 (1988): 57–76.

Harreld, Donald J. *High Germans in the Low Countries: German Merchants and Commerce in Golden Age Antwerp.* Leiden: Brill, 2004.

Heckscher, William S. "Bernini's Elephant and Obelisk." *Art Bulletin* 29 (1947): 155–82.

Herrlinger, Robert. "Dryander, Johannes." *Neue Deutsche Biographie* 4 (1959): 142–43.

Hessus, Helius Eobanus. *De victoria Wirtembergensi.* Erfurt: Saxus, 1534.

Hind, Arthur M. *An Introduction to a History of Woodcut.* 2 vols. New York: Dover, 1963.

Hirsch, August. "Dryander, Johannes." *Allgemeine Deutsche Biographie,* 5:440. Leipzig: Duncker and Humblot, 1877.

Hirsch, Rudolf. *Printing, Selling, and Reading, 1450–1550.* Wiesbaden: Otto Harrassowitz, 1967.

Hochstadt, Steven. "Migration in Preindustrial Germany." *Central European History* 16 (1983): 195–224.

Hsia, R. Po-chia. *Social Discipline in the Reformation: Central Europe 1550–1750.* New York: Routledge, 1992.

Huffines, Marion Lois. "The Original Manuscript of Ulrich Schmidl: German Conquistador and Chronicler." *The Americas* 34 (1977): 202–6.

Impey, Oliver, and Arthur MacGregor. *The Origins of Museums: The Cabinet of Curiosities in Sixteenth- and Seventeenth-Century Europe.* Oxford: Clarendon Press, 1985.

Jagusch, Britta, ed. *Mit dem Glauben Staat machen: Hessens prägende Zeit; Landgraf Philipp der Großmütige; 1504–1567.* Frankfurt am Main: Medienhaus, 2004.

Johnson, Christine R. *The German Discovery of the World: Renaissance Encounters with the Strange and Marvelous.* Charlottesville: University of Virginia Press, 2008.

Johnson, Harold B. "Portuguese Settlement, 1500–1580." In *Colonial Brazil,* edited by Leslie Bethell, 1–38. Cambridge: Cambridge University Press, 1987.

Johnson, Hildegard B. *Carta Marina: World Geography in Strassburg, 1525.* Minneapolis: University of Minneapolis Press, 1963.

Jutte, Robert. "Household and Family Life in Late Sixteenth-Century Cologne: The Weinsberg Family." *Sixteenth Century Journal* 17 (1986): 165–82.

Kellenbenz, Hermann. "Der Norden und die Iberische Halbinsel von der Wikingerzeit bis ins 16. Jahrhundert." In *Kleine Schriften,* edited by Hermann Kellenbenz. Stuttgart: Steiner, 1991.

Kiening, Christian. *Das wilde Subjekt: Kleine Poetik der Neuen Welt.* Göttingen: Vandenhoeck and Ruprecht, 2006.

Kiple, Kenneth F., and Stephen V. Beck, eds. *Biological Consequences of European Expansion, 1450–1800: An Expanding World: The European Impact on World History 1450–1800.* Aldershot, Hampshire: Variorum, Ashgate Publishing, 1997.

Klarer, Mario. "Cannibalism and Carnivalesque: Incorporation as Utopia in the Early Image of America." *New Literary History* 30 (1999): 389–410.

Koenigsberger, H. G. "The Empire of Charles V in Europe." In *The Reformation (1520–1559),* edited by G. R. Elton, 339–76. Cambridge: Cambridge University Press, 1990.

Koerner, Joseph Leo. *The Moment of Self-Portraiture in German Renaissance Art.* Chicago: University of Chicago Press, 1993.

König, Hans-Joachim. "Newly Discovered Islands, Regions, and Peoples: The Letters of Christopher Columbus, Amerigo Vespucci, and Hernán Cortés." In *America: Early Maps of the New World,* edited by Hans Wolff, 103–8. Munich: Prestel, 1992.

Kupčík, Ivan. *Munich Portolan Charts "Kunstmann I–XIII" and Ten Further Portolan Charts.* Munich and Berlin: Deutscher Kunstverlag, 2000.

Larner, John. *Marco Polo and the Discovery of the World.* New Haven, CT: Yale University Press, 1999.

Las Casas, Bartolomé de. *The Devastation of the Indies: A Brief Account.* Translated by Herma Briffault. Baltimore: John Hopkins University Press, 1992.

Leaver, Robin A. *Luther's Liturgical Music: Principles and Implications.* Grand Rapids, MI: Eerdmans Publishing, 2007.

Legassie, Shayne Aaron. "Differently centered worlds: The traveler's body in late medieval European narrative (1350–1450)." Ph.D. diss., Columbia University, 2007.

Leite, Serafim, SJ, ed. *Monumenta Brasiliae.* 5 vols. Rome: Monumenta Historica Societatis Iesu, 1956–1968.

Léry, Jean de. *History of a Voyage to the Land of Brazil, Otherwise called America.* Translated by Janet Whatley. Berkeley: University of California Press, 1990.

Lescarbot, Marc. *Histoire de la Nouvelle-France* [1618]. Reprint, Marc Lescarbot. *The History of New France.* 3 vols. Toronto: The Champlain Society, 1907.

Lester, Toby. *The Fourth Part of the World: The Race to the Ends of the Earth and the Epic Story of the Map That Gave America Its Name.* London: Profile Books, 2009.

Lestringant, Frank. *Cannibals: The Discovery and Representation of the Cannibal from Columbus to Jules Verne.* Translated by Rosemary Morris. Cambridge: Polity Press, 1997.

———. "The Euhemerist Tradition and the European Perception and Description of the American Indians." In *The Classical Tradition and the Americas,* edited by Wolfgang Haase and Meyer Reinhold, 173–88. Berlin: Walter de Gruyter, 1993.

———. "Introduction." In *Le Brésil d'André Thevet: Les singularités de la France Antarctique (1557),* edited by Frank Lestringant, 7–38. Paris: Éditions Chandeigne, 1997.

Letts, Malcolm Henry Ikin, ed. and trans. *Hans Staden: The True History of His Captivity, 1557.* London: G. Routledge and Sons, 1929.

Lockhart, James. *The Men of Cajamarca: A Social and Biographical Study of the First Conquerors of Peru.* Austin: University of Texas Press, 1972.

Lopes, Marília dos Santos. *Wonderful Things Never Yet Seen: Iconography of the Discoveries.* Translated by Clive Gilbert. Lisbon: Livros Quetzal, 1998.

Lovejoy, Paul. "Extending the Frontiers of Transatlantic Slavery, Partially." *Journal of Interdisciplinary History* 40 (2009): 57–70.

Lowden, John. *The Making of the Bibles Moralisées.* 2 vols. University Park: Pennsylvania State University Press, 2000.

Luther, Martin. *Geistliches Gesang-Büchlein.* Wittenberg: Josef Klug, 1524.

Lyncker, Karl. "Geschichte der Stadt Wolfhagen." *Zeitschrift des Vereins für hessische Geschichte und Landeskunde.* Cassel: J. Bohne, 1855.

Maack, Reinhard, and Karl Fouquet, eds. *Hans Stadens Wahrhaftige Historia.* Marburg an der Lahn: Trautvetter and Fischer, 1964.

Machiavelli, Niccolò. *The Prince*. Translated by J. G. Nichols. London: Oneworld Classics, 2009.

Mancall, Peter, ed. *Travel Narratives from the Age of Discovery: An Anthology*. New York: Oxford University Press, 2006.

Mandeville, John de. *The Travels of Sir John Mandeville*. Translated by C.W.R.D. Moseley. Hammondsworth, Middlesex: Penguin Books, 1983.

Marchant, Alexander. *From Barter to Slavery: The Economic Relations of Portuguese and Indians in the Settlement of Brazil, 1500–1580*. Baltimore: Johns Hopkins University Press, 1942; reprint, Gloucester, MA: Peter Smith, 1966.

Martel, H. E. "Hans Staden's Captive Soul: Identity, Imperialism, and Rumors of Cannibalism in Sixteenth-Century Brazil." *Journal of World History* 17 (2006): 51–69.

Massing, Jean Michel. "The Quest for the Exotic: Albrecht Dürer in the Netherlands." In *Circa 1492: Art in the Age of Exploration*, edited by Jay A. Levenson, 115–19. Washington, DC: National Gallery of Art, and New Haven, CT: Yale University Press, 1991.

Mathew, K. S. *Indo-Portuguese Trade and the Fuggers of Germany: Sixteenth Century*. New Delhi: Manohar, 1997.

———. *Portuguese Trade with India in the Sixteenth Century*. New Delhi: Manohar, 1983.

Matos, Jorge Semedo de. "A navegação atlântica dos portugueses em 1500." *Oceanos* 39 (1999): 82–99.

Maxwell, Mary Jane. "Journeys of faith and fortune: Christian travelers in the fifteenth and early sixteenth-century Dar al-Islam." Ph.D. diss., Washington State University, 2004.

McCusker, John J. "The Demise of Distance: The Business Press and the Origins of the Information Revolution in the Early Modern Atlantic World." *American Historical Review* 110 (2005): 295–321.

McLean, Matthew. *The Cosmographia of Sebastian Münster: Describing the World in the Reformation*. Aldershot: Ashgate, 2007.

Megenberg, Conradus de. *Naturbuch*. Frankfurt am Main: Christian Egenolff, 1540.

Menk, Gerhard. "Die beiden Widmungsschreiben Hans Stadens an die Grafen von Waldeck und Hanau: Bildungs- und hilfswissenschaftliche Betrachtungen zur Stadenforschung." *Zeitschrift des Vereins für Hessische Geschichte und Landeskunde* 94 (1989): 63–70.

Menninger, Annerose. "Hans Stadens 'Wahrhaftige Historia': Zur Genese eines Bestsellers der Reiseliteratur." *Geschichte in Wissenschaft und Unterricht* 47 (1996): 509–25.

———. *Die Macht der Augenzeugen: Neue Welt und Kannibalen-Mythos, 1492–1600*. Stuttgart: F. Steiner, 1995.

Metcalf, Alida C. *Go-betweens and the Colonization of Brazil: 1500–1600*. Austin: University of Texas Press, 2005.

———. "Hans Staden: The Consumate Go-between." In *Die Warhaftige Historia von 1557: Das erste Brasilienbuch, Wolfhagener Kongress zu 450 Jahren Hans-Staden-Rezeption*, edited by Franz Obermeier and Wolfgang Schiffner, 71–86. Kiel: Westensee-Verlag, 2008.

———. "Mapping the Traveled Space: Hans Staden's Maps in *Warhaftige Historia*." *E-Journal of Portuguese History* 7 (2009): 1–15.

Meurer, Peter. "Cartography in the German Lands, 1450–1650." In *Cartography in the European Renaissance*. Vol. 3, bk. 2 of *The History of Cartography*, edited by David Woodward, 1172–245. Chicago: University of Chicago Press, 2007.

Midelfort, H. C. Erik. *A History of Madness in Sixteenth-Century Germany.* Stanford, CA: Stanford University Press, 1999.

Miller, Joseph C. *Way of Death: Merchant Capitalism and the Angolan Slave Trade, 1730–1830.* Madison: University of Wisconsin Press, 1988.

Montaigne, Michel de. *The Complete Essays of Montaigne.* Translated by Donald M. Frame. Stanford, CA: Stanford University Press, 1958.

Monteiro, John M. "The Crises and Transformations of Invaded Societies: Coastal Brazil in the Sixteenth Century." In *South America.* Vol. 3 of *The Cambridge History of Native Peoples of the Americas,* edited by Frank Salomon and Stuart Schwartz, 973–1023. Cambridge: Cambridge University Press, 1999.

Moryson, Fynes. *An Itinerary Containing His Ten Yeeres Travell through the Twelve Dominions of Germany, Bohmerland, Sweitzerland, Netherland, Denmarke, Poland, Italy, Turky, France, England, Scotland and Ireland* [1617]. Glasgow: James MacLehose and Sons, 1908.

Mouette, Stéphane. "Les balbutiements de la colonisation française au Brésil (1524–1531)." *Cahiers du Brésil Contemporain* 32 (1997): 7–18.

Münster, Sebastian. *Cosmographei.* Basel: Henric Petri, 1550. Reprint facsimile edition, Amsterdam: Theatrum Orbis Terrarum, 1968.

———. *Cosmographia.* Basel: Henric Petri, 1544.

———. *Geographia.* Basel: Henric Petri, 1540. Reprint facsimile edition. Amsterdam: Theatrum Orbis Terrarum, 1966.

Nagler, G. K. *Die Monogrammisten.* 6 vols. Nieuwkoop: B. de Graaf, 1966.

Neuber, Wolfgang. "Die Drucke der im Original deutschen Amerikareiseberichte bis 1715: Synopse, Bibliographie und marktgeschichtlicher Kommentar." *Frühneuzeit-Info* 2 (1991): 12–34.

———. *Fremde Welt im europäischen Horizont. Zur Topik der deutschen Amerika-Reiseberichte der Frühen Neuzeit.* Berlin: Erich Schmidt, 1991.

———. "Travel Reports in Early Modern Germany." In *Early Modern German Literature, 1370–1700,* edited by Max Reinhart, 737–60. Rochester, NY: Camden House, 2007.

Oberacker, Karl Heinrich. *Der deutsche Beitrag zum Aufbau der brasilianischen Nation.* São Paulo: Herder, 1955.

Obermeier, Franz. "Die Geschichte der Ulrich-Schmidel-Forschung." *Jahresbericht des Historischen Vereins für Straubing und Umgebung* 107 (2005): 129–65.

———. "Hans Stadens Brasilienbuch im 450. Jahr seines erstmaligen Erscheinens, der verkannte Klassiker?" In *Die Warhaftige Historia—das erste Brasilienbuch, Akten des Wolfhagener Kongresses zu 450 Jahren Hans-Staden-Rezeption,* edited by Franz Obermeier and Wolfgang Schiffner, 6–52. Kiel: Westensee-Verlag, 2008.

———. "Hans Staden und Ulrich Schmidel im Brasilianischen São Vicente. Dokumente zu Hans Stadens Zweiter Brasilienreise und Ulrich Schmidels Rückreise nach Europa." *Jahresbericht des Historischen Vereins für Straubing und Umgebung* 107 (2005): 73–127.

———, ed. *Hans Staden. Warhaftige Historia: Zwei Reisen nach Brasilien (1548–1555) / História de duas viagens ao Brasil.* Translated by Joachim Tiemann and Guiomar Carvalho Franco. Kiel: Westensee, 2007.

———. "Die Illustrationen in Stadens Warhaftige Historia von 1557." *Jahrbuch Martius Staden* 53 (2006): 35–50.

————. "As relações entre o Brasil e a região do Rio de La Plata no século XVI nos primeiros documentos sobre Assunção (Asunción) e Santa Catarina." *Jahrbuch für Geschichte Lateinamerikas* 43 (2006): 317–41.

————, ed. *Ulrich Schmidel, Reise in die La Plata-Gegend, 1534–1554.* Kiel: Westensee Verlag, 2009.

————. "A viagem ao Brasil de Hans Staden e seu relato." In *Hans Staden,* edited by Franz Obermeier, 289–307. Kiel: Westensee, 2007.

Obermeier, Franz, and Wolfgang Schiffner, eds. *Die Warhaftige Historia—das erste Brasilienbuch, Akten des Wolfhagener Kongresses zu 450 Jahren Hans-Staden-Rezeption.* Kiel: Westensee-Verlag, 2008.

Obeyesekere, Gananath. *Cannibal Talk: The Man-Eating Myth and Human Sacrifice in the South Seas.* Berkeley: University of California Press, 2005.

Oliveira, Cristóvão Rodrigues de. *Lisboa em 1551, Sumário.* Edited by José da Felicidade Alves. Lisbon: Livros Horizonte, 1987.

Oliveira, Fernando. *Arte da guerra do mar.* Lisbon: Arquivo Histórico da Marinha, 1937.

Pagden, Anthony. *European Encounters with the New World: From Renaissance to Romanticism.* New Haven, CT: Yale University Press, 1993.

Palencia-Roth, Michael. "The Cannibal Law of 1503." In *Early Images of the Americas: Transfer and Invention,* edited by Jerry M. Williams and Robert E. Lewis, 21–63. Tucson: University of Arizona Press, 1993.

Panofsky, Erwin. *Albrecht Dürer.* 2 vols. Princeton, NJ: Princeton University Press, 1945.

Pedersen, Kennet. "European Indians and Indian Europeans: Aspects of Reciprocal Cultural and Social Classification in the Brazilian East Coast in the Early Period of Contact." *Etnologiska Studier* 38 (1987): 382–416.

Pereira, Duarte Pacheco. *Esmeraldo de Situ Orbis* [1505–1508]. Translated and edited by George H. T. Kimble. London: Hakluyt Society, 1937.

Pérez-Mallaína, Pablo E. *Spain's Men of the Sea: Daily Life on the Indies Fleets in the Sixteenth Century.* Translated by Carla Rahn Phillips. Baltimore: Johns Hopkins University Press, 1998.

Pfister, Christian, and Rudolf Brázdil. "Climatic Variability in Sixteenth-Century Europe and Its Social Dimension: A Synthesis." *Climactic Change* 43 (1999): 5–53.

Phillips, Carla Rhan. *Six Galleons for the King of Spain: Imperial Defense in the Early Seventeenth Century.* Baltimore: Johns Hopkins University Press, 1986.

Pieroni, Geraldo. *Os excluídos do reino: A Inquisição portuguesa e o degredo para o Brasil-colônia.* Brasília: Editora Universidade de Brasília, 2000; São Paulo: Imprensa Oficial do Estado, 2000.

Pistor, Julius. "Hans Staden zu Homberg und sein Reisebuch." In *Festschrift der deutschen Anthropologischen Gesellschaft zur XXVI. allgemeinen Versammlung zu Cassel,* 1–18. Cassel: Fischer and Co., 1895.

Pohle, Jürgen. *Deutschland und die überseeische Expansion Portugals im 15. und 16. Jahrhundert.* Münster: Lit Verlag, 2000.

Purchas, Samuel. *Hakluytus posthumus, or Purchas his Pilgrimes: Contayning a History of the World in Sea Voyages and Lande Travells by Englishmen and Others.* 20 vols. Glasgow: J. MacLehose and Sons, 1905–7.

Quinn, David. "Artists and Illustrators in the Early Mapping of America." *Mariner's Mirror* 72 (1986): 244–73.

Reichart, Folker. *Ludovico de Varthema Reisen im Orient.* Sigmaringen: Jan Thorbecke, 1996.

Reis, João José, and Flávio dos Santos Gomes. *Liberdade por um fio: História dos quilombos no Brasil.* São Paulo: Companhia das Letras, 1996.

Reske, Christoph. *Die Buchdrucker des 16. und 17. Jahrhunderts im deutschen Sprachgebiet. Auf der Grundlage des gleichnamigen Werkes von Josef Benzing.* Wiesbaden: Harrassowitz, 2007.

Roncière, Charles de la. *Histoire de la Marine Française.* 6 vols. Paris: Librairie Plon, 1910.

Rowlands, Alison. "The Conditions of Life for the Masses." In *Early Modern Europe: An Oxford History,* edited by Euan Cameron, 31–62. New York: Oxford University Press, 1999.

Sadlier, Darlene. *Brazil Imagined: 1500 to the Present.* Austin: University of Texas Press, 2008.

Said, Edward W. *Orientalism.* New York: Vintage Books, 1979.

Sandman, Alison. "Mirroring the World: Sea Charts, Navigation, and Territorial Claims in Sixteenth-Century Spain." In *Merchants and Marvels: Commerce, Science, and Art in Early Modern Europe,* edited by Pamela H. Smith and Paula Findlen, 83–108. New York: Routledge, 2002.

Santa Cruz, Alonso de. *Islarió general de todas las islas del mundo.* Edited by Antonio Blázquez. 2 vols. Madrid: Imprenta del Patronato de Huérfanos de Intendencia é Intervención Militares, 1918.

Saunders, A. C. de C. M. *A Social History of Black Slaves and Freedmen in Portugal, 1441–1555.* Cambridge: Cambridge University Press, 1982.

Scammell, G. V. "Indigenous Assistance in the Establishment of Portuguese Power in Asia in the Sixteenth Century." *Modern Asian Studies* 14 (1980): 1–11.

Schachtner, Petra. "Johannes Dryander und die Aufwertung der angewandten Mathematik zur Universalwissenschaft." In *Melanchthon und die Marburger Professoren (1527–1627),* edited by Barbara Bauer, 789–821. Marburg: Völker and Ritter, 2000.

Schedel, Hartmann. *Liber chronicarum.* Nuremberg: Anton Koberger, 1493.

Schedel, Hartmann, and Stephan Füssel. *Chronicle of the World: The Complete and Annotated Nuremberg Chronicle of 1493.* Cologne: Taschen, 2001.

Schmidel, Ulrich. *Relatos de la conquista del Río de la Plata y Paraguay, 1534–1554.* Madrid: Alianza Editorial, 1986.

Schmidt, Benjamin. *Innocence Abroad: The Dutch Imagination and the New World, 1570–1670.* Cambridge: Cambridge University Press, 2001.

Schmölz-Häberlein, Michaela, and Mark Häberlein. "Hans Staden, Neil L. Whitehead, and the Cultural Politics of Scholarly Publishing." *Hispanic American Historical Review* 81 (2001): 745–51.

Schreffler, Michael J. "Vespucci Rediscovers America: The Pictorial Rhetoric of Cannibalism in Early Modern Culture." *Art History* 28 (2005): 295–310.

Schulze, Manfred. *Fürsten und Reformation: Geistliche Reformpolitik welticher Fürsten vor der Reformation.* Tübingen: Mohr, 1991.

Schwartz, Seymour I. *Putting "America" on the Map: The Story of the Most Important Graphic Document in the History of the United States.* Amherst, NY: Prometheus Books, 2007.

Schwartz, Stuart B. *Sugar Plantations in the Formation of Brazilian Society: Bahia, 1550–1835.* Cambridge: Cambridge University Press, 1985.

Shevlin, Eleanor F. "'To Reconcile Book and Title, and Make 'em Kin to One Another': The Evolution of the Title's Contractual Functions." *Book History* 2 (1999): 42–77.

Silva, Luciano Pereira da. *A astronomia de 'Os Lusíadas.'* [1913–1915]. Reprint, Lisbon: Instituto Camões, 2002.

Singer, Charles. "Brain Dissection before Vesalius." *Journal of the History of Medicine and Allied Sciences* 11 (1956): 261–74.

Smith, Margaret M. *The Title-Page: Its Early Development, 1460–1510.* London and New Castle, DE: The British Library and Oak Knoll Press, 2000.

Smith, Pamela H., and Paula Findlen. "Commerce and the Representation of Nature in Art and Science." In *Merchants and Marvels: Commerce, Science, and Art in Early Modern Europe,* edited by Pamela H. Smith and Paula Findlen, 1–28. New York: Routledge, 2002.

———, eds. *Merchants and Marvels: Commerce, Science, and Art in Early Modern Europe.* New York: Routledge, 2002.

Smith, Robert. "Dürer as Christ?" *Sixteenth-Century Journal* 6 (1975): 26–36.

Smoller, Laura A. "Playing Cards and Popular Culture in Sixteenth-Century Nuremberg." *Sixteenth Century Journal* 17 (1986): 183–214.

Sobral, Luís de Moura. "The Expansion and the Arts: Transfers, Contaminations, Innovations." In *Portuguese Oceanic Expansion, 1400–1800,* edited by Francisco Bethencourt and Diogo Ramada Curto, 390–459. Cambridge: Cambridge University Press, 2007.

Sousa, Pero Lopes de. *Diario da navegação de Pero Lopes de Sousa, 1530–1532.* 2 vols. Rio de Janeiro: Typographia Leuzinger, 1927.

The Spanish Letter of Columbus: A Facsimile of the Original Edition Published by Bernard Quaritch in 1891. London: Quaritch, 2006.

Spinks, Jennifer. "Wondrous Monsters: Representing Conjoined Twins in Early Sixteenth-Century German Broadsheets." *Parergon* 22 (2005): 77–112.

Springer, James J. "Review: Untitled." *Anthropological Quarterly* 53 (1980): 148–50.

Staden, Hans. *Warhaftige Historia und Beschreibung eyner Landschafft der wilden nacketen grimmigen Menschenfresser Leuthen in der Newenwelt America gelegen.* Marburg: Andreas Kolbe, 1557.

———. *Warhaftige Historia und Beschreibung eyner Landschafft der wilden nacketen grimmigen Menschenfresser Leuthen in der Newenwelt America gelegen.* Frankfurt: Wiegand Hans, 1557.

———. *Warhaftige Historia und Beschreibung eyner Landschafft der Wilden / Nacketen / grimmigen Menschenfresser Leuthen in der Newenwelt America gelegen.* Kassel: Verlag and Schwarz, 1978. http://gutenberg.spiegel.de/autoren/staden.htm.

Stagl, Justin. "Die Apodemik oder 'Reisekunst' als Methodik der Sozialforschung vom Humanismus bis zur Aufklärung." In *Statistik und Staatsbeschreibung in der Neuzeit, vornehmlich im 16.-18. Jahrhundert,* edited by Mohammed Rassem and Justin Stagl, 131–204. Paderborn: Ferdinand Schöningh, 1980.

Steinberg, Sigfrid H. *Five Hundred Years of Printing*. New edition. Edited by John Trevitt. London: British Library; New Castle, DE: Oak Knoll Press, 1996.

Stewart, Alison G. *Before Bruegel: Sebald Beham and the Origins of Peasant Festival Imagery*. Aldershot, Hampshire; Burlington, VT: Ashgate, 2008.

Stöffler, Johannes. *Cosmographicae aliquot descriptiones*. Marburg: 1537.

Strauss, Gerald. *Sixteenth-Century Germany: Its Topography and Topographers*. Madison: University of Wisconsin Press, 1959.

Strauss, Walter L. *The Illustrated Bartsch*. Vol. 13, *(Commentary) German Masters of the Sixteenth Century: Erhard Schoen [and] Niklas Stoer*. New York: Abaris Books, 1984.

Sullivan, Margaret A. "The Witches of Dürer and Hans Baldung Grien." *Renaissance Quarterly* 53 (2000): 333–401.

Tedeschi, Martha. "Publish and Perish: The Career of Lienhart Holle in Ulm." In *Printing the Written Word: The Social History of Books, circa 1450–1520,* edited by Sandra Hindman. Ithaca, NY: Cornell University Press, 1991.

TenHuisen, Dwight E. Raak. "Alterity and hagiography in the early modern captivity narrative: *Naufragios, Wahrhaftige Historia,* and *Peregrinação.*" Ph.D. diss., University of Illinois at Urbana-Champaign, 2005.

———. "Providence and Passio in Hans Staden's *Warhaftig Historia.*" In *Foreign Encounters: Case Studies in German Literature before 1700,* edited by Mara R. Wade and Glenn Ehrstine, 213–54. Amsterdam and New York: Editions Rodopi, 2005.

Thevet, André. *Le Brésil d'André Thevet: Les singularités de la France Antarctique (1557).* Edited by Frank Lestringant. Paris: Éditions Chandeigne, 1997.

———. *Les singularités de la France Antarctique.* Paris: 1558.

Thornton, John. "The Portuguese in Africa." In *Portuguese Oceanic Expansion, 1400–1800,* edited by Francisco Bethencourt and Diogo Ramada Curto, 138–60. Cambridge: Cambridge University Press, 2007.

Toulouse, Sarah. "Marine Cartography and Navigation in Renaissance France." In *Cartography in the European Renaissance.* Vol. 3, bk. 2, of *The History of Cartography,* edited by David Woodward, 1550–68. Chicago: University of Chicago Press, 2007.

Treadway, Emma. "Vespucci's Earthly Paradise and the Four-Finger Map." Unpublished paper submitted to Alida Metcalf.

Tzanaki, Rosemary. *Mandeville's Medieval Audiences: A Study on the Reception of the Book of Sir John Mandeville (1371–1550).* Aldershot, Hampshire: Ashgate, 2003.

Unckel, Bernhard. "Die Entwicklung des Schulwesens der Stadt Marburg seit der Reformation." In *Marburger Geschichte. Rückblick auf die Stadtgeschichte in Einzelbeiträgen,* edited by Erhart Dettmering and Rudolf Grenz, 237–75. Marburg: Magistrat, 1982.

Unger, Richard. *Ships on Maps: Pictures of Power in Renaissance Europe.* New York: Palgrave Macmillan, 2010.

Varthema, Lodovico de. *The Itinerary of Ludovico di Varthema of Bologna: From 1502–1508.* Translated by John Winter Jones. London: The Argonaut Press, 1928.

———. *Reisen im Orient.* Translated by Folker Reichert. Sigmaringen: Thorbecke, 1996.

Verdi, Richard. *The Parrot in Art: From Dürer to Elizabeth Butterworth.* London: Scala Publishers, 2007.

Vesalius, Andreas. *De humani corporis fabrica.* 2nd ed. Basel: Per Joannem Oporinum, 1555.

Vespucci, Amerigo. *Lettere di viaggio.* Edited by Luciano Formisano. Milan: Arnoldo Mondadori Editore, 1985.

Villas-Bôas, Luciana. "Anatomy of Cannibalism: Religious Vocabulary and Ethnographic Writing in the Sixteenth Century." *Studies in Travel Writing* 12 (2008): 7–27.

———. "Travel writing and religious dissent. Hans Staden's *Warhaftig Historia* in print." Ph.D. diss., Columbia University, 2006.

———. "Wild Stories of a Pious Travel Writer: The Unruly Example of Hans Staden's *Warhaftig Historia* (Marburg 1557)." In *Foreign Encounters: Case Studies in German Literature before 1700,* edited by Mara R. Wade and Glenn Ehrstine, 187–212. Amsterdam and New York: Editions Rodopi, 2005.

Vogel, Susan. "Africa and the Renaissance: Art in Ivory." *African Arts* 22 (1989): 84–104.

Vogler, Günter. *Europas Aufbruch in die Neuzeit, 1500–1650. Handbuch der Geschichte Europas.* Stuttgart: Eugen Ulmer, 2003.

Vogt, John. *Portuguese Rule on the Gold Coast, 1469–1682.* Athens: University of Georgia Press, 1979.

Voigt, Lisa. *Writing Captivity in the Early Modern Atlantic: Circulations of Knowledge and Authority in the Iberian and English Imperial Worlds.* Williamsburg, VA: Omohundro Institute of Early American History and Culture, 2009.

Völker, Stefan, and Barbara Bauer. "Medizin and Chemie." In *Melanchthon und die Marburger Professoren (1527–1627),* edited by Barbara Bauer, 533–43. Marburg: Völker and Ritter, 2000.

Waldseemüller, Martin. *Die älteste karte mit dem namen Amerika aus dem jahre 1507 und die Carta marina aus dem jahre 1516 des M. Waldseemüller (Ilacomilus).* Edited by Joseph Fischer and Franz von Wieser. Innsbruck: Wagner; London: H. Stevens, Son, and Stiles, 1903.

———. *Carta Marina Navigatoria Portugallen Navigationes Atque Tocius Cogniti Orsis Terre Marisque.* [Strasbourg?], 1516.

———. *Cosmographiae introductio.* Translated by John Hessler. London: Giles, 2008.

———. *Universalis cosmographia secunda Ptholemei traditionem et Americi Vespucci aliorum que lustrations.* [Strasbourg?], 1507.

Wallis, Helen. Introduction to *The Maps and Text of the Boke of Idrography Presented by Jean Rotz to Henry VII: Now in the British Library.* Edited by Helen Wallis. Oxford: Roxburghe Club, 1981.

———. "The Role of the Painter in Renaissance Marine Cartography." In *Imago et mensura mundi: atti del IX Congresso internazionale di storia della cartografia,* edited by Carla Clivio Marzoli, 2 vols. Rome: Instituto della Enciclopedia Italiana, 1985.

Walther, Rolf. "Fremde Kaufleute in Sevilla im 16. Jahrhundert." In *Weltwirtschaft und Wirtschaftsordnung. Festschrift für Jürgen Schneider zum 65. Geburtstag,* edited by Rainer Gommel and Markus A. Denzel, 45–56. Stuttgart: Steiner, 2002.

Whatley, Janet. Translator's introduction to Jean de Léry, *History of a Voyage to the Land of Brazil, Otherwise called America,* xv–xxxviii. Berkeley: University of California Press, 1990.

Whitehead, Neil L. "The Ethnographic Lens in the New World: Staden, de Bry, and the Representation of the Tupi in Brazil." In *Early Modern Eyes,* edited by Walter S. Melion and Lee Palmer Wandel, 81–103. Leiden, the Netherlands, and Boston: Brill, 2010.

————. "The Häberleins and the Political Culture of Scholarship." *Hispanic American Historical Review* 81 (2001): 3–4.

———— "Hans Staden and the Cultural Politics of Cannibalism." *Hispanic American Historical Review* 80 (2000): 721–51.

Whitehead, Neil, and Michael Harbsmeier, eds. *Hans Staden's True History: An Account of Cannibal Activity in Brazil.* Durham: Duke University Press, 2008.

Wiesner, Merry E. *Women and Gender in Early Modern Europe.* 2nd ed. Cambridge: Cambridge University Press, 2000.

Winckelmann, Johann Justus. *Der Americanischen Neuen Welt Beschreibung, beneben einer wunderbaren Schifffahrt und Reise-Beschreibung Brasiliens zusammen getragen durch Hans Just Wynckelmann.* Oldenburg: Heinrich Conrad Zimmer, 1664.

Winter, Heinrich. "The Origin of the Sea Chart." *Imago Mundi* 13 (1956): 39–44.

Wintroub, Michael. "Civilizing the Savage and Making a King: The Royal Entry Festival of Henri II (Rouen, 1550)." *Sixteenth Century Journal* 29 (1998): 465–94.

Wolff, Hans, ed. *America: Early Maps of the New World.* Munich: Prestel, 1992.

Woodward, David, ed. *Cartography in the European Renaissance.* Vol. 3 of *The History of Cartography.* Chicago: University of Chicago Press, 2007.

————. "Techniques of Map Engraving, Printing, and Coloring in the European Renaissance." In *Cartography in the European Renaissance.* Vol. 3, bk. 1 of *The History of Cartography,* edited by David Woodward, 591–610. Chicago: University of Chicago Press, 2007.

Wright, William J. *Capitalism, the State, and the Lutheran Reformation: Sixteenth-Century Hesse.* Athens: Ohio University Press, 1988.

————. "Reformation Contributions to the Development of Public Welfare Policy in Hesse." *Journal of Modern History* 49 (1977): 1145–79.

Zagorin, Perez. "The Historical Significance of Lying and Dissimulation." *Social Research* 63 (1996): 863–912.

————. *Ways of Lying: Dissimulation, Persecution, and Conformity in Early Modern Europe.* Cambridge, MA: Harvard University Press, 1990.

Zika, Charles. "Cannibalism and Witchcraft in Early Modern Europe: Reading the Visual Images." *History Workshop Journal* 44 (1997): 77–105.